NEUROECONOMICS
THE DISRUPTIVE PATH

Author: Sebastián Laza

Year: 2018

INDEX

INTRODUCTION 7

THE HUMAN BRAIN 20

1. THE NERVOUS SYSTEM 23
2. THE TRIUNE BRAIN 28
3. BRAIN AREAS OF INTEREST FOR NEUROECONOMICS 42
4. METHODS TO STUDY THE BRAIN 44
5. APPLICATIONS TO ECONOMICS 51

RATIONALITY AND ECONOMIC THEORY 59

1. THE CLASSICS 60
2. THE FIRST NEOCLASSICALS 63
3. THE SECOND NEOCLASSICALS 68
4. ROBBINS: 72
5. HUTCHISON 77
6. J.M.KEYNES 79
7. OTHER ALTERNATIVE APPROACHES TO THE DOMINANT VIEW: AUSTRIANS, HISTORICISM AND AMERICAN INSTITUTIONALISM 87
8. FRIEDMAN AND MONETARISM. RATIONAL EXPECTATIONS AND NEW CLASSICAL ECONOMICS 96
9. NEW KEYNESIANS AND REAL BUSINESS CYCLE ECONOMISTS 107

10. SIMON 113
11. BEHAVIORAL ECONOMICS AND EXPERIMENTAL ECONOMICS 116
12. NEUROECONOMICS 121

ADVANCES IN NEUROECONOMICS..........126

1. ALLAIS'S PARADOX 129
2. THE ANOMALIES 132
3. NEUROECONOMICS AND ULTIMATUM GAME 139
4. NEURAL PURCHASING PREDICTORS 142
5. THE THEORY OF MIND................................145
6. OXYTOCIN AND TRUST 149
7. SOMATIC MARKERS AND DECISION MAKING 153
8. THE UTILITY OF MONEY 159
9. DELIBERATIVE VS AFFECTIVE......................161
10. RISK AND UNCERTAINTY 167
11. GAME THEORY AND NEUROECONOMICS..171
12. INTERTEMPORAL DECISIONS 181
13. GLIMCHER'S TWO STAGES MODEL...........188
14. BASAL GANGLIA AND AVERSION TO CHANGE: CRITICISM TO THE EXTREME LIBERAL 200
15. NOTIONS IN NEUROFINANCE....................207
16. REWARD PREDICTION ERROR 213

NEUROECONOMICS AND EPISTEMOLOGY 217

1. NOTIONS ABOUT EPISTEMOLOGY 219
2. THE LOGICAL DEDUCTIVISM IN ECONOMICS 224
3. POPPER AND THE FALSIFIABILITY CONDITION 240
4. THE POPPERIAN FALSIFIABILITY CRITERIUM IN ECONOMICS 245
5. CHANGE OF PARADIGM WITH NEUROECONOMICS? 262
6. NEUROECONOMICS CHANGE TO LAKATOS: HARD CORE OR PROTECTIVE BELT? 267
7. APOLOGISTS AND DETRACTORS OF NEUROECONOMICS 268

CONCLUSIONS 282

BIBLIOGRAPHY 290

NOTAS 309

ABOUT THE AUTHOR

Sebastián Laza is an argentine economist, graduated from the National University of Cuyo (Mendoza, Argentina), specialized in the interrelation between Neuroscience and Economics, with postgraduate courses on the subject at the National University of La Plata (Buenos Aires, Argentina), National Research University, Higher School of Economics (Moscow, Russia) and Duke University (USA).

The aforementioned author is Professor and Executive Director of the Diplomate in Applied Neurosciences in Management and Economics at the National University of Cuyo (Mendoza, Argentina).

Sebastián Laza is also the Coordinator of Neuroeconomics Area of Instituto Latinoamericano de Neurociencias Aplicadas (http://Neurosciences.online/), directed by the renowned neuropsychologist PhD Roberto Bataller.

He has previously written three books in Spanish on the subject: Neuroeconomía, Racionalidad y Epistemología (2015), Introducción a la Neuroeconomía (2016) y Neuroeconomía, Disrupción y Cambio (2018).

Additionally, he maintains the blog Neuroeconomía (http://seblaza.blogspot.com.ar/) with numerous articles on the fields of Neuroeconomics and Behavioral Economics, freely accessible to the general public.

THANKS

A warm thank you to the doctors Nestor Braidot and Roberto Bataller, intellectuals and experts of first international level in Neuroapplications to Business and Economics, with which I have been trained in these subjects. Undoubtedly, the motivational support of both has been fundamental in deciding to write a text referring to a completely new subject, and with very little standardized bibliography.

Also a strong recognition (at a distance) for the remarkable professor Vasily Klucharev, of the National Research University, Higher School of Economics (Moscow, Russia), academic director of a wonderful program on Neuroeconomics that I had the possibility to access, that helped me to better structure all my previous knowledge on the subject.

I must also acknowledge that this work could not have been carried out without the understanding of my road mate Ana María Castro, and of our two small children, Nicolás and Clara, who stoically tolerate my family distractions due to this editorial projects.

Finally, the gratitude to my parents, Raimundo Laza (already deceased) and María Angélica Milani, who always encouraged me towards intellectual effort and perseverance.

INTRODUCTION

The human being makes decisions in a context of limited rationality, that is, subject to a huge amount of biases that lead him to behave, in many cases, in a suboptimal way from the point of view of what Neoclassical Economics prescribes. Behavioral Economics has been showing this phenomenon clearly for at least four decades, with Nobel Prizes Simon, Kahneman and Thaler as main banners.

However, in recent years, the disruptive confluence of Neuroscience, Psychology and Economics has built a hybrid field called Neuroeconomics, which with methods different from the traditional ones has added even more evidence about biases and limited rationality: human decisions related to consumption, investment, saving, among many others, are not based exclusively on the calculating and maximizing ratio of neoclassical homo economics (pre-frontal cortex), but rather more uncontrollable and automatic elements often come into play, such as emotions, feelings, intuitions and biases (limbic system).

Kahneman, winner of the Nobel Prize in Economics in 2002, describes: *"the most important characteristic of a human being is not that he reasons poorly, but often acts instinctively; and the behavior is not guided by the calculations that can be made, but by what is seen at the moment when the decision has to be made"*.[1]

But it happens that these human "fragilities" (the departure from full rationality when making economic decisions), so frequent in our daily behavior, until very recently were very little taken into account at the time of analyzing and modeling economic processes. For example, Vernon L. Smith, also Nobel Prize in Economics in 2002, states that until recently, economics was considered a non-experimental science that had to rely on observation of the real world more than in laboratory experiments, and cites the following words of the renowned Paul Samuelson: *"Due to the complexity of human and social behavior we cannot hope to have the precision of the physical sciences, chemists and biologists. As astronomers, we should content ourselves with observing."*

However, and luckily, we now know that this appreciation of Samuelson was wrong, and over the years the evolution of neuroscientific technology has allowed us to overcome limits that were believed impossible to achieve.

In this way, during the last fifteen years, neuroscientists and "open minded" economists around the world are focusing their research precisely on the interaction between the rational and the emotional brain, when people make decisions related to scarcity and money, giving rise to a new field of study called Neuroeconomics. Let's look at some recent definitions of this hybrid term:

Says Paul Zak[2]:

Neuroeconomics is an emerging transdisciplinary field that uses neuroscientific techniques to identify the neural substrate associated with economic decisions. "Economic" should be interpreted here in the broadest sense, as any decisional process (human or non-human) that is given by the evaluation of alternatives.

According to Paul W. Glimcher and Aldo Rustichini[3]:

Neuroeconomics has tried to put together the theory and methodology of diverse areas such as economics, psychology, neurology, cognitive science, cognitive neurology, mathematics, statistics, behavioral finance and decision theory to create a model of human behavior that not only explains, but also predicts how people make decisions.

According to Kevin McCabe[4]:

Neuroeconomics is an interdisciplinary research program whose goal is to build a biological model of decision making in economic environments. Neuroeconomists are asking how the embodied brain allows the mind (or group of minds) to make economic decisions.

Words more, words less, the above definitions explain that by Neuroeconomics we mean all those efforts to try to elucidate the true mechanisms that underlie our economic decision making, which until now economists have almost always been very rational. And to this new way of investigating economics, majority of scientific community already grants it the character of a "respectable research program".

Refining the concept a bit more, today we talk about two different Neuroeconomics, or rather, two different research programs within the same field, which we should already be clear from the beginning of this work:

- Behavioral Economics in the Scanner (BES)
- Neurocellullar Economics (NE)

In this book we will analyze both branches, although a little more the BES branch, the most advanced in terms of field research, which is the version of Neuroeconomics that tries to empirically test the concepts of Behavioral Economics. The other branch, the NE, opens a bit of Behavioral Economics to understand the mechanisms by which the brain comparatively evaluates possible alternatives with scarce resources, and that, under the guidance of Paul Glimcher, is increasingly gathering scientific respect.

Neuroeconomics has aroused great expectations since its inception. For example, let's mention a reflection by Colin Camerer, when this research program started (year 2000):

COLIN CAMERER

"Something tells me that within ten years, the entire digital universe is going to seem like pretty mundane stuff compared to the new technology that right now is but a mere glow radiating from a tiny number of American and Cuban (yes, Cuban) hospitals and laboratories. It is called

brain imaging and anyone who cares to get up early and catch a truly blinding twenty-first-century dawn will want to keep an eye on it...If I were a college student today, I don't think I could resist going into neuroscience. Here we have the two most fascinating riddles of the twenty-first century: the riddle of the human mind and the riddle of what happens to the human mind when it comes to know itself absolutely."[5]

The ten years have passed and, realistically, still the important advances in Neurosciences have not manifested markedly in Social Sciences, particularly economics; remember that traditional (highly rationalist) thinking is still strong in our science. Additionally, neuroimaging (brain imaging), as an econometric research instrument, has still some problems that need to be overcome, which do not invalidate it, but which do require the complement of other field instruments, such as Transcranial Magnetic Stimulation (TMS), and other techniques that we will also mention later. However, the seeds for change are already scattered, and in this Neurosciences have been determining.

What is clear is that today, thanks to all these advances, the human brain can be analyzed by making decisions in real time: purchase, investment, negotiation, etc., and with a high degree of detail. And you do not need to be a futurologist to predict that, sooner or later, economists should at least become familiar with these issues, as is already happening in Management with Neuromarketing, Neuromanagement and Neuroleadership. That is to say, the change will come, that is inevitable. What nobody knows yet is how deep it will be within economic science, it will depend a lot on the methodological subject in economics (epistemological), of the dominant and emerging research programs, a topic to which we will dedicate an entire chapter in this book.

In another fact that is not minor, today the vast majority of economists are aware of the high degree of mathematization that our science has acquired. Studying economics - both at the undergraduate and graduate levels - has become increasingly complex. And although several are proud and fully in agreement with this course, many others note the abuse that has been committed in recent years with the excessive mathematization of economic theory, mathematization that hides behind, underlying - as we economists like to say - the strong neoclassical rationalist thought that still survives within economic theory, which seems not even have known that modernity and positivism / rationalism, as paradigms in Social Sciences, were long ago replaced by postmodernity, the complex systemic and so many innovations that could have improved it.

That is, today many economists are wondering if it was really worth such a degree of theoretical mathematization to understand the economic functioning of the world. And this luck of boredom, also plays in favor of many economists begin to "look with affection" to Neurosciences and the possibility of analyzing and modeling human beings making economic decisions, via methods other than hypothetical-deductive, so rationally logical and so based on mathematics and its abstractions, that it was always quite remote from real man, flesh and blood.

Today Economics can use the contributions of Neurosciences to access the black box (the mind) of economic agents -consumers, investors, savers, etc.-, instead of relying so much on the equations and their ultra-maximizing assumptions. It is not a small thing of what we are talking about.

But traditional thinking, ultra-rationalist and maximizing, has been and is powerful and influential in economics and will be difficult to qualify, let alone dethrone. Most economists who are below 45 years of age have heard from their professors that our science is converging more and more towards "the micro fundamentals of macroeconomics", meaning that it was not going to be seen with seriousness that theoretical economist who raised some macro postulate without putting together his theoretical model from the micro, obviously the micro of the neoclassical homo economicus, the one that Neurosciences today discredit.

Let us quote the following criticism of utilitarianism (the cornerstone of neoclassical economics) by the brilliant historian of economic analysis J. Schumpeter:

SCHUMPETER

"The psychology actually used [...] was always individual psychology, introspective, and the most primitive type, rarely endowed - if it ever was - of more than a few simple hypotheses about the reactions of the individual psyche. This procedure was called empirical [...]. There was nothing "experimental" or inductive, and in reality it was not very realistic, despite the programmatic statements, the war cries and the invocations of Francis Bacon."[6]

However, the discourse of high rationality in terms of economic theory, even in our days, has many adherents, most of them framed in the so-called classic / neoclassical / new classics schools and all its branches and sub-branches, both micro level as macro.

But these attacks of Neuroeconomics and Behavioral Economics, although they are the strongest, are not the first against the ultra-maximizing rationality. Throughout the history of economic analysis there have been high-sounding voices to the dominant discourse, mainly from the so-called Keynesian School, where both JM Keynes and his followers emphasized that economics does not always walk along paths of high rationality and that for example, sometimes there are situations of collective panic, which imply paralysis of investment and consumption even under conditions that should allow rational men to return to a situation of equilibrium, that is to come out of a crisis.

In short, behind the Keynesian thought and its ramifications lies the idea that individuals and companies are not 100 percent maximizing, for different and debatable reasons, but not always maximizing. And therefore, the Keynesians have always tried to model human economic behavior by contemplating these "presumably irrational" avatars, unlike mainstream thinking.

And while Keynesianism has been powerful in its critical potential - and also in its ability to influence politics - it has been weak at the theoretical level; although it is necessary to recognize that, specifically in the subject rationality, it did not count on the weapons that today Cognitive Neuroscience offer to base their ideas.

But beyond this kind of "unfulfilled promise" of Keynesianism in the task of "thoroughly" modifying the current theory, today the hopes of improvement have passed to Behavioral Economics and especially to Neuroeconomics, particularly when more and more economists, worldwide, begin to familiarize themselves with the advances that come from the Cognitive Neuroscience.

For example, Nobel Prize Simon has been key in this crusade with his theory of "bounded rationality" back in the '70s, which were the basis of what we now call Economics of Behavior.

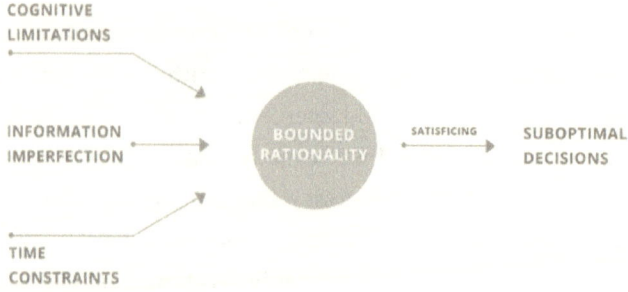

COMPLEX PROBLEMS

COGNITIVE LIMITATIONS

INFORMATION IMPERFECTION → BOUNDED RATIONALITY → SATISFICING → SUBOPTIMAL DECISIONS

TIME CONSTRAINTS

And since Neuroeconomics, today it is clearly shown that the decision that drives a purchase is not a completely rational process, but in most cases is relatively automatic and derived from metaconscious forces, that is, people incorporate many more things to the purchase decision that the simple cost-benefit analysis that we use in micro-and now also in macroeconomics-, issues beyond the reason that obviously are not calculated and more than obviously cannot be mathematized in the traditional way.

And to illustrate a little more, we are going to mention other ideas-force that come from Neuromarketing, which are perfectly applicable in Economics, especially in everything related to the consumption function at the macro level or to the theory of demand at the micro level[7]:

"According to scientists, the brain areas of rationality cannot function isolated from the areas of biological-

emotional regulation. The two systems communicate and affect the behavior jointly, and consequently, the behavior of the people ".

"Moreover, the emotional system (the oldest area of the brain) is the first force that acts on mental processes, therefore determines the direction of decisions."

"The fragrance of a perfume, for example, can evoke different sensations. If the client associates it with painful experiences or with a person with whom he does not sympathize, it is very likely that he will not buy it, even when the price-quality-brand ratio is reasonable ".

"These and other associations, like most mental processes, are verified in the metaconscious plane and force us to find new tools that allow us to access that disordered set of emotions, memories, thoughts and perceptions that determine the decisions of purchase and consumption, and that most of the times the client does not know ".

These ideas, coming from Neuromarketing, are just a sample of how far apart human beings are from full rationality in consumer decision-making, and as a consequence of that, also from the economic-maximizing models of functions. The creative question of Neuroeconomics is going to be given by the way in which it incorporates the "non-rational" variables into the models, which allow modeling "more human" consumers. The challenge is great.

And to mention one more example of the potential contributions of Neuroeconomics to traditional theory, let's take the case of Game Theory, very fashionable in recent times. In a paper written by the neuroeconomists Camerer, Loewenstein and Prelec[8], it is argued that economic theory has assumed (without implying an interest in Neuroscience) that agents possess a ToM module (Theory of Mind), and that they can "to mentalize" (deduct from the actions of other agents, and quite correctly, what their preferences and beliefs are). However, since the modern advances in Neuroscience, there is accumulated evidence that "mentalizing" is a specialized skill and modularized in specific brain regions, and that this ability effectively exists, but in varying degrees of person to person, while game's theory generalizes for all type of economic actor.

Game theory is based on the assumption that people are capable of predicting the actions of others. The most fundamental concepts in that field - Nash equilibrium, late induction, and iterated elimination of dominated strategies - are based on this assumption. These concepts require that people be able to see the game from the perspectives of other players, for example, that they understand the motives and beliefs of others. However, traditional economists (unlike neuroeconomists) know little or nothing about what allows people to "put themselves in the shoes of others" and about how this ability interacts with their own preferences and beliefs. In fact, experimental evidence suggests that many people do not obey the traditional concepts of game theory and often behave as if they - counter-objectively - believe that others are going to play with dominant strategies.

In this way, today Social Neuroscience and particularly Neuroeconomics provide new ideas about the neural mechanism that underlies our ability to represent intentions of others, beliefs, and desires, and also about the ability to share the feelings of others, called "empathy"; it is then from these new approaches where game's theory should rethink their assumptions.

At this point, we believe the purpose of this work is clear: to illustrate some of the main advances that Cognitive Neuroscience have been showing towards the decision-making process - mainly what has been discovered about our emotional brain (limbic system) and its complex interaction with our most rational areas (prefrontal cortex) - and, what is even more important, also illustrate the enormous possibilities that are opening up today in Economics to find an answer to many of the anomalies existing in the traditional theory, giving richness to the debate on possible changes in the dominant research program, although this hypothesis may seem too ambitious for the current achievements of Neuroeconomics, although it does not take away future possibilities.

THE HUMAN BRAIN

Currently, the continuous advances in Neuroscience allow us to know which brain centers are activated during most of the episodes of our daily life. The different brain structures that we humans have allow us to accept or reject the different alternative courses of action that are presented to us at each moment, analyzing their convenience or not, but in a broad sense (permanent interaction between the deliberative system and intuitive system), and not under the simple hyper-rational cost-benefit calculation of the Neoclassical Economics, which considers the selfish human being, with unlimited will and unlimited analysis power, which is quite far from reality.

This chapter is responsible for making a brief introduction about the anatomy and functioning of the nervous system of human beings and about the main techniques available today to approach their study (neuroimaging, transcranial magnetic stimulation, among the main ones), these last instruments today of very high utility for advances in Neuroeconomics, although still perfectible.

To introduce ourselves in the subject, and following the very complete introduction of Alfredo Navarro[9], the first thing we must know is that the human brain is made up of approximately one hundred billion cells -neurons- connected in a very complex way, formed by a body from which two types of extensions emerge: the axon and the dendrites. The axon is a filiform prolongation that can reach great distances, whose end dilates forming the synaptic ending, which adheres to the dendritic spines of neighboring neurons. The dendrites are several small and short extensions that have tiny protuberances called dendritic spines.

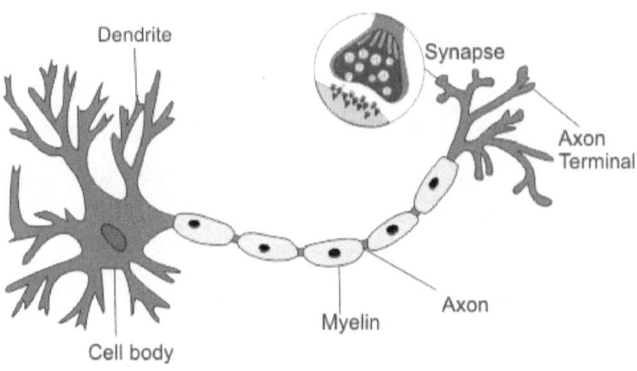

Neurons are surrounded by cells of the glia, which serve as support, contribute to the arrival of blood flow, coat the myelin axons, phagocytosis the remains of neurons that are destroyed and transmit the information by means of electrical impulses by the axon -presynaptic- to the dendrite of the postsynaptic neuron. The electrical impulse passes from one neuron to another through the synapse, with the participation of chemical substances, the neurotransmitters, released in the synaptic endings of the axon. There are many neurotransmitters with different specific functions in the neuronal circuit.

The endings of axons have been called biological transducers, because they convert electric energy into chemical energy. This involves the synthesis of neurotransmitters, their storage in synaptic buttons and their release produced by nerve impulses in the synaptic junction, acting also as receptors in the membrane of the post-synaptic neuron. Once the function is completed, the neurotransmitters are reacquired by the neuron that secreted them. There is a large amount of neurotransmitters: dopamine, noradrenaline, acetylcholine, etc., whose secretion is determined by the function of the different brain sectors. For example, dopaminergic neurons, which release dopamine at the terminal pole of the axon, project to many regions of the brain, committed to goal-directed behavior and motivations, including the striatum, the nucleus accumbens, and the pre-frontal cortex, participating in the emotional activity and in the act of selection. It is supposed that the release of dopamine regulates the plasticity of the neurons that produce decision actions, such as those of the prefrontal cortex.

Neurotransmitter molecules bind to specialized sites of the postsynaptic neuron. The sites are complex protein molecules located in the neuronal membrane, which expand and change their shape when they bind to the ligand (in this case, a neurotransmitter). This change in shape allows the entry of positive ions that depolarizes the postsynaptic membrane by exciting the cell. The communication between the neurons is reached when the neurotransmitter released from the presynaptic neuron affects the postsynaptic neuron by exciting or inhibiting it. Many thousands of postsynaptic sites in the dendrites of a neuron can respond with depolarization or hyperpolarization for a few milliseconds.

1. **The Nervous System**

The nervous system is constituted by the nervous tissue of the organism and the associated support elements. From a structural or anatomical point of view, the nervous system is divided into two; the Central Nervous System (CNS) and the Peripheral Nervous System (SNP). The CNS is made up of the brain and the spinal cord, while the SNP includes specialized nerves, ganglia and receptors.

On the other hand, from the functional point of view, the nervous system is divided into the Somatic or Voluntary Nervous System and the Autonomic Nervous System (ANS), involuntary or visceral. The somatic system is the part of the nervous system that responds or relates the organism to the external environment, whereas the autonomous system is in relation to the organic internal environment, performing internal regulation and adaptation functions. This system in turn includes the sympathetic nervous system (composed of thoracic and lumbar nerves) and the parasympathetic nervous system (constituted by cranial and sacral nerves). The sympathetic and parasympathetic sectors of the autonomic nervous system are functionally antagonistic. Both the Somatic Nervous System and the Autonomous System are interrelated and cooperate with each other, they do not act independently.

The function of the nervous system is to receive the stimuli that come from both the external and internal environment of the organism, organize this information and cause the appropriate response to occur.

The stimuli coming from the external environment are received by the receptors located in the skin, destined to capture general sensations such as smell, touch, pressure and temperature, and by receptors that capture special sensations such as taste, sight, smell, heard, position and movement. The signals (or impulses) that reach the peripheral nervous system, are transmitted from these receptors to the central nervous system, where the information is recorded and processed conveniently. Once registered and processed, the signals are sent from the central nervous system to the different organs in order to provide the appropriate answers.

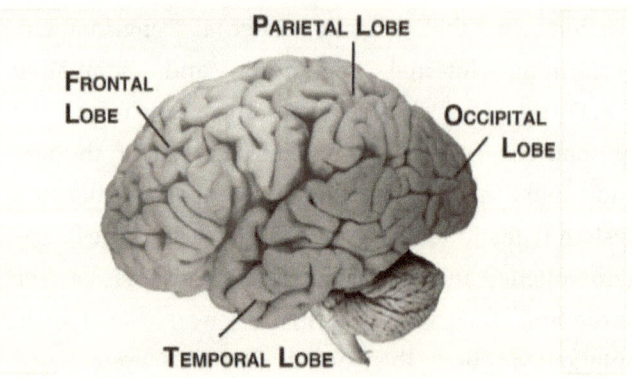

The spinal cord is responsible for carrying the signals (nerve impulses or information) from the different regions of the body to the brain and brain to the different segments of the body, it is also responsible for controlling the reflex activities.

The brain is the body responsible for controlling thought, memory, emotions, touch, sight, appetite and all the processes that regulate our body. It is divided into brain, diencephalon, brainstem and cerebellum:

Brain:

- Processes sensory information, controls and coordinates movement, behavior and may come to give priority to homeostatic bodily functions, such as heartbeat, blood pressure, fluid balance and body temperature; although, the region in charge of carrying out the automatic process is the medulla oblongata.
- In humans it has an approximate surface of 2 m², and it fits in the skull because it is folded in a very peculiar way.
- It is the only conscious structure of the brain, that is, the one that deals with voluntary functions.
- In its outermost layer, the cortex, the sensory reports are analyzed, the data are processed and the appropriate voluntary motor orders are elaborated for each case.
- Is responsible for higher functions specially developed in the human being, such as language, learning, creativity, will, memory, thinking and interpretation of sensations and emotions.
- It is the only organ completely protected by a bony vault and lodged in the cranial cavity.

- It consists of two hemispheres, the right and the left, both divided by the longitudinal fissure.

Diencephalon: it is composed of:

- Corpuscular Body: Connection between the two cerebral hemispheres.

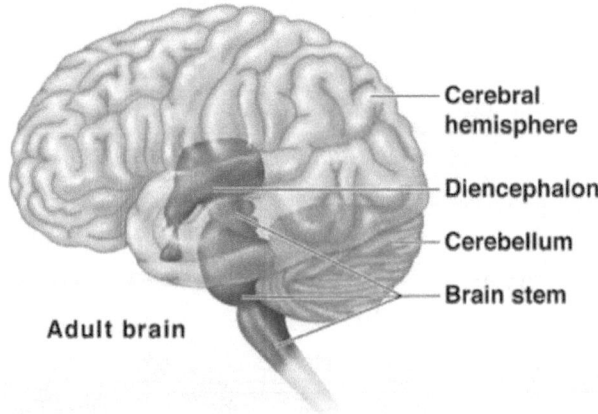

Adult brain

- Thalamus: It is a sensory relay station between several body areas and the cerebral cortex. It acts, therefore, as a filter of sensitive reports and only passes those that matter. This function is very relevant, since the brain could not process all the stimuli. We can pay attention only to what we are interested in at each moment or that requires a quick response because it constitutes a threat or a danger, therefore, the thalamus intervenes in the warning and awakening mechanisms.
- Hypothalamus: The hypothalamus is one of the busiest parts of the brain, and is mainly

related to homeostasis. It is responsible for the regulation of body temperature, balance, sleep cycle, appetite and sexual arousal. Controls involuntary functions, such as thirst, response to pain, levels of pleasure, anger, etc. It also regulates the functioning of the sympathetic and parasympathetic nervous systems, which means that it regulates things like pulse, blood pressure, respiration, and physiological activation in response to emotional circumstances (it controls the secretion of some neurons by the pituitary gland).

Brain stem: it is formed by:

- Mesencephalon: it is divided into two parts that contain different structures, in its dorsal region are the colliculi (rostral and caudal) which are related to visual and auditory function respectively. In its ventral region we can see the peduncles where we find the real origin of two cranial nerves.
- Protuberance: Consists of intertwined transverse and longitudinal white nerve fibers that form a complex network attached to the cerebellum. This intricate system of fibers connects the medulla oblongata with the cerebral hemispheres and contains many of the control areas for the movements of the eyes and face.
- Spinal bulb: is actually an extension of the spinal cord. The impulses between the spinal cord and the brain are conducted through the

medulla oblongata by major nerve fiber pathways, both ascending and descending. It is the part of the brain that controls many vital functions, such as heartbeat, breathing, swallowing and dilation and contraction of blood vessels. It is, therefore, the control center of all these involuntary processes related to the functioning of the body. The bulb also controls numerous vegetative protective reflexes, such as coughing, vomiting, hiccups and sneezing.

Cerebellum:

It is one of the parts that deals with functions that we perform unconsciously, but they are essential for life. It is responsible for maintaining balance and coordinating voluntary movements. It receives information about the situation of the skeletal muscles, as well as the orders they receive from other structures of the nervous system.

That is, he knows the state of the muscle, the tendons and the joints and the effort that is going to be asked, and can therefore make the necessary adjustments so that the corporal movements are smooth and precise. In addition, he participates in the control of body posture and receives information from the eyes and ears.

2. **The Triune Brain**

The theory of the "triune brain" arises from the results of the research of Roger Sperry and Paul MacLean, mainly during the decade of the '80s. The neurophysiologist Paul MacLean developed a model of the brain structure of the human being, known as the "triune brain", according to which the human brain is made up of three chemically and physically different structures:

- The reptilian system (instinctive) that is related to patterns of behavior, sense of belonging and territoriality, as well as the system of beliefs and values that is received from the first formation (the crocodile that we carry inside).

- The limbic brain system, also called "emotional brain", associated with our ability to feel and desire (all mammals share this brain system).

- The neocortical system, formed by the left hemisphere and the right hemisphere, also called "rational brain" or thinking brain, the most distinctively "human" part.

These three parts, anatomically and functionally well differentiated and with a different physical and chemical structure, are superimposed on a perfect representation of the ascending evolution of life. The three levels conform a whole, are interrelated and in turn are capable of operating independently. According to Mac Lean, each of them has its own functions.

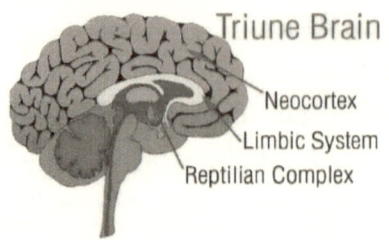

Reptilian System

According to Mac Lean, it is the most "old" part evolutionarily speaking. It is so named because it is a brain similar in structure and function to that currently presented by reptiles.

It is composed of the cerebellum, responsible for the modulation of muscle movement and postural balance, the spinal cord, which manages important functions of the body, such as the cardiovascular system and breathing; and the basal ganglia, involved in the control of movement and other routine actions.

It would become the basic brain, the so-called intelligence of the routines, customs, habits and behavior patterns of the human being. This part of the brain regulates the instincts essential for the survival of the species

This brain level bases its reactions on the known and is not prone to any type of innovation. It is oriented towards action and learns by repetition. It has little capacity to adapt to changes. Their behaviors, in most cases, are unconscious and automatic. People act from this structure in response to their vital needs.

Limbic System

It is a complex set of structures that are above and around the thalamus, is the portion of the brain located immediately below the cerebral cortex. It includes the hypothalamus, the hippocampus, the amygdala, the thalamus, the olfactory bulbs and the septal region.

These structures are found in all mammals and are the seat of affectivity. In this way, in the limbic system the different emotions (sorrows, anguish, intense joys, fear, aggression, etc.) are processed, and it is a key area for Neuroeconomics, due to its great influence in the effective decision making of the people, that often do not coincide with those hypothesized by traditional economics manuals.

The limbic system is composed of several nuclei with specific activity:

- The accumbens, involved in the process of gratification -food, monetary gains, anticipation of gratifications-, key nucleus in the conversion of motivation into action-. It is thought that this nucleus has an important role in reward, laughter, pleasure, addiction and fear; Knutson and others[10] explain that images of brains taken with functional magnetic resonance imaging (fMRI) during certain experiments showed a spontaneous increase in activation of the nucleus accumbens of the brain just before running a financial risk in the game.
- The lateral amygdala: affection and solidarity;

- The amygdala media: aggressiveness. And if the amygdala is removed (not to be confused with the tonsil of the throat), the animals become very docile and do not respond to things that would have caused them anger before. Also when they are removed, animals also become indifferent to stimuli that might otherwise have caused them fear and even sexual responses, therefore there are more things in it than just anger. Patients with the injured amygdala are no longer able to distinguish the expression of a face or if a person is happy or sad;
- The insula: displeasure due to inequality of unfair treatment, very active when faced with an offer considered unfair or excessive price;
- The septum: feeling of pleasure, especially sexual;
- The hippocampus: plays an important role in converting short-term memory into long-term memory. If the hippocampus is damaged, a person cannot build new memories, and lives in a strange place where everything he experiences simply fades away, keeping older memories intact before damage. This unfortunate situation is pretty well described in the wonderful movie Memento;
- The cingular gyrus related to free will;
- The hypothalamus with visceral and hormonal functioning;
- The sensory thalamus that performs the processing of external stimuli.

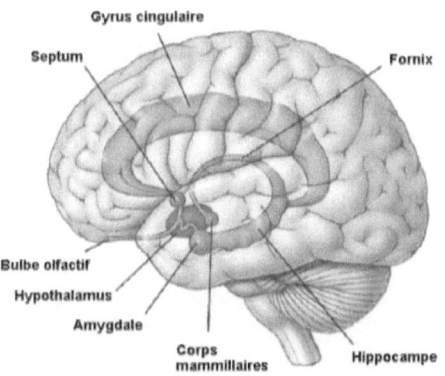

The limbic system is oriented towards emotion and learns by association, which is why it is fundamental for the development of memory. When for example we feel a familiar smell and transport ourselves to a situation of the past, we are using the limbic system. Researchers J. F. Fulton and D. F. Jacobson of Yale University also provided evidence that learning ability and memory require an intact amygdala: they put chimpanzees in front of two bowls of food. In one of them there was an appetizing mouthful, the other was empty. Then they covered the bowls. After a few seconds the animals were allowed to take one of the closed containers. The healthy animals took without hesitation the bowl that contained the appetizing bite, while the chimpanzees with the injured amygdala chose at random; the appetizing morsel had not aroused in them any excitement in the amygdala, and that is why they did not remember it either.

Neocortex

The cerebral cortex is not only the most accessible area of the brain: it is also the most distinctively human. Most of our thinking or planning, and language, imagination, creativity and capacity for abstraction, comes from this brain region. Thus, the neocortex enables us to solve algebra equations, to learn a foreign language, to study anything, besides other things.

The neocortex is the place where the superior cerebral functions are carried out. It is the center for the generation and resolution of problems, analysis and synthesis of information, the use of analogical reasoning and critical and creative thinking (rational brain).

Sperry, Gazzaniga and Bogen[11], considered the division of the cerebral cortex into two hemispheres (left and right) with specific functions. Although the structure of the cerebral hemispheres is symmetrical (with the lobes that emerge from the brain stem and with sensory and motor zones in both), certain intellectual functions are performed by a single hemisphere. The neurologist Roger Sperry, discovered that both sides of the brain are different and that they tend to divide the main intellectual functions.

The dominant hemisphere of a person usually deals with language and logical operations, while the other hemisphere controls emotions and artistic and spatial abilities. In almost all right-handed people and in many left-handed people, the dominant hemisphere is the left hemisphere.

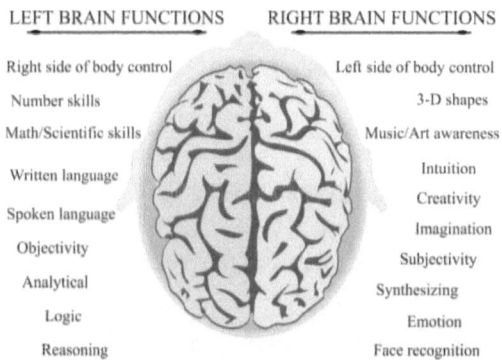

LEFT BRAIN FUNCTIONS	RIGHT BRAIN FUNCTIONS
Right side of body control	Left side of body control
Number skills	3-D shapes
Math/Scientific skills	Music/Art awareness
Written language	Intuition
Spoken language	Creativity
Objectivity	Imagination
Analytical	Subjectivity
Logic	Synthesizing
Reasoning	Emotion
	Face recognition

The individuals in which the right predominates are more spontaneous, disorderly, charlatans and no notion of time. They learn without a plan and love teamwork. Instead, those who use the left most are calm, orderly, organized, with a good memory and prefer individual work.

The left hemisphere is associated with processes of logical reasoning, functions of analysis-synthesis and decomposition of a whole in its parts, logic, cause and effect, hypothetical reasoning, precision and accuracy. While in the right hemisphere, there are associative, imaginative and creative processes, associated with the possibility of seeing globalities and establishing spatial relationships, synthesis and integration.

Both hemispheres are connected through millions of nerve fibers by a structure called the corpus callosum, which allows reciprocal interaction between them.

In something that is very important for Neuroeconomics, we must not lose sight of the fact that the cortex "does not decide alone" and that the "three brains" interact with each other. Following McLean's example, it is as if a crocodile, a horse and a human being coexisted in our heads and that "decisions" were made by the three (although not always in common agreement).

For example, the waking state of the cerebral cortex depends on the impulses it receives from the thalamus (which is part of the limbic system, that is, the horse). So if something awakens our interest and enthusiasm, we quickly pay attention to it; while if something bores us, the thalamus stops sending impulses to the cortex and we feel drowsy. That is to say, it will normally be the inner horse that will decide what is interesting and what is not.

"We see only what we know", is attributed to the great Goethe. Through this analysis of the structure of the brain we begin to understand that objectivity depends on an adequate management of our cognitive system. Because if our "inner horse" does not want to see something, it will simply make the cerebral cortex ignore it.

Therefore to access a truly objective vision of reality it is necessary to have a state of alert, which activates the ability to "realize" from the neocortex, with sufficient motivation, to save the resistances of the limbic system, which associates each stimulation with subliminal emotional memory of all our experience and self-control, to overcome the barrier of the instinctive impulse that leads us to act without having processed reality.

Actually the empowerment of the human mind tends to balance, the rational does not replace the emotional, but complements it and tends to influence the development of it. Human behavior is the result of the permanent interaction between two systems: the Deliberative System (System 2) that values options with a broad perspective based on an objective and an Affective System (System 1) that contains emotional and motivating impulses.

Deliberative behavior develops primarily in the prefrontal cortex and emotional behavior develops in the limbic system, especially the insula and amygdala. But as we pointed out earlier, both systems interact. There are nervous connections between the limbic system and the prefrontal cortex, through which one influences the other. For example, if the affective system informs the sensation of hunger in the deliberative system, it stimulates the decision to eat. Depending on the relative influence of the two systems, in certain circumstances, the same person can be led to form different before similar situations.

It is also interesting to distinguish, again following Alfredo Navarro[12], a prominent Argentine economist, between automatic processes and controlled processes. The brain implements most of the time automatic processes, which are performed without mental effort and does not involve cognitive activity. For daily functioning, behavior is conditioned by emotional tone systems, which allow to regulate properly the usual deliberative system. Consequently, human behavior is a result of the interaction of controlled and automatic processes and affective and cognitive systems. The controlled processes are activated when a person is faced with a problem, which supposes a subjective feeling of effort, as it is to remember the necessary steps to solve it (evaluate the purchase of a house or solve a mathematical equation).

Automatic processes do not access consciousness and occur almost effortlessly, facilitate quick responses and in certain types of tasks, such as visual identification, for example, give the brain a remarkable power. Not being accessible to the conscience, the automatic processes have little introspective penetration, since the individual usually does not know why he proceeded in the way he did.

The automatic cognitive processes are concentrated in the occipital, parietal and temporal regions of the brain. The amygdala is a region of important automatic affective responses. The controlled processes operate primarily in the orbital and prefrontal regions of the brain. Recall that the prefrontal cortex is considered the executive region par excellence.

Automatic, affective or cognitive processes are latent all the time, even during sleep. Controlled processes occur in special circumstances in the face of unexpected events. Man's behavior then takes place between reasons and passions (cognitive and affective processes). Affective processes induce the attitude to act or stop doing it. Cognitive processes analyze if something is true or false, but to influence behavior must operate through the affective system. However, in many circumstances knowledge is able to control emotion. Automatic processes, not accessible to consciousness, are developed in parallel.

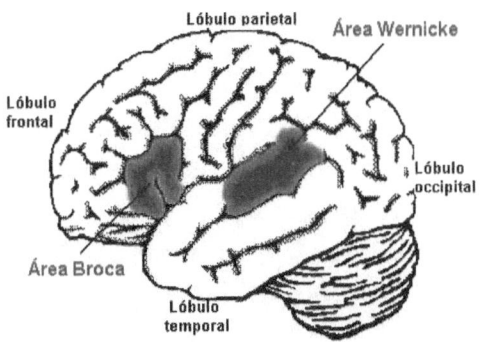

If the brain must perform two actions simultaneously, look for a balance that reconciles the final result. They also have specialization, since different parts of the brain have different functional structures and properties, operating in coordination as functionally specialized systems, for example the areas of Broca and Wernicke for the expression and understanding of language, the amygdala for the sense of smell, the fear and anger.

They also have coordination, that is to say, that in order to carry out a task correctly, they use the specialized systems and often resort to the prefrontal area - control region of the processes - until, over time, they perfect the activity by concentrating it in specialized areas in the process in question. Due to the limitations of controlled processes, the brain permanently automates the processing of tasks. If the use of specialized systems is repeated, anatomical changes in the corresponding area may occur after some time.

Emotion plays a dominant role in behavior. Many people can express their liking or disgust for something more quickly than identifying that something. The distinction between affective and cognitive processes, between automatic and controlled processes is useful to try to understand the wonderful functioning of the brain, but it is good to understand that behavior in all circumstances and judgments, is always the result of the interaction of all these processes.

The importance of affectivity in decision making becomes clear when we feel intimately what we know we are doing. The mechanism of interaction between affective and cognitive systems in the control of behavior is still quite unknown. Human behavior is then the result of the interaction of two systems: the deliberative system that values options with a broad perspective based on an objective and an affective system that contains emotional and motivating impulses.

Deliberative behavior develops primarily in the prefrontal cortex and emotional behavior develops in the limbic system, especially the amygdala and the insula. But as we pointed out earlier, both systems interact. There are nervous connections between the limbic system and the prefrontal cortex, through which one influences the other. For example, if the emotional-affective system informs the feeling of hunger in the deliberative system, it stimulates the decision to eat.

But also the deliberative system can influence the affective system trying to control the motivations of it. However, the influence of the emotional system on the deliberative is powerful, while the control of the conscience over the emotions is weak. The attempts of the deliberative system to overcome emotional impulses need a cognitive effort, or what we usually call willpower. Depending on the relative influence of the two systems, in certain circumstances, the same person may behave differently in similar situations.

3. Brain Areas of Interest for Neuroeconomics

Prefrontal cortex: ventromedial orbit-frontal

Integrates the somatic / emotional states with the present information of the decision making, including the learning in previous situations and allows to evaluate the long-term consequences of the choice made.

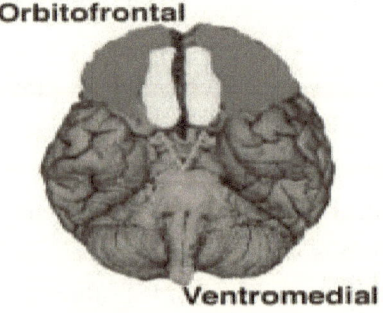

Dorsolateral prefrontal cortex

This area plays an important role in executive functioning (including working memory) and attention. It stands out for its importance in integrating sensory data from different sources of information and planning behavior. It is the area "par excellence" of the self-control of the "emotional limbic horse". Yoga and meditation help to enhance the use of this region.

Dorsolateral

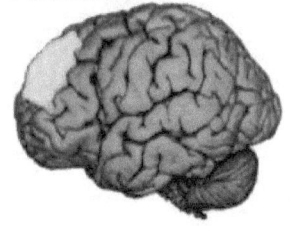

Amygdala

Intervenes in detecting signals anticipating danger or threat. In this way, stimuli are associated with their consequences, if they are negative, and this information is used to make decisions in similar situations. It processes emotional content in disadvantageous decisions and intervenes in the learning of those decisions.

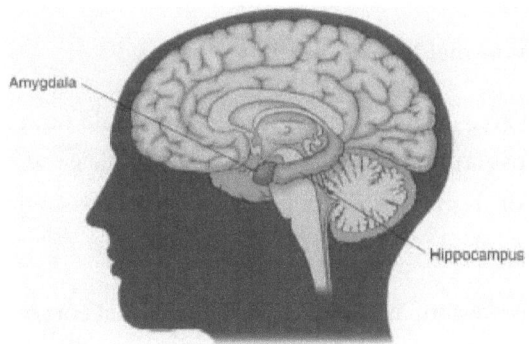

Anterior cingulate cortex

It is associated with the anticipation of the consequences of an election and is activated in situations that require resolving conflicts between options. Intervenes in the monitoring of one's behavior, evaluating and inhibiting inappropriate responses. Together with the orbitofrontal, it has greater activation in tasks of risk or uncertainty.

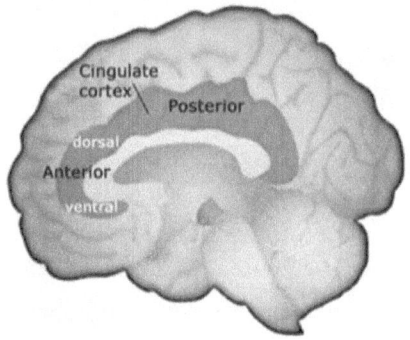

The anterior cingulate cortex monitors the process and inhibits responses, especially in situations of uncertainty.

In summary:

In the decision-making process, it intervenes:

⊚ An impulsive system, driven by the amygdala (and also the insula): indicates pleasure or displeasure, attraction or repulsion, depending on the possible options.

⊚ A reflexive system, managed by the prefrontal cortex (especially dorsolateral): detects the future consequences set in motion by those same options.

4. Methods to Study the Brain

Scientific technologies are not just tools used by scientists to explore areas of interest. The new tools also define new scientific fields and erase old limits.

The telescope created astronomy by elevating science from pure cosmological speculation. The microscope made similar advances possible in biology. The same is true in Economics. Its limits have been constantly changing by tools such as mathematical, econometric, and simulation methods. Also, the current surge of interest in neurology by psychologists emerged largely thanks to new methods available to study the human brain, and such methods can productively blur the limits of economics and psychology. This section reviews some of these methods.

Brain Imaging

The brain scan is currently (along with the relatively new Transcranial Magnetic Stimulation) the most popular neuroscientific tool. Most brain imaging projections involve an analysis of what happens in people while performing different tasks-tasks of "control" and "experimental" tasks. The difference between the images taken while the subject is performing the two tasks provides an image of the regions of the brain that are activated depending on the task.

There are three basic methods of brain scanning. The oldest is the electroencephalogram (EEG), which uses electrodes attached to the scalp to measure electrical activity related to stimuli or behavioral responses.

Secondly, we have Positron Emission Tomography (PET), which is an old scanning technique (given the accelerated and changing terms of neurology), but which is still useful. The PET method measures the blood flow in the brain, which is a Proxy of neurological activity, since the neurological activity in a region leads to an increased flow of blood in it.

The most modern, and currently the most popular, method is the Functional Magnetic Resonance Imaging (fMRI), which tracks the blood flow of the brain using changes in magnetic characteristics due to the oxygenation of the blood (the BOLD signal"). Direct simultaneous recording of neurological processing and fMRI responses confirm that the blood signal reflects inputs of neurons and their processing.

WHAT IS FMRI?

- **BRAIN IMAGING METHOD** for obtaining **3D** images related to **activity in the brain**.

- fMRI measures the ratio of oxygenated haemoglobin to deoxygenated haemoglobin in the blood, at various locations in the brain.

- Performs brain activation studies by measuring **BRAIN-OXYGEN-LEVEL DEPENDENT (BOLD)** signal.

Additionally, we can include a fourth method within what is brain scanning, the Magnetic Brain Encephalogram Method (MEG), which measures the magnetic fields generated by the different electrical activities of the brain with a unit of time of one millisecond, but which is only used to study superficial regions of the brain, and therefore is a method of great potential to investigate processes of neuronal physiology that occur faster in the unit time and in smaller brain volumes.

Although fMRI is increasingly becoming the method of choice, each of the descriptions here has pros and cons. For example, the EEG has an excellent temporal resolution (of the order of one millisecond) and is the only one of those used with humans that directly monitors neurological activity, for example, blood flows. However, the spatial resolution is poor and can only measure activity in the outer part of the brain, although with an increase in the number of electrodes. Interpolation methods, and the combined use of EEG and fMRI to measure brain-external signals and brain-internal signals at the same time, are techniques that have been used a lot.

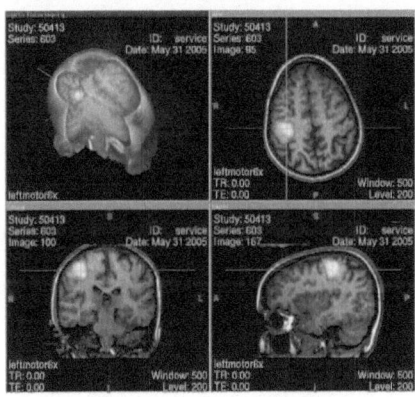

For Economics, an important advantage of the EEG is that it is relatively non-invasive and easy to transport. Portability allows non-invasive measurements of people while they are performing their daily tasks.

Comparing, PET and fMRI methods provide better spatial resolution than the EEG method, but a poorer temporal resolution, ranging from a few seconds (fMRI) to one minute (PET). In short, brain imaging still provides only a crude picture of brain activity. Neurological processes occur on a scale of 0.1 millimeters in 100 milliseconds (milliseconds), but the spatial and temporal resolution of a typical scanner is only 3 millimeters and a few seconds. It is to be expected that with the advance of neuroimaging technology, brain scanning will become increasingly deep and fast, and therefore being increasingly useful to Applied Neurosciences, including Neuroeconomics.

The Diffusion Tensor (DTI)

The image projection by Diffusion Tensor (DTI) has allowed obtaining detailed images of the white matter fibers that connect the different brain regions. The DTI method is a variant of fMRI, which allows us to explore the way in which the rapid flow of water moves in the axon, revealing the trajectory of the nervous stimulus that connects one neuronal region with another. These images are used to understand the functioning of neuronal circuits and are an important complement for fMRI, which only shows activity in isolated brain centers. The brain, as we have seen, is composed of different anatomical regions, which are not autonomous, but constitute a cohesive and integrated system organized in a mysterious pathway, so it is impossible to understand how the brain works, studying only one particular region in time.

Transcranial Magnetic Stimulation (TMS)

A relatively new method called Transcranial Magnetic Stimulation (TMS) uses magnetic pulses to temporarily interrupt brain function in specific regions. The differences in cognitive and behavioral functioning that result from such interruptions provide clues as to which regions control the various functions. The theoretical advantage of TMS over brain imaging (fMRI for example) is that TMS leads to causal inferences about the functioning of the brain rather than the purely associative evidence provided by the techniques of imaging. Unfortunately, the use of TMS is currently limited to the cortex (for example it is particularly useful for studying visual processes in the occipital lobe, in the back of the head).

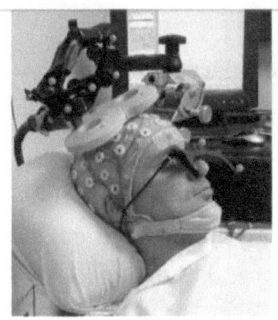

From the point of view of Neuroeconomics, Neuromanagement and other branches that study economic decision-making, TMS is one of the techniques that have better future, since, combined with fMRI, it will allow deciphering chains of causality of the functioning of the human brain, both in the aspects of economic valuation (the total or marginal utility that we give to each possible alternative) and also of decision (when it is finished choosing the most useful alternative).

Measurement of the Solo-Neuron

Even the most subtle techniques of brain imaging measure only activity of "circuits" consisting of thousands of neurons. The measurement on a single neuron, tiny electrodes that are inserted in the brain, has produced striking results, relevant to economics. One limitation of this technique is that, since the insertion of the wires damages the neurons, it is largely restricted to the animals. Studying animals is informative about human beings since many brain structures and functions of non-human mammals are similar to those of human beings (reptilian brain, limbic system).

As the measure of neuron alone is largely restricted to non-human animals, this technique has a small coverage of the basic emotional and motivational processes, which are shared in humans and non-humans, but it does not say anything about higher level processes, such as language and knowledge. That is its great limitation.

Psychopathologies and brain damage in humans

Chronic mental illness (schizophrenia), developmental disorders (autism), degenerative diseases of the nervous system, accidents and strokes that damage localized regions of the brain help to understand how the brain works[13]. When patients with known damage in an area X perform a certain task worse than "normal" patients, but do others equally well, one can deduce the certain function that fulfills area X. Patients who have undergone neurosurgical procedures such as lobotomy (used in the past to treat depression) or radical brain bisection (an extreme remedy for epilepsy, now rarely used) have provided valuable data to Neurosciences.

Psychophysical Measure (Psychophysical Measurement)

An old and simple technique is the measurement of psychophysiological indicators such as heart rate, blood pressure, the galvanic skin response (for example, sweating on the palms), and dilation of the pupils (the pupils dilate in response to the excitement, for example a monetary reward). These measures are easy, very unobstructive and quick. The disadvantage is that these measurements can fluctuate for many reasons (for example body movement) and also various combinations of emotions lead to similar psychophysiological responses. These measures are often useful in combination with other techniques or in patients with lesions that are likely to have very diverse physiological reactions (for example psychopaths do not show normal reactions of fear before a possible monetary loss). The facial muscles can also be used to measure, joining the small electrodes to the smiling muscles and the frowning muscles (between the eyebrows).

5. Applications to Economics

The Ultimatum Game

In game theory, decisions are made keeping in mind what the other player is going to do once one has chosen, therefore the forecast of what the other person will do influences what one decides.

Within strategic decisions, the ultimatum game has been one of the pioneering exercises in neuroeconomic experimentation. Let's briefly see what happens in the brain of the participants while the simulation is taking place.

In this version, one of the most widespread of the ultimatum game[14], there are 2 players (A and B). 100 A is given to player A and he is asked to share them with player B, whose identity is ignored. A must make an offer. The rules of the game and the bet are known by both and establish that player B can accept the offer and receive what he has accepted, or can refuse and both players receive nothing. The question is how much A will offer, so as not to run out of anything.

The results of this experiment show that more than 50% of people are willing to offer half the sum. What is the reason for this to happen if, rationally speaking, any person is willing to have something before anything, in this way an offer of a single weight should rationally be accepted. The data say, however, that offers of 20% of the amount, or lower, have more than 20% chance of being rejected. This would lead us to think that the decision is not so rational and that there is an emotional component (indignation before an offer that is considered unfair) that intervenes in the decision making process.

What happens in the brain of player B?

By means of functional magnetic resonance it has been possible to show that 3 regions are activated:

• The anterior part of the insula responsible for the automatic control of visceral sensations and the corresponding automatic responses. The insula is found in the place where the brain transforms physical reactions into feelings, such as feeling anxious when the heart accelerates. The insula is a complex center of connection and interoperability between the limbic system and the neocortex. It is linked to gustatory and olfactory elaboration and the evaluation and representation of negative emotional states such as anger and disgust (both physical and moral, such as the ultimatum game). It is very likely that while this area is activated player B will be considered offended and, disgusted by the lack of loyalty and reject the offer.

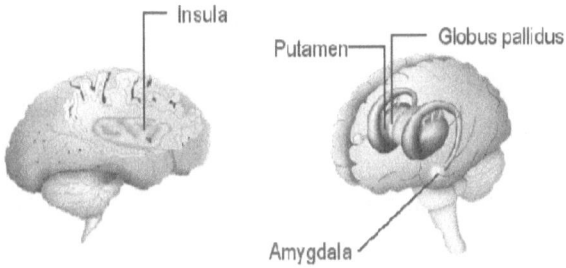

• The dorsolateral area of the prefrontal cortex that is found in the anterior portions of the frontal lobe of the neocortex is also activated. This region, as explained above, is dedicated to cognitive (rational) control, to make us pursue the objectives we have set for ourselves and to maintain working memory. It could be said that the frontal lobe is a center of rationality, which tends towards the maximization of utility, speaking in microeconomic language. Therefore, if this area is activated more than the insula, player B will be tempted to accept the offer whatever it is (a weight is better than none).

• The third area is the anterior cingulate cortex. This is activated when individuals have to make important decisions among several options and when they are about to make a mistake. It is considered that the anterior cingulate cortex develops the revealing role of cognitive conflicts and detector of conflicts and discrepancies (as for example internal contradictions between cognitive motivations and emotional motivations). In recent years, the anterior cingulate cortex of the brain has been well studied because it plays an important role in brain processes of great complexity. Faced with an unfair offer almost certainly the anterior cingulate cortex of player B will be activated because it records a mental conflict (on the one hand the displeasure of accepting such a miserable offer - the use of their feelings - and the increase of their wealth however small it may be for the other - the use of reason -).

What happens when Player A is a computer and not a person?

Given an offer to player B very low (say less than 20% of the amount in play), the effect that occurs in your brain is less activation of the insula, caused by the fact that no intentions are attributed (fair or unfair) to the computer (it's just a machine). Therefore, the dorsolateral prefrontal cortex is activated leading to an acceptance of the offer, whatever this may be. And since no conflict occurs, the anterior cingulate cortex remains inactive (unlike what happened when Player A was a person).

Other Studies Applied to Economics

Continuing with simple examples, in order to understand what Neuroeconomics is about, let us take the study of Knutson and collaborators[15], made with the current technical procedures, during the purchase of a product, taking into account the factors that normally play in it, namely: the presentation of the product and the price and the purchase decision or not, and on the other hand the desire of the product, the price that the interested party is willing to pay and the possibility of not buying, we obtain the following results: the preference of the product active the nucleus accumbens -process of gratification-, the difference -in less- of price, activates the average prefrontal cortex-rational calculation, good business-, and if the decision is not to make the purchase, the insula is activated -the loss of money-.

Neural Predictors of Purchases

- Knutson, Rick, Wimmer, Prelec and Loewenstein, Neuron, 2007
  - Investigates how people process preference and price when buying
  - Decision to purchase
    - Tradeoff between pleasure of acquisition and pain of paying
    - Positive and negative anticipatory affect
  - Determine the distinct neural components of the purchase decision process in individuals

Then, the product vision and the purchase prediction activate the nucleus accumbens, but the anticipation of monetary loss -pain- activates the insula. The activation of the prefrontal cortex is greater the lower the price compared to what we were willing to spend. In all cases the studies show a higher concentration of blood and oxygen in the areas corresponding to the nuclei, which when activated stand out clearly in the image obtained. Remember that the gray matter constitutes 40% of the brain mass, which consumes 94% of the total oxygen of the brain due to the electrical pulses -potential action- that allow neurons to communicate with others.

Another example of the functioning of these neural circuits is given by Camerer, Loewenstein and Prelec[16]: what happens if a dinner plate is approached by a sushi plate? His eyes look at the sushi, and through the optic nerves the stimulus goes to the occipital visual cortex where forms, lines, etc. are reproduced.

From here the impulse goes to the inferior temporal visual cortex, which through a very complicated mechanism of stored memory of the representation of objects, makes it possible to recognize sushi. This image follows its course to the orbito-frontal cortex, which values the recognized object to the information the utility is added.

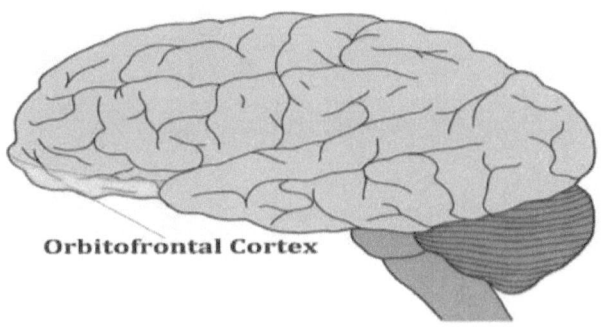
Orbitofrontal Cortex

But the evaluation depends on the personal story about the sushi - if previously produced discomfort the amygdala works, if there is appetite the hypothalamus is activated (sensitive to the sensation of hunger). If there is appetite and you like sushi, the motor cortex guides the arm to bring the food to the mouth. If there is information about the risk of eating raw fish, there are two alternatives: eating it, if socially there is no other remedy, or hiding it in the napkin when the host does not look. This thought involves anticipated feelings, memories stored in the hippocampus, involvement of the limbic system and planning in the prefrontal cortex."

So far a brief overview of the main aspects that are scientifically handled today around the brain, its operation and the techniques most used to scrutinize the human black box. In the next chapters, we leave a bit of the purely neuropsychological aspects to get fully into Neurosciences applied to Economics, its field research in decision making and its methodological implications (Epistemology).

RATIONALITY AND ECONOMIC THEORY

The assumption about the high rationality of economic agents has been key to the construction of modern economic theory, which began to take shape, as a separate science, approximately with the neoclassical (Jevons, Walras, etc.) during the nineteenth century. In terms of Lakatos, one of the most influential epistemologists of the twentieth century, all science has a hard core, which is very difficult to refute, to modify, and in which there are certain premises that nobody usually discusses, and all accept them as basal foundation from where the current models start. And the premise of rationality that prevailed in economics is that of the hyper-maximizing human being, always tending towards quasi-perfect cost-benefit evaluations as the basis of each economic decision; this is perhaps the fundamental assumption on which the neoclassicals built modern economic theory, and which is still valid today, beyond the numerous criticisms received over the past two centuries, with the School of Behavioral Economics and Neuroeconomics among the most recent critics.

Throughout this chapter we will try to walk the evolutionary path that has transited the concept of rationality in economic theory, emphasizing both the holders of the traditional premise (the vast majority of theorists) and its main critics for at least the last century, from JM Keynes to the Nobel prizes Simon and Kahneman, and from Hutchison to modern neuroeconomists like Glimcher, Camerer, Zak, etc., to name but a few of the most important critics. And to face the difficult task of analyzing the historical path that the concept of rationality has followed, we will take, as a framework for the analysis, mainly three works:

- The wonderful work of Mark Blaug, *The Positive Economy Methodology*, one of the highest authorities in Epistemology of Economics in recent decades[17].
- The historical division of economic schools made by the Argentine economist Alfredo Navarro in his very interesting work *Neuroeconomía y Metodología: Algunas Reflexiones Iniciales*[18].
- The brilliant analysis on economic schools of the Spanish economist Blanca Sanchez Robles, in *La Economía. Concepto y Método*[19].

1. The Classics

The first economists began their task when psychology still did not exist, which is why they acted in some way as psychologists. Hume's work[20] is largely devoted to analyzing human knowledge from a perspective that we would consider today as a field of psychology, and it is not precisely a simplified and monolithic vision that serves as a support for the neoclassical model, but rather, applying introspection, describes a much more complex and real human being.

In this line of thought is the work of Adam Smith "Theory of Moral Sentiments"[21], which is a detailed (if basic) analysis of human psychology. Following the Platonic distinction, Adam Smith differentiates two systems in the human being, one affective, linked to the passions and the most primitive feelings, and another superior, which controls, in the manner of an impartial spectator, the first:

When I strive to examine my own behavior, when I endeavor to pronounce judgments on it, either to approve it or to condemn it, it is evident that in such cases it is as if I were divided into two different persons, and that I, the examiner and the judge, I embody a man different from the other me, the person whose conduct is examined and judged. The first is the spectator ... The second is the agent, the person that I designate as myself, and from whose behavior I tried to form a feeling, as if it were a spectator's. The first is the judge, the second the person who is judged...

When we are about to act, the avidity of passion will rarely allow us to consider what we do with the dispassion of an intelligent person...

In the "Wealth of Nations", according to Nobel Prize winner Simon[22], *"the rationality that Smith describes is that of common sense every day. This follows from the idea that people have reasons to do what they do, and that this does not depend on an elaborate calculation of utility."*

But not all the outstanding classics thought the same way as Smith, at least not in regard to how to model human beings when trying to do economic theory. For example, let's take Stuart Mill and his concept of homo economicus[23]. The main ideas in this regard are the following: first, Mill recognizes that there is a part of human behavior where obtaining wealth is not the main objective. Now, there are other departments of human affairs where the acquisition of wealth is the main purpose; Economics deals with this second category, so that it abstracts from all human passions and motives except the desire for wealth and the aversion to work. The man thus described is a fictitious man, and Mill himself is aware that the economic sphere is only a part of human behavior. However, he recommends that economics proceed to abstract and work with this fictitious man, who seeks to obtain "the greatest possible amount of wealth with the minimum possible work and self-denial".

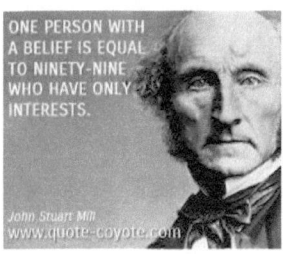

And in general, it is pertinent to note that along with Stuart Mill, two other classic theorists, also important at the time, such as Senior and Cairnes, coincide in the search for maximum wealth with the least possible effort as one of the driving principles of the man. The coincidence is not accidental, but responds to the influence in the England of s. XIX exercised the philosophical current of utilitarianism.

In this way, classical economists seem to have no unanimity about how human rationality should be taken when doing economics, on the one hand there were, among others, David Hume and Adam Smith, the latter called the "father of Economics", who introduced the principle of personal interest, but with the above-mentioned limitations (especially in his "Theory of the Moral Sentiments"), but on the other hand there were Mill, Senior, Cairnes, among others, closer to the utilitarian currents that were going to impact fully in the subsequent school, the neoclassical ones.

2. The First Neoclassicals

The considerable influence that utilitarianism exercised in the economic theory elaborated in the s. XIX, facilitated the assumption of rationality, understood as maximizing pleasure and minimize pain, gradually introduced into Economics to be described in detail by Stuart Mill (although, as we said, a classic author, not a neoclassical) in his characterization of the homo economicus.

Subsequently, already in what we know as "the neoclassical model", said hyper-maximizing homo economicus reached a more formalized approach thanks to the theory of marginal utility, associated with names such as Jevons, Edgeworth, Sidgwick, Wicksteed or Marshall (some calls early neoclassical, and others like Marshall second neoclassical). If the hypothesis of rationality is added the additional hypothesis of perfect information, one of the pillars of neoclassical economics is reached: the methodological individualism, where the agents are optimizing and identical to each other, because to act consists of calculating the alternative that maximizes satisfaction and, automatically, choose it.

In general, this "neoclassical model" is based on a theory of human behavior that has worked more or less satisfactorily. The basic idea is that economic agents act rationally and therefore optimize their utility in a predictable way when they consume, and produce efficiently, by combining production factors in the best possible way.

The principle of rationality can be considered from two different angles: the normative, which implies establishing what are the characteristics that a behavior must have to be classified as rational, and the descriptive, which analyzes the observed behavior to determine if it can be classified as rational. When is a behavior rational? When from a set X (x1, x2, x3, ..., xn), if we have preferred x1 to x2 and x2 to x3, we will always prefer x1 to x3, and when at the same time we seek to maximize our own interest. That is, with the neoclassical, economic theory chooses a very clear course towards supposing a human rationality far removed from the one initially assumed by Adam Smith and David Hume, which, as already mentioned, placed both eminently cognitive and emotional as determinants of economic decision making.

But as we said above, the "breeding ground" of the concept of homo economicus was already among the classics (rather, some classics, those that were already strongly utilitarian like J.S.Mill, not Adam Smith for example). Take then the case of Neville Keynes, another classic, who highlights how the use of the hyper-rationality assumption in the economic literature has been confusing and ambiguous.

While for Stuart Mill and Cairnes it is only a hypothetical and therefore fictitious simplification, for Senior, who maintains a position even closer than the others to that of utilitarianism, it is a postulate of more real content. Neville Keynes is rather in the tradition of Senior and, in a way, goes a step further by stating that the economic behavior that pursues self-interest dominates in reality the motives of altruism and benevolence. In short, for Stuart Mill the economist elaborates his theories as if man were selfish, while for

Neville Keynes and Senior the economist works knowing that man is selfish.

To close the topic of the first neoclassicals, we can highlight that it is with Jevons when important changes occur in the way of making economic theory: first, the focus of Macroeconomics is shifted to Microeconomics; secondly, the hedonistic principles - which already underlay the conceptions of Stuart Mill, Senior and Cairnes, etc. - are consolidated in a much more explicit way. -; and finally, the use of the mathematical method in the scientific development of our discipline is postulated. These ideas are present in some definitions of Economics - somewhat vague - that can be found in his writings; thus, he describes it as "a calculation of pleasure and pain" and as "a kind of mathematics that calculates the causes and effects of human activity".

But before continuing with the neoclassicals, let's understand the context. Jevons wrote sometime[24]:

"I hesitate to say that men will ever have the means of measuring directly the feelings of the human heart."

That is, from this sentence it is clear that Jevons and many of the other neoclassicals took the hyper-rational premise almost with resignation, because of the scientific impossibility of measuring the emotional. But luckily Jevons was wrong and the modern Neurosciences (early 21st century) can effectively measure the emotional at the time of making decisions - through neuroimaging techniques - and has discovered, among other things, the following[25]:

- *"According to scientists, the brain areas of rationality cannot function isolated from the areas of biological-emotional regulation. The two systems communicate and affect the behavior jointly, and consequently, the behavior of the people ".*
- *"Moreover, the emotional system (the oldest area of the brain) is the first force that acts on mental processes, therefore determines the direction of decisions."*
- *"The latest advances in Neuroscience have shown that consumer decision-making is not a rational process. That is, customers do not consciously examine the attributes of a product or service to acquire it. "*
- *"In most cases, the selection process is relatively automatic and derives from habits and other metaconscious forces, among which history,*

> *personality, neurophysiological characteristics and the physical and social context that surrounds us all gravitate".*

- *"The fragrance of a perfume, for example, can evoke different sensations. If the client associates it with painful experiences or with a person with whom he does not sympathize, it is very likely that he will not buy it, even when the price-quality-brand ratio is reasonable."*

We will return to these issues of applied neuroscience and its impact on traditional economic theory at the end of this chapter.

3. The Second Neoclassicals

In general, the second generation of neoclassical, basically is dedicated to deepening and refining the contributions of the first generation, that is, to build the concepts, graphics and mathematical deductions that even today are studied in undergraduate courses at universities around the world; but little added to the debate on the hypothesis of rationality to be used, that issue is practically no longer questioned.

That is, already between the second half of the nineteenth century and the first of the twentieth century, approximate age of the second neoclassical, it was no longer argued that the theoretical Economics was based mainly on three well-marked assumptions, namely:

- People have rational preferences towards results, which can be identified and associated with a value.
- Individuals maximize utility and firms maximize profit.
- People act independently based on complete and relevant information.

By neoclassical seconds it is generally located, within what is the nineteenth century, Alfred Marshall (1842-1924), follower of Jevons (English school), Friedich von Wieser (1851-1926) and Eugene von Bohm-Bawerk (1851) -1914), great followers of Carl Menger (Austrian school) and Vilfredo Pareto (1848-1923), successor of Walras (Swiss school). In the 20th century, the most influential neoclassicals are often referred to as Friedrich von Hayek (Austrian school), Lionel Robbins (English school) and Milton Friedman (USA) - the latter two, given their exponential theoretical influence, we are going to give special paragraphs in this chapter.

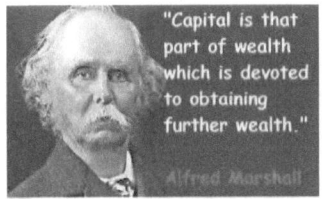

His formulations, like all those of the first neoclassical school, revolve around the principle of diminishing marginal utility. In general, neoclassicals consider that economic analysis should start from the analysis of human needs and the laws that determine the use of available resources to satisfy them. Unlike the classical school considers that the value of the goods is determined by the desire and need, and not by the cost of production or the amount of work that has been used to produce them.

Definition

- The law of diminishing marginal utility describes a familiar and fundamental tendency of human behavior.
- "The law of diminishing marginal utility states that, "as a consumer consumes more and more units of a specific commodity, utility from the successive units goes on diminishing".

To mention some of the most important contributions of the second generation of neoclassicists, let us take Alfred Marshall, the result of his theoretical efforts was the so-called "neoclassical synthesis", the basis of the economic theory of the time (and even of the current one). In 1890 he published his capital work, Principles of Economics, where he combined concepts of classical economics such as wealth, production, labor, capital or value with contributions from the marginalist school as utility and marginal utility. To the agents of production (land, labor, capital) added a new factor, that of industrial organization.

In the second edition, he presented the functioning of markets, an analysis of supply and demand and presented his theory of general equilibrium, the formation of supply, the incidence of monopolies and the distribution of national wealth. The most important problems analyzed were the formation of prices and the distribution of income.

In the first case, it established as determinants of the value of a good both the cost of production and the utility. From the value of the good, the formation of prices would be given by the confluence of supply and demand; the first, determined by production costs, and the second, by marginal utility.

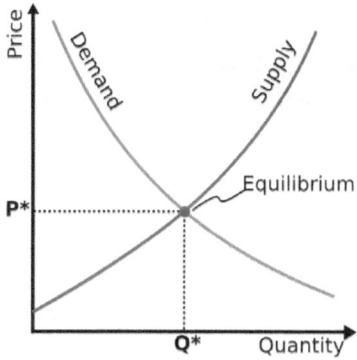

It also established a relationship between price and quantity demanded whose graphical syntax (supply and demand curves) is still valid today. That is to say, as we said above, the second neoclassicals refined the theory and left it very similar to the current one, which today criticizes Neuroeconomics in several aspects, but little contributed to the debate emotions versus reason in decision-making, there already the first neoclassicals made strong contributions, which the latter did not put into discussion.

Marshall was perhaps the brightest British economist of his day. He was also an outstanding professor and exerted a great influence on the economists who read him or had him as a professor (case of J.M.Keynes in Cambridge). His major contribution to economics was to systematize classical economic theories and the development of the concept of marginal utility. He stressed the importance of thorough analysis and the need to adapt the theories to new developments.

4. Robbins:

As time goes by, a way of grounding economics based on an ad-hoc psychology - an eminently rational human being - which we remember had begun in the 18th century with some classics, not all of them, was clearly defined, and it reaches its culmination with the paradigmatic work of Robbins (1932) "Nature and Significance of Economic Science"[26], which defines a methodology that brings together a series of ideas that floated in the English Economics, and that integrates with the Austrian School, with whose most representative exponents was in contact in his visit to Vienna in the twenties. His thesis is that economic agents, who are faced with unlimited ends to which they have to allocate scarce resources, act rationally, optimizing their utility as consumers and their efficiency as producers.

It does not analyze the possibility that these ideas are subjected to empirical verification, since they are part of the basic assumptions that we access through introspection, and because they are obvious they cannot be subjected to any "test". There is only one system in the human brain, the deliberative, and there is no place for the passions and other functions of the affective system. In this way, an ad-hoc psychological basis is defined, totally unreal, although it must be recognized: made to measure for the economic science and the mathematical instruments available at that time. Formulating economic models based on maximizing mathematics was the task to which the great majority of twentieth-century theorists turned, all under the hyper-rationalist paradigm that today Neuroeconomics and Behavioral Economics, among other movements, are trying of, if not dethrone, at least nuance.

The way in which Robbins considers human rationality for the purpose of doing economics could even be considered as an antecedent to the famous thesis of the irrelevance of assumptions, which Friedman develops more deeply and forcefully years later. Although the methodological positions of Robbins and Friedman are different, similarities can be found between both contributions in relation to this question, since in the end both Robbins and Friedman affirm that starting from unrealistic assumptions does not deprive the conclusions of the economic models. In turn, this proposition gives a greater degree of legitimacy and acceptability to economic theory, whose implications in this way can be accepted by different schools of economists, even if the respective views of human being maintained by the latter are different.

But his contributions do not remain there, since Robbins is also one of the main responsible for the cost - benefit marginalist calculation, in its hyper - rational version, to penetrate the great majority of human activities and not only in the cold world of business. Lionel Robbins in his controversial "Essay on the Nature and Significance of Economic Science" (1932) argued that the traditional approach (until then) suffered from a serious limitation, since there are aspects of economic life that are not related to welfare material, but with aspects that could be described as "immaterial", activities that do have to be framed in economic science.

Robbins solves this apparent paradox by focusing the scope of economics not on a type of human actions but on one aspect of all or, at least, a large part of human actions. What is this aspect? For Robbins, it is the one that is most directly related to what, in a radical way, constitutes the essence of the economic problem: scarcity, which in turn derives from the opposition of a multiplicity of ends and limited means. The economic aspect of human's activity is that limited means can be used in different ways and, consequently, it is necessary to choose the ends that are considered primordial.

And in turn, continuing with Robbins' argument, as a consequence of the election, the concept of opportunity cost immediately arises. Ultimately, economics is conceived as a way of approaching any problem in which scarcity and choice emerge: it can be applied not only to cases of production and distribution of goods, services and productive factors, as has been traditional, but also to the analysis of other social phenomena in which the logic of rationality - as the choice of the optimal means to achieve ends - becomes evident. This approach, on the one hand, reflects, as we have already said, the great influence that the Austrian School had on Robbins - in particular through Mises and Hayek - and on another the influence of an English economist, Wicksteed. Indeed, Wicksteed suggested that the marginalist calculation should apply not only to economics - as postulated by Jevons and Marshall - but to all human activity.

For Robbins economics "is the science that studies human behavior as a relationship between ends and scarce means, susceptible to alternative employment", without doubt, a definition that had a remarkable echo in the profession and introduced an important change in the approach of the nature and scope of economics. In effect, thus understood, economics is the general science of human behavior according to the economic principle, a discipline that can encompass, in the final analysis, all the domains of human action, as long as the problem to be solved can be posed as an optimization in an environment conditioned by the limitation of some resource.

With regard to the present, it can be said that the definition of Robbins is accepted by a large part of the economists, and in fact it is included in a large number of available Economics manuals. Not in vain he has managed to gather in the definition three key ideas of economic science, such as scarcity, choice and opportunity cost. The underlying epistemological approach is also being imposed among many authors: to understand economics in this way provides a starting point for studies carried out through the application of economic logic to social phenomena such as the birth of law, delinquency or the family. The works of two economists awarded with the Nobel Prize in recent years, Ronald Coase (in 1991) and Gary Becker (in 1992) can be mentioned here.

In short, with Robbins, that is, in the middle of the 20th century, theoretical economics achieves two very important things that ended up shaping it as we see it now:

- The economic models must or should start from the assumption of hyper-calculating human beings, and of the good ones, that is, hyper-maxi / minimizers.
- This way of understanding economic decision-making should not be left only for the analysis of business issues, governments and other economic good, but should also

apply to all those areas where there are situations of scarcity of resources for alternative purposes.

5. Hutchison

This way of seeing economics (Robbins') still has a fairly widespread acceptance, despite the fact that critical voices have existed and exist. One of the first and best known is that of Hutchison (1938), who, inspired by Popper, maintains the need to falsify all the theories that claim to be scientific. His work The Significance and Basic Postulates of Economic Theory[27] is a positivist critique of Robbins' main postulates, fundamentally in two aspects: he considers the use of introspection to be inadequate in order to obtain the postulates of the theories, and advocates for a higher degree of utilization of empirical procedures in economics. It can be considered, finally, as a change of tendency with respect to the previous verificationist methodology and as the explicit introduction of the contribution of Popper (falsificationism) in the economic methodology.

Let's see the following paragraph of the aforementioned work by Hutchison:

If one conceives of Gossen's Law as an empirical generalization one can, when wants to, go to the facts of economic behavior to test it. On the other hand, simply to rely on dogmatic assertions even when supported by phrases like "inner feelings of necessity" or "a priori facts", is to commit scientific suicide. It must really be explained in what precise way this "inner feeling of necessity" with which psychological method justifies its propositions differs from the "inner felling of necessity" which political fanatics and the like always discover in support of their doctrines...

We have seen that within Economics the "optimistic procedure of beginning with highly simplified" isolated "abstractions, in the hope of gradually making more realistic by removing the simplifying assumptions, is apt to come to a dead end, and that if one wants to get beyond a certain high level of abstraction one has to begin more or less from the beginning with extensive empirical research...

This vision of Hutchison, very much in agreement with what today sustains Neuroeconomics, however, was criticized first by Knight (1940)[28], who insists - with arguments similar to those made by Robbins years ago-, in the impossibility of that the starting point of economics are assumptions susceptible to contrast since in human behavior there are important unobservable facets. Knight also defends the advisability of maintaining a position of methodological dualism between economics and the natural sciences. It seems that the criticism influences in Hutchison, because this one, years later, opts for the methodological dualism, in front of his monist position externalized in 1938.

Later, in the 1950s, Machlup (a supporter of economic theory being elaborated mainly by logical deductive procedures) affects Knight's criticism and accuses Hutchison of ultra - empiricist for pretending that economic theory is based on empirically testable hypotheses. Hutchison subsequently defends himself by asserting that the empirical testing requirements he had formulated in 1938 refer primarily to the final propositions, not to the assumptions. Machlup's point, however, seems accurate, because the complete reading of the original work of Hutchison seems to suggest that the requirements of empirical testing also refer to assumptions, mainly that of ultra-rationality.

HUTCHISON

In short, regardless of whether or not Hutchison recanted what he said in 1938, his criticism is valid since, at that time, it was difficult to submit the basic principles (the true human rationality) to empirical verification, and those who denied his need as Knight, Robbins and many others were mainly inspired by the impossibility of doing so, something that has been substantially modified today, with the advance of Neurosciences. In other words, today it would be easier for Hutchison to defend his position, and perhaps he would never have retracted.

6. J.M.Keynes

John Maynard Keynes also departs from the concept of rationality when he asks how it can be that even when the rational analysis of investment projects shows its inconvenience, economic agents decide to invest despite the high probability that the project will not turn out to be profitable and that can bankrupt the investor. It supposes that this is due to the "animal spirits", which are something like waves of optimism and pessimism that envelop society alternately and that move us to action for the pleasure of doing things, beyond what the cold cost-benefit calculation says. In addition, the inflexibility of falling wages, the monetary illusion, the inability of businessmen to adequately formulate their expectations and the trap of liquidity - all Keynesian concepts - are manifestations of the withdrawal of full rationality on the part of the economic agents, who make economics diverge naturally from full employment and public policies that restore it are necessary.

The contribution of Keynes to economic science is very important, basically because of the degree of influence he had and still has today in applied macroeconomic policy, especially in the short term. And of course, it helped to introduce into current economic theory certain aspects that make the true rationality of man, not the ad-hoc that Robbins enthroned, and that comes from the utilitarians. That is why we are going to do a more detailed analysis of this economist.

To begin with, it is said that Macroeconomics was born as something separate with Keynes, that is, it begins to differentiate the micro from the macro. During the nineteenth century and the first decades of the twentieth century the vast majority of neoclassical economists - Jevons, Walras and Menger, and their disciples Marshall, Edgeworth and Pareto - focused mainly on the study of microeconomic issues, although it is true that some of they were also interested in topics of a macro nature. With respect to the aggregate functioning of economics, there was a certain consensus regarding some basic principles, among which the validity of the Quantitative Theory of Money - in its Marshallian version, for example - was the validity of the price and wage flexibility guaranteed by the full employment and the effectiveness of Say's Law.

But in 1936 John Maynard Keynes published The General Theory of Employment, Interest and Money[29], one of the most influential economics books of the 20th century. The appearance of Keynes's book was of crucial importance due to two reasons. In the first place, this work supposes the birth of the Macroeconomics in its current form where Keynes - and from it, later the Keynesian economists -

elaborates macroeconomic models proper, characterized by a particular way of adding markets, goods and economics agents. Second, the subsequent dissemination of the ideas contained in the General Theory by authors such as Samuelson and Hicks broke the existing agreement on macroeconomic issues referred to above (the flexibility of prices and wages, Say's law, etc.).

> ### The Classical theory- Criticism
> - **John Maynard Keynes** was the main critic of the classical macro economics.
> - In his book '*General Theory of Employment, Interest and Money*' he out-rightly rejected the Say's Law of Market that supply creates its own demand.
> - He severely criticized that cuts in real wages help in promoting employment in the economy.
> - He also opposed the idea that saving and investment can be brought about through changes in the rate of interest.
> - In addition to this, the assumption of full employment in the economy is not realistic.

Two types of factors can be distinguished that contribute to the development of Keynesian thought: on the one hand, the high unemployment rates in England and the United States in the 1930s, which led economists to question the causes and remedies of this pathology. Second, Marshallian microeconomics was also being questioned by economists such as Joan Robinson, Chamberlin, Kahn, and Harrod. In short, John Maynard Keynes knew how to elaborate the theoretical framework that supported and justified, in a more or less coherent way, two beliefs that were accepted by economists and that classical economics of orthodox and hyper-rationalist tendency was not able to adequately explain:

- on the one hand, that the observed unemployment was involuntary;
- on the other, that fluctuations in aggregate demand had a strong impact on income and employment.

In particular, the General Theory linked both ideas and offered a plausible diagnosis and remedy of mass unemployment: the cause of unemployment was the insufficiency of effective demand. The solution, on the other hand, was in the stimulation of the latter. Keynes supports his analytical construction on principles radically opposed to those that maintain the classics, a term with which Keynes designates, disdainfully, all those who accept the basic premises on money, prices, wages and Say's Law detailed above.

The alternative principles on which Keynes works are the following: first, he does not accept the Quantitative Theory of Money because the demand for money is not directly related to rent (for the reason transaction) but also, inversely, to the type of interest (Keynes - great speculator in the stock market - highlights the speculation motive to demand money); secondly, it postulates that there are certain rigidities in prices and wages, and in particular that the nominal salary is rigid due to institutional aspects such as the unions or the monetary illusion of the workers; and, finally, defends the invalidity of Say's Law since it is the demand that creates its own offer and not the other way round (or, in other words, nothing guarantees that the saving equals the investment at the level of full employment).

The conjunction of these premises gives rise to one of the crucial implications of the General Theory: economics can be placed for long periods of time in a situation of equilibrium with unemployment (that is, the most irrational that can be for the classics); given that nominal wages are rigid and that Say's Law is a fallacy, economics alone will not return to the level of full employment. Therefore, the active intervention of economic policy becomes necessary. However, Keynes doubts the effectiveness of monetary policy given that, in his conceptual apparatus, investment is rigid and the demand for money -at low interest rate levels- is quite elastic with respect to the interest rate, which is why the prescription of economic policy is also immediate: the impulse of the aggregate demand must be carried out by means of an expansive fiscal policy (and, therefore, opposed to the orthodox dogma of the balanced budget).

At this point we are already appreciating the way in which Keynes begins to refute the dominant hyper-rationalist / maximizing economic theory until now:

- first, using macro variables instead of micro variables;
- second, from an acute and controversial reasoning, obviously introspective - there was no neuroimaging or EMT - about how human

beings, especially businessmen and consumers, make certain decisions: prices and wages are rigid in the short term, the expansive monetary policy in extreme situations has no effect on the expectations of economic agents, entrepreneurs sometimes invest without necessarily looking at profitability in the short term; in short, a whole series of aspects that Keynes observed happened in economics (and that the traditional theory did not contemplate), and that when beginning to be debated, and inserted in the theoretical models, they began to bring a little closer to the man of economic theory the man of flesh and bone, the real human being, not Robbins.

The publication of the General Theory, and the certain air of ambiguity with which it was written, generated an enormous volume of works that tried to unravel the authentic message of Keynes. The work of Patinkin (1956)[30], which analyzes both Keynesian and Neoclassical thought in detail and depth, must be highlighted, so that, on the one hand, it provides a clear exposition of Keynes' theory; on the other hand, it shows the logical coherence of neoclassical propositions. In any case, and as we have already said, the influence of the Keynesian contribution was immense, both in the academic field and in that of economic policy. Certainly, most economists, during the 1950s and 1960s, developed their contributions within the framework of Keynesian thought, theoretically refining or empirically contrasting some of their propositions. In the applied field, the ideas of Keynes - and in particular the prominence attributed to fiscal policy - constituted the new orthodoxy that replaced the traditional one in most of the Western countries.

The interpretation of Keynes's thought that can be considered dominant is the so-called neoclassical synthesis of Hicks and Modigliani, popularized in its graphic version by the IS-LM curves. The model accurately captured the central message of the Keynesian contribution: the fact that prices and wages adapt slowly (that is, irrationally for the classics) to the mismatches between supply and demand. On the other hand, the qualification of neoclassical was due to the fact that the economic environment was perfectly Walrasian: markets were competitive; there were no externalities or imperfections in the information available to agents. The IS-LM model soon achieved great success: in fact, it has exercised an undeniable influence on the profession and has been incorporated into the vast majority of Macroeconomics textbooks for its (apparent) simplicity, elegance and versatility; it also continues to be used in recent manuals. The model suffers, however, from certain limitations that hinder its understanding and generate confusion in those who study it in depth, as is its timeless nature since it is a model of comparative statics and, therefore, not explicitly dynamic, and also its omission of the role of expectations. In addition, it is surprising that it is a Walrasian general equilibrium model in which there are rigid prices and salaries, at least in the short term.

But beyond the limitations mentioned, it is undeniable, from Keynes, the advance of economic theory to consider in their models much more realistic assumptions about how consumers, investors, and economic actors in general reason and make their decisions, against the excessive oversimplification of the Jevons, Marshall, Robbins and all those who, for intellectual and scientific convenience, assumed machine-men at the time of putting together the theoretical models of economic decision-making.

7. Other Alternative Approaches to the Dominant View: Austrians, Historicism and American Institutionalism

Before analyzing Friedman's thought, that is, to return to the dominant view of neoclassical theory, although rejuvenated (methodologically by Friedman); then we will "take a look" to three schools of medium influence (compared with the neoclassical and its Keynesian rival), but that cannot be ignored in any way in what makes theoretical contributions, at least in what makes methodology and rationality in economics. Both historicism and institutionalism always maintained deep criticisms of neoclassical thought, and with very interesting arguments; while the Austrians, although closer to orthodoxy, also have interesting methodological contributions to the debate.

✓ The Modern Austrians

The so-called modern Austrian Economics, takes as models no longer both Menger and Bohm-Bawerk (although they influence), but mainly Von Mises and

Von Hayek. The current continuators of Austrian thought are inspired, for example, by Hayek's attack on scientism or methodological monism, and his emphasis on the principle of methodological individualism, and also on the consecrated work of Von Mises *Human Action*. Other influential (to a lesser extent than Mises and Hayek) members of the Austrian Economics have been the well-known economists Schumpeter, Morgenstern, Machlup and Haberler, among others.

Mises argues that what gives economics its unique position in the orbit of pure knowledge and the practical use of such knowledge, is the fact that its complete theorems are not susceptible to verification or falsification in the field of experience, but the ultimate measure of the correction or not of an economic theorem is only the reason, without any help from experience.

"Most of the tyrants, despots, and dictators are sincerely convinced that their rule is beneficial for the people, that theirs is government for the people."
-Ludwig von Mises

In this sense, the modern Austrians are not very different from the neoclassical ones, both being equally a priori, that is to say, being quite far from what today Neuroeconomics postulates, in terms of working with more verifiable hypotheses in reality, since Neuroimaging and other modern techniques (such as Transcranial Magnetic Stimulation) allow it.

Mises also insists on what is called methodological dualism, or the essential disparity of approach between Social and Natural Sciences (a barrier that Neuroeconomics today is trying to tear down, since part of Neurosciences - or natural sciences - to then enter in the Social Sciences) and, in something that is quite peculiar and peculiar to Austrian thought, advocates the radical rejection of any kind of quantification, either of the premises or of the implications, of economic theories.

How Austrians Understand the Business Cycles?

- Macroeconomic Propositions have Microeconomic Foundations
- Austrian Business Cycle Theory (Capital-Based Macroeconomic Theory)
- Böhm-Bawerk built upon the TIME PREFERENCE ideas of Carl Menger → there is always a difference in value between present goods and future goods of equal quality, quantity, and form. Moreover, the value of future goods diminishes as the length of time necessary for their completion increases.
- Austrian Economics understand that "K" is never homogeneous.
- Inter-temporal consumption.

In summary, the main ingredients of the modern Austrian methodology, inspired by Hayek and Mises, and currently "aggiornada" by Rothbard, Kirzner and Lachmann, among others, are:

- absolute insistence on methodological individualism as a priori postulate;

- deep mistrust towards macro aggregates (GDP, inflation, unemployment, etc.);
- firm disapproval of any quantitative contrast of economic predictions and, in particular, the categorical rejection of everything that sounds by far to Mathematical Economics and Econometrics;
- the belief that there is much more to learn from the study of how market processes converge towards equilibrium, rather than the endless neoclassical analyzes of the properties of the final states of equilibrium.

In this last point, to study the processes, the Austrians agree enough with the American Institutionalism, and obviously today with Neuroeconomics, since, in the latter case, one of its main contributions is to allow economics to take more concepts of Biology and leave aside those of Physics, the last much more mechanistic (final equilibria), while the former more oriented to the evolutionary processes.

The Austrians also distance themselves from the neoclassicals because of their emphasis on the radical subjectivism of human beings, which has a much broader meaning than that which refers merely to tastes. The Austrians, following this idea, emphasize utility and reject costs as a relevant element in the determination of economic value. This last aspect constitutes the most marked rupture with the English variant (Marshall and Jevons) of the neoclassical theory of value. As the costs are subjective, since they are opportunity costs (utility to which it is renounced), and therefore only perceived by the one that makes an election, in the end everything is reduced to the individual subjectivity, that is to the utility of the one who decides. This line of thought is opposed to the strict Marshallian tradition that associates costs with events, and that therefore, considers costs as something objective.

- ✓ American Institutionalism

This group tries to explain economic events through the identification of their corresponding place in a scheme of relationships, which is supposed to characterize the system as a whole. They constitute what have been called schematic models. The builders of these models reject all forms of atomism and refuse to abstract from any part of the system; their working hypotheses are relatively concrete and close to the economic system that is described, and if they somehow generalize, they do it by means of the elaboration of typologies; his explanations emphasize comprehension rather than prediction.

The most prominent figures of this school are Veblen, Commons, Mitchell, Ayers and Myrdal, among others, emerging as a think tank in the late nineteenth century in the United States, especially in the hands of Veblen. Currently Samuels and Boulding stand out among the leading modern institutionalists.

Veblen sympathized with the views of the English historicists (use of empirical deductive generalizations rather than deductive logic, the latter so typical of traditional thinking in economics), but went further than the British historicists in terms of methodology and consistency.

It is basically Veblen's methodological contribution that makes his critique of capitalism durable and singularly important. This author considered that the material circumstances that surround humans are the most significant factor in determining their propensities and preconceptions about the world. A worldview is premised on the material conditions of any particular epoch, and institutions (ways of doing and thinking things, distributing rewards, etc.) appear to support a given set of material circumstances.

The interactions postulated by Veblen between the technological institutions (technicians, engineers and certain workers), on the one hand; and the ceremonial institutions (companies, banks, businessmen), on the other, are the main reasons for the change in their system. And additionally, he argued that the orthodox neoclassical vision of the economic system and the theoretical superstructure that it sustained, were sterile and useless. However, he never argued that neoclassical analysis was not valid, given his assumptions.

The main criticism to Institutionalism was the lack of a specific methodology, unlike orthodox economics. The institutionalists used a lot of "story telling", similar to what Applied Economics is today within orthodoxy. However, since the activity of telling stories lacks a definite logical structure and therefore of scientific rigor, their stories will be easy to verify and practically impossible to falsify. This activity is so persuasive because it almost never runs the risk of being wrong.

However, what is interesting about Institutionalism for Neuroeconomics is its insistence on analyzing evolutionary processes, that is, the tendency towards new equilibria, and not the simple photographic visions of current equilibria, so typical of neoclassical orthodox analysis. According to Veblen, the neoclassical school tries to find natural laws that later turn into absolute truths, while there is a process of economic, evolutionary life (similar to the one studied by biology in nature), which awaits a theoretical explanation, to that orthodoxy does not contribute practically nothing. Today Neuroeconomics, a century after these visionary arguments of Veblen, tends to give traditional economic theory the bridge to move to analyze the economic dynamics and systemic change, and not the profuse amount of stable equilibria to which we are accustomed, both at the micro level of specific markets, and the general equilibrium. The theory of evolution, initiated by biologists (mainly Darwin), should be continued by the researchers of culture, and especially by economists, Veblen opined, more than 100 years ago.

Institutions and Institutional Theory-significance

- Politics, profoundly by rules, steers political behaviour in different directions.
- Since the 1980s, political scientists have developed a renewed interest in the study of political institutions based on the assumption that "institutions matter",
- a set of constitutional-legal rules and structural arrangements within which politics take place (as well as informal institutions) are crucial determinants of the shape of politics and policy outcomes (Lijphart 2002).
- For others, institutions are rules or norms by which people live either abiding or breaching them

✓ Historicism

The historical movement, which dates from the second half of the 19th century, also makes significant criticisms of the methodology of the neoclassical research program. The economists of this school incarnated a strong reaction against deductivism, abstract methods, analytical models and unverified hypotheses (for example the maximizing rationality of homo economicus), so characteristic of the orthodox model and today so criticized by Behavioral Economics and Neuroeconomics In this way, and in what makes his feature more peculiar, the historicists advocated an economic science that would describe man and his institutions as they are organically raised in certain places and times.

Friedrich List can be considered as the forerunner of this school. His originality in economic theory and his method consisted in the systematic use of historical comparison as a means to demonstrate the validity of economic propositions and in the introduction of new and useful points of view, unlike the economic orthodoxy of liberalism classic.

The German historical school is usually divided into two groups of authors: the "old" and the "young"; the latter being much more radical in their methodological criticisms than the former. The "old" are represented mainly by Roscher, Knies and Hildebrand; while the "young" by Schmoller, perhaps the most famous historicist in the history of economic analysis. While the old historicist school questioned the absolutism of orthodox theory, the young school rejected the theory as a whole. Schmoller contrasted the method of the Neoclassicals and Austrians (especially Menger), who defended and used the abstract-deductive argument, with the historical-inductive method of the German school, which he considered superior.

The main criticism of historicism was its anti-rationalism, since it refused to deduce general rules from reason, insisting instead on the observation of historical variation. Thus, at a theoretical level, it offered no principle to guide or limit human action.

The Austrian economist Carl Menger was one of the harshest critics of German historicism, which led to the famous "war of methods", which the remarkable J. Schumpeter once called "meaningless".

8. Friedman and Monetarism. Rational Expectations and New Classical Economics.

While Friedman, Lucas and the new classics in general have not achieved much in what makes to bring the human being of economic models (hyper-rational) to real human being (bounded rationality, simplifying Behavioral Economics), it is also useful highlight their main contributions because they served to mark and correct a series of important errors that had the original Keynesian modeling, which of course does not opaque, in our opinion, the revolutionary for the economic theory of several of the contributions arising from the writings of J.M.Keynes.

In the 1960s and 1970s the foundations of the neoclassical synthesis (the IS / LM model from Keynesian thought) began to falter. The attacks came, on the one hand, from theoretical contributions such as those of Friedman (1968) and Phelps (1967). The poor microeconomic basis of the IS / LM model, the explicit absence of dynamic considerations and the omission of the role of expectations were questioned. With respect to the first of these aspects, the fundamental incongruity of the neoclassical synthesis was ever more palpable: the no instantaneous adjustment of prices in a perfectly competitive (Walrasian) environment.

In addition, both Friedman[31] and Phelps[32] argued that *economic authorities could not exploit indefinitely the trade-off between inflation and unemployment, since ultimately there is a natural rate of unemployment that is not a function of the growth of the money supply but can be considered the unemployment rate consistent with the actual conditions existing in the labor market. It can be reduced if obstacles in the labor market are eliminated, if friction is reduced. It can be increased if additional obstacles are introduced. The purpose of this concept is to separate the monetary aspects of non-monetary aspects in the situation of unemployment,* Friedman said, in one of his critical writings on Keynesianism[33]. On the other hand, the supply shock that overtook the world economy after the oil price increases of 1973 and 1979, and which resulted in high rates of inflation and unemployment, could not be satisfactorily explained within the Keynesian research program, that based the economic fluctuations on the displacements of aggregate demand and advocated an inverse - and not direct - relationship between price increases and unemployment. And while it must be recognized that the Keynesian models, once they were conveniently modified to allow displacements of the aggregate supply, returned to provide plausible explanations for these phenomena, we must also recognize that the disenchantment of the economists with the neoclassical synthesis was already considerable and led to the rise of other schools, such as monetarism.

Milton FRIEDMAN

Milton Friedman is the main representative of the monetarist school of thought, which also includes Brunner, Meltzer, Cagan and Laidler. Friedman, on the one hand, recovers for macroeconomics the importance of long-term analysis through, for example, his theory of consumption based on permanent income. On the other hand, it reformulates the Quantitative Theory of Money and argues that both the demand for money and its speed are stable functions of a certain number of variables. The implication of these hypotheses is that money can cause variations in output and employment in the short term but generates long-term inflation, with people realizing and distrusting the monetary emission increases. In other words, the Phillips curve presents a trade-off between unemployment and inflation in a close temporal horizon but, if the period considered is extended, it becomes a vertical line at the level of unemployment of the natural rate. A crucial assumption to give rise to this result is that it is necessary to explicitly consider the expectations of the agents, which in Friedman's case are elaborated in an adaptive way.

The implications of economic policy derived from this theoretical approach are different from those proposed by Keynes: the monetarists argue that the leading role of economics must be driven by the private sector, while the excessive activity of the government is counterproductive; Therefore, the deregulation of economic activity, the less expansive - or even balanced - budgets and the replacement of the discretion of monetary policy with the rules are preferable.

As we can see, despite their important contributions, Friedman and his acolytes continued to think of extremely calculating human beings (albeit in an adaptive way) and in markets with very few failures - which make the role of government almost null-, which is equivalent to say that the private agents are so good calculators in their economic decisions that they facilitate the system of decentralized economy (extreme capitalism) takes to the societies towards its maximum well-being, that is to say, the government more than helping, hinders. In this last point the monetarist theory is quite criticized, as it demonstrates the modern theory of the market failures, today with a lot of acceptance among the economists and that has already given even Nobel prizes, as it is the case of Stiglitz.

- ✓ Friedman and his justification for using unrealistic assumptions

The prolific (and notoriously influential) academic Milton Friedman also has very important contributions in regard to methodology in economics, that is, how theoretical models are scientifically constructed, which serve and which do not, among other important methodological issues. And one of Friedman's fundamental ideas, which has also been remarkably influential among economists for the last 50 years, is that of the irrelevance of the realism of assumptions: it does not matter that the theoretical models start from premises far removed from reality, what is important is that their predictions are relatively accurate; simplifying enough, this condition is what defines for Friedman if a theory is useful or not in economics.

These ideas come from the year 1953, when Milton Friedman publishes the article The Methodology of Positive Economics[34], one of the key works in the economic methodology of this century, since as we said exerts great influence on economists, and in turn is very controversial. It is a difficult and complex work, which suffers from a certain ambiguity, and which justifies the feeling of vagueness that some economists experience when they read the work. The reason for this inaccuracy may be that Friedman did not seek to carry out a methodological theorization of a speculative nature - he is not a philosopher of science - but, rather, to provide concrete solutions to certain problems.

Continuing with his line of argument, according to Friedman, *it is proven that truly important and significant hypotheses have "assumptions" that are clearly inadequate representations of reality and, in general, the more significant the theory, the less realistic the "assumptions" will be (in this sense). The reason is simple. A hypothesis is important if it "explains" much through little, that is, if it abstracts the common and crucial elements from the mass of concomitant circumstances, since its true success shows that the latter are irrelevant to the phenomena that must be explained*[35].

But, in addition, from the previous statement it can also be inferred that the lack of realism is not only an obstacle for science but can be an advantage. Friedman's thought suggests that the most accurate theory will explain and predict more with less: that less refers to the assumptions, which should capture the essential economic relationships but be simple, so that they are not lost in the tangle of accessory details. Recall that Friedman's article was born, among other things, as a defense of the neoclassical theory of the firm, where although it is true that employers do not calculate the cut-off point between marginal cost and marginal revenue to determine the optimal amount offered so that profits are maximized, supposing that they do it is useful and produces results that are observed in practice.

Instrumentalism vs realism

- Friedman's *as if* doctrine
- « Good models have to necessarily be artificial, abstract, patently unreal » (Lucas, 1981)
- « Of course, that model does not not represent reality and that is not its purpose » (Bliss, 1975)
- « It is better to be precisely wrong rather than roughly right »
- Ex.: The use of the Gaussian copula function to price CDO (collaterized debt obligations) was based on an index of CDS (credit default swaps) market prices instead of looking at true default rates.

In our view, Friedman's thought - very successful among the community of theoretical economists - is at least scientifically dangerous. So, following their advice, build economic models assuming that economic agents are ultra-optimizers (hypothesis quite far from reality, as demonstrated by Neurosciences today) would not be bad, the important thing is that the model explains and forecasts well the reality, that is, that serves to interpret what happens in economics and what will happen. We agree with Samuelson that this type of reasoning constitutes a sort of juggling, and what's more, following Friedman's thinking, it can be deduced that to be a good theoretician in economics, luck (or intuition) would be highly necessary.

And if this instrumentalist vision of assumptions has worked reasonably well during a time when human feelings and thoughts could not be measured (that is, until very recently) would it not be a scientific sin to continue defending it in a context that has changed so much from the rise of Neurosciences? Why continue with "Friedman's consolation" of "assumptions do not matter, the predictive capacity matters", if now, with Neurosciences, it is possible to make assumptions about human rationality much more accurate, and model accordingly. And while models based on a more real rationality would gain in complexity, surely their predictions would be more robust. This topic will be taken up in the last chapter, when we talk about the change or not of paradigm in economics based on the findings of Neuroeconomics.

✓ Rational Expectations and the New Classical Economics

Returning to Macroeconomics, Friedman's approach implied a return to the propositions of classical and neoclassical economists. But in 1972, the Nobel Prize Robert Lucas goes one step further by developing a model, called imperfect information, where expectations are considered rational. The assumption of rational expectations is not original to Lucas, since it had already been elaborated by Muth (1961)[36], but Lucas's contribution popularizes and diffuses it among economists. In fact, the assumption of rational expectations is the natural continuation of the microeconomic budget of rationality (the ultra-maximizing, that today critics Neuroeconomics) in the agents, and it is logical that this rationality is also present when the future is explicitly taken into consideration.

Three years later, Sargent and Wallace (1975)[37] argue that, under the assumption of rational expectations, systematic economic policy cannot always reduce unemployment: it is another criticism of one of the basic implications of the Keynesian model, the discretionary use of the stabilization policy to boost or contract economic activity, since in the analysis of Sargent and Wallace only economic policies not anticipated by the agents are effective. The Phillips curve can be vertical even in the short term (unlike what Friedman proposed) if the agents are able to correctly predict future policy measures.

Rational Expectations

- The theory of rational expectations states that expectations will not differ from optimal forecasts using all available information.
  - *It is reasonable to assume that people act rationally because it is is costly not to have the best forecast of the future.*

The previous statement is completed with the so-called criticism of Lucas (1976), according to which a change in the rules of economic policy generates a change in the expectations of the agents and, therefore, in the parameters of the macroeconometric models, so that the predictive capacity of the latter is invalidated if the impact of alternative policies is to be evaluated. One can already speak, then, of a new school of macroeconomic thought, the New Classical

Economics, whose most relevant contributions are articulated around three principles: the continuous equilibrium in the markets -because prices and wages are flexible-, a more microeconomic foundation careful about the optimizing behavior on the part of agents, and the formation of expectations in a rational way (which is something like incorporating into the decision process all the available information, even if it is not perfect, and with it making the intertemporal economic calculation maximizing, and in function of it to decide).

In short, what this School of Rational Expectations does is to refine the ideas of monetarism a little more, therefore, from Neuroeconomics the same criticisms that we did for Friedman and can be summarized in that they suppose fully economic agents maximizers, optimizers, both short-term and long-term - due to the inclusion of expectations now - what goes wrong with the latest neuroscientific findings, which speak of the important role of emotions and bias in decision-making, and that in all cases justify a combined maximization of cognitive (rational) and emotional well-being at the same time, not of the cognitive only.

At this point of our exposition, and in order to make even clearer the erroneous assumption of rationality of Lucas (and also of Friedman), we repeat some of the latest neuro scientific findings, especially those related to the consumption function of the macro models[38]:

- ✓ *"According to scientists, the brain areas of rationality cannot function isolated from the areas*

> *of biological-emotional regulation. The two systems communicate and affect the behavior jointly, and consequently, the behavior of the people ".*

- ✓ *"Moreover, the emotional system (the oldest area of the brain) is the first force that acts on mental processes, therefore determines the direction of decisions."*
- ✓ *"The latest advances in Neuroscience have shown that consumer decision-making is not a rational process. That is, customers do not consciously examine the attributes of a product or service to acquire it."*
- ✓ *"In most cases, the selection process is relatively automatic and derives from habits and other metaconscious forces, among which history, personality, neurophysiological characteristics and the physical and social context that surrounds us all gravitate".*

To conclude with the topic of rational expectations, a clarification seems to be necessary to dispel very common misunderstandings: at present, the assumption of rational expectations is not exclusive to the models of the New Classical Economics or the Theory of the Real Cycle. On the contrary, models can be found designed by economists who do not belong to either of these two schools and who, nevertheless, adopt as a premise the generation of expectations in a rational way. It can even be said that "the widespread acceptance of the axiom of rational expectations is perhaps the greatest change in the Macroeconomics of the last two decades"[39], which in our opinion is dangerous, especially today that Cognitive Neurosciences contradict these assumptions.

9. New Keynesians and Real Business Cycle Economists

After the Keynesian emergence and the critiques of Friedman, Lucas and other orthodox, it seems that the initially dominant pre-Keynes paradigm, that is, the hyper-optimizer of the neoclassicals, would have emerged again in the last decades, and more strengthened, since to overcome Keynes's criticisms, traditional theoretical models had to be significantly improved (today it is modeled with expectations, with intertemporality, with dynamic mathematics, among other refinements). Likewise, there has been a fairly respectable place for the so-called New Keynesians - followers of Keynes, but who use advanced mathematical instruments - although in our opinion the ideas of the "New Classics" have had a better reception in the profession.

In what follows we will review how it has been - after so much debate - the macro at present, since it has peculiar features that seem relevant to mention. Indeed, criticisms of the neoclassical synthesis (the IS-LM model based on the ideas of Keynes), the contributions of the monetarists and members of the New Classical Economics and the advances in the fields of Mathematics and Econometrics have influenced notably in the way macroeconomics are developed, so that the following characteristics can be distinguished in the macroeconomic models that are currently being designed:

- The microeconomic foundation is much more careful, but it remains hyper-rationalist. The starting assumption of the models is usually the optimizing behavior of the agents, so that most of them start from the presentation of a utility function (preferences) and a production function (technology).
- The models are solved in a dynamic environment, so their solution requires the mastery of differential equations or finite differences.
- Attention is paid to the formation of expectations by agents, and these expectations are generally rational.
- The empirical testing of the models also plays a key role.

From the loss of prestige of the neoclassical synthesis (the IS-LM model with the ideas of Keynes), the macroeconomists have been progressively divided into two main groups. If it is argued that, ultimately, the weakening of the IS-LM model was due to the contradiction with the coexistence of a Walrasian economic environment with incomplete nominal adjustments in prices - which in turn means that money produces real effects (money matters) - the macroeconomists had, from here, basically two options. One of them is the one advocated by the economists of the Real Cycle, which consists of completely preserving the Walrasian traits to the point of reviving the proposition of monetary neutrality (money does not matter), which supposes the abandonment, not only of the synthesis neoclassical but also many of the messages of Keynesian macroeconomics. The second option is that of those economists who do not share the previous principles, mainly because they do not accept that the labor market is continuously in Walrasian equilibrium, and also because they want to preserve the implication of the non-neutrality of money. These are the Neo-Keynesian economists.

These ideas imply a new difference between the macroeconomists of the 1950s and 1960s (Keynesians versus monetarists) and the current ones. The controversy among economists in the 1950s and 1960s centered on issues such as the relative effectiveness of monetary and fiscal policies. Today, however, the main object of discrepancy is the ability or not of money to influence the real variables, or, alternatively, what is the cause of the economic cycle. Basically, it is a debate about how economic agents interpret and assimilate the introduction of new money into economics (a subject of perceptions, very much related to the discussion about what human rationality is really like), and it is also a debate about whether Economies really need to be stimulated via changes in the currency to slow down the economic cycle.

The schools of the Real and Neo-Keynesian Cycles do not exhaust all possibilities. If it is argued that the fundamental criterion for classifying the main macroeconomic schools is the answer to the two crucial questions - the validity of the classical dichotomy (or alternatively, the neutrality of money), and the existence of non-Walrasian features (markets that are not always balanced) in economics - four groups can be found in the current macroeconomic landscape. According to this classification, there are:

- a first large group of theories that question the classic dichotomy - or, in other words, argue that money is not neutral - but conceive economics as Walrasian: this group includes most of the developments up to the second the mid-1970s, like the Keynesian, the monetarist, and even Lucas's imperfect information model, with all the differences we noted earlier among them;
- the second group is made up of the so-called coordination failure models, where it is argued that in economics there are important non-Walrasian traits, but they believe in the validity of the classical dichotomy. In these types of theories, multiple equilibria, self-fulfilling prophecies and sunspots are frequent. This set of economists, however, is not excessively numerous;
- the two remaining groups are, in effect, the economists of the Real Cycle and the New Keynesians.

Real Business Cycle Theory

- Explored by John Muth (1961) and others.
- Fluctuations and output and employment are the results of a variety of real shocks that hit the economy
- Markets adjust to these shocks rapidly and always remain in equilibrium
- The ups and downs are caused by technology or other similar shocks to the supply side of the economy.
- Highlights the importance of *supply side of business*.
- Reflects the outcome of rational decisions made by many individuals.
- Minimizes the role of nominal fluctuations and money.

The most important authors within the Real Cycle Theory are Kydland, Prescott, Long and Plosser, Black, among others. The starting point of their models, as already mentioned, is an economy of eminently Walrasian features: markets are competitive, there are no externalities, there is no asymmetric information or other types of imperfections (that is, economic agents with advanced computer skills), almost of robots, extremely far from the real man, of flesh and bone, and therefore very far from what today postulates Neuroeconomics). It can be said, therefore, that these models are a replica of the old Ramsey model.

However, it is necessary to add some source of fluctuations to the model, since in the absence of these the model tends to a situation of steady state in which there are no cycles in economic activity. Since one of the fundamental implications of this type of model is that money does not affect production or employment, the origins of the shocks must be of a real nature: in particular, changes in technology or variations in government purchases. In this context, economic cycles are the efficient response of economics to the aforementioned shocks.

The New Keynesians, on the other hand, cover a wide spectrum of positions, although the feature that unites them is the belief that the fluctuations of economics reflect inefficient agent behavior, where there is some type of market failure, example, agents with limited computational capabilities to optimize and more, sometimes not directly optimizing, as shown by Neuroeconomics today, or at least not optimizing in the traditional way.

> ### The Name
> - The name "New Keynesian Theory" was introduced by Michael Parkin (1982).
> - One of the earliest uses of the term "new-Keynesian Economics" was in an article by Ball, Mankiw, and Romer (1988).
> - "New" is used instead of "neo" to distinguish from "Neoclassical Synthesis Keynesian Economics" (a term used by Samuelson and others), and also to show it is the counter-argument to the New Classical Economics.

Some of the most prominent members among the Neo-Keynesians are Akerlof, Yellen, David Romer, Blanchard, and Mankiw. Likewise, they all start from the idea that unemployment and economic fluctuations are crucial problems. They take from the New Classical Economics the dedication in the microeconomic foundation of the models, and obviously it had to be that way, because despite being wrong the use of the optimizing micro-as Neurosciences demonstrate today-is currently part of the dominant paradigm. A group of works states that small price rigidities at a microeconomic level can lead to a significant impact on the aggregate macroeconomic. Generally, the companies that make up economics in these models operate in a monopolistic competition regime.

Another set of articles, in which Stiglitz and Bernanke stand out, among others, focus on the problem of market imperfections in existing information asymmetries, particularly in capital markets. Finally, those contributions that support unemployment from a microeconomic point of view are also relevant, considering the labor market as non-Walrasian and affected by rigidities. In synthesis, from the point of view of Neuroeconomics, Neo-Keynesian models may be a little more realistic (from the point of view of rationality assumptions) than those of the Real Cycle.

10. Simon

Leaving a bit of the Macroeconomics, and returning a little to the direct questions to the assumption of the neoclassical optimizing hyper-rationality, Simon gives account of his questions to the principle of rationality in the decisions of the entrepreneurs, from a series of works that made him the winner of the Nobel Prize[40]. Define his idea of "bounded rationality" in the following terms:

The task, then, was to replace the classical model with one that describes how decisions could be made (and probably actually were) when the alternatives of search had to be sought out, the consequences of choosing particular alternatives were very imperfectly known both because of limited computational power and because of uncertainty in the external world, and the decision maker did not possess a general and consistent utility function for comparing heterogeneous alternatives.

Several procedures of rather applicability and wide use have been discovered that transform intractable decisions into tractable ones. One procedure already mentioned is to look for satisfactory choices instead of optimal ones. Another is to replace abstract, global goals with tangible subgoals, whose achievement can be observed and measured. A third is to divide up the decision -making tasks among many specialists, coordinating their work by means of a structure of communications and authority relations. All of these, and others, fit the general rubric of "bounded rationality" ...

Simon then opens a gate for the reformulation of the firm's theory and business decisions, which attempts to modify the neoclassical model. Instead of optimizing in the way that neoclassical theory assumes, economic agents set a goal. When they achieve it, even if it is not optimal, they feel satisfied with it and do not seek to optimize. The men of flesh and bone have limited capacities to acquire knowledge and to make calculations, and to predict the behavior would require the participation of psychologists and sociologists, in addition to the economists.

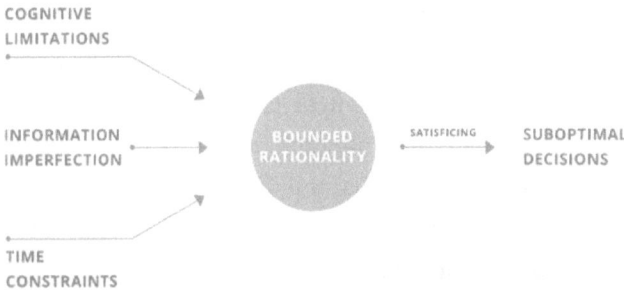

And in line with Simon's concept of limited rationality, we have Akerlof with his concept of cognitive dissonance, which also illustrates us about behaviors contrary to the supposed individual rationality that governs economic decision making, for example in situations where, those who make decisions, do not know their preferences well, or are too influenced when they act as part of closed groups to external points of view. The due obedience, which leads someone to do things that displease him for pleasing the superior, is an extreme example.

However, it must be recognized that, after all that has been said in previous pages about the enormous degree of current penetration of micro fundamentals and rational expectations in macroeconomics, and even though Simon has won a Nobel prize in economics, it would seem that the concept of limited rationality has not yet been very successful in changing the course of traditional modeling, and therefore of the dominant paradigm. But it is also a valuable, and extremely realistic, attempt by Simon.

11. Behavioral Economics and Experimental Economics

The revival of Psychology within Economics is translated into the current of thought that is mainly covered under the denomination of Behavioral Economics, which is disseminated and generalized with the awarding of the Nobel Prize in Economics in 2002 to Kahneman, who receives it in conjunction with Vernon Smith, whose branch, although related to the previous one, is called Experimental Economics. Both notables theoretical define two types of cognitive processes: System 1, which they call intuition and System 2, reasoning:

"The operations of System 1 are fast, automatic, effortless, associative, and often emotionally charged; they are also governed by habit, and are therefore difficult to control or modify. The operations of System 2 are slower, serial, effortful, and deliberatively controlled: they are also relatively flexible and potentially rule-governed" ...**Utility cannot be divorced from emotion, and emotions are triggered by changes. A theory of choice that complete ignores feelings such as pain of losses and the regret of mistakes is not only descriptively unrealistic, it also leads to prescriptions that do not maximize the utility of outcomes as they are actually experienced...**[41]

To be rigorous, and beyond their great coincidences, the substantial difference between Behavioral Economics and Experimental Economics is that the first is based on the assumption that incorporating psychological principles will improve economic analysis, while the second presupposes that incorporating methods of psychology (for example controlled experiments) will only improve the testing of economic theory. Then we will devote a few paragraphs mainly to Behavioral Economics, which is, of the two branches, the one that has had the most impact at the theoretical contributions level in Economics.

In a landmark book on Behavioral Economics, Camerer and Loewenstein (2004)[42] summarize the main findings of this current. The method used by economists and psychologists working in the aforementioned line is mainly the active experiment, that is to say the one that is carried out on a group of chosen people, to which they are subjected to questions related to the subject under study, it is repeatable and it can be analyzed statistically, although the other methods used by Economics in general are also used. However, what distinguishes this current is the use of knowledge that comes from psychology to analyze economic behavior.

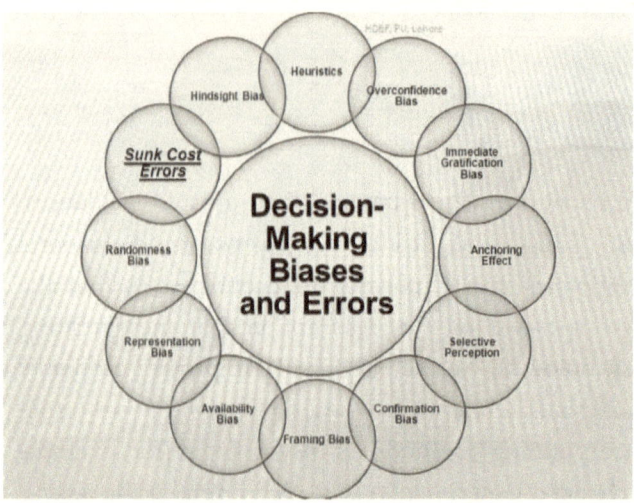

In a very interesting work, the Peruvian economist Ernesto López[43] points out some of the current conceptual contributions of Behavioral Economics. Following Mullainathan and Thaler (2000)[44], he asserts that behaviorists criticize the neoclassical economic paradigm, since it is based, in terms of its assumptions about agents, on three attributes, at least highly debatable:

- unlimited rationality;
- unlimited will;
- Unlimited selfishness.

With regard to the attribute of unlimited rationality, and making a bit of history, it is necessary that, as early as 1955, Herbert Simon, whom we mentioned in the previous section, criticized the economic models that adopted the assumption of agents with unlimited capacities for processing information, which led him to coin the term bounded rationality to describe a more realistic view of human capacity for information processing.

We have already stressed that, according to this vision, human beings face restrictions of mental capacity and time and, therefore, will not always be able to solve complex problems optimally. Consequently, a "rational" strategy against these restrictions may be the adoption of practical rules that allow people to economize in the use of time or their mental faculties. But, just as this rational strategy can facilitate complex decisions, it can also lead to systematic errors, that is, repeated ones, as shown by Kahneman and Tversky[45].

Deviations from the assumption of rationality can occur with respect to judgments -based on beliefs- of the agents, which leads to situations of overconfidence, anchoring, extrapolation and judgments about the probability of future events based on limited but available information. They can also occur with respect to agent options, described by the prospect theory of Kahneman and Tversky. Two important concepts in this theory are those of "aversion to losses" and "mental accounting". The concept of "aversion to losses" suggests that people are more sensitive to decreases in their well-being than to increases in it, or in other words, it has been empirically verified that, in many cases, the decrease in utility associated with a loss is greater than the increase in utility associated with an equivalent gain.

For its part, the concept of "mental accounting" coined by Thaler[46], refers to situations in which agents, in the face of repetitive events with uncertain results, treat them as independent results and adopt a strategy for each of them, instead of to consider them as a single pool of events and adopt a general strategy. An example of mental accounting, collected by Camerer[47], is the behavior of taxi drivers in New York City. As in many other countries, many New York taxi drivers pay a fixed rent for the use of a taxi, and keep the rest of the income they earn. In this situation, the "rational" strategy of optimization would be to work more during the days of high demand (days with bad weather, or days when there is a big event in the city) and slightly less during days of low demand.

However, if the drivers evaluated each day independently, and compared the income of the day with a pre-established standard, they could end up working more hours, precisely in the days of low demand, something quite unsound from the neoclassical theory, but which is precisely the most usual empirical finding.

In relation to the second attribute, that of unlimited will, there are numerous examples of situations in which it can be affirmed that agents effectively know what is best for them, but do not opt accordingly due to problems of self-control. These deviations occur in the case of addictions, but also in usually less severe cases, such as bad eating habits, sedentary lifestyle or simple procrastination (leave for tomorrow what can be done today), something that usually happens to the majority of people.

Finally, the attribute of unlimited selfishness is also rebuttable and, happily, innumerable examples of altruistic behavior can be found, including the relative success of many national collections and volunteerism in charities.

Undoubtedly, it is quite clear, after all these examples, that behaviorists reason and theorize following a line of argument very similar to Simon's ("bounded rationality"), and obviously in tune with Neuroeconomics, but with the difference that their models were born based on psychological research, and not on Cognitive Neuroscience, unlike Neuroeconomics, which has stronger solid science foundations. However, behavioral contributions have been growing, and with a high degree of acceptance of mainstreams (several Nobel prizes), especially today that their theoretical developments are being provided with foundations in Cognitive Neurosciences, which gives them more rigor.

12. Neuroeconomics

While the conception of the neoclassical model starts from the idea that human beings have well-defined objectives that they try to obtain, the first findings of Neuroeconomics confirm the idea that in a person there are at least two decision centers, one from the "deliberative" system, located in the cerebral cortex, and another "affective" system, located in the inner part of the brain, that is, in its limbic part; and both systems interact permanently.

We return this way to the beginning, when Adam Smith (from introspection, not from Neurosciences) spoke of a confrontation between our passions and what he calls "impartial spectator" (Smith used a well-directed psychology, but very rudimentary). Although the neoclassical model starts from the premise that consumers optimize their utility and entrepreneurs maximize their profits, in a scenario of perfect information, this has not been the case at the beginning of economic science on the one hand (Adam Smith and others classics), and on the other there have been divergent opinions with that model for a long time (the aforementioned Hutchison, J.M.Keynes, Simon, among others mentioned throughout this chapter).

However, it is generally recognized that the neoclassical model has worked reasonably well, although we believe it must be discussed again in its fundamental premise (quasi-perfect optimizing rationality) in order to build a better economic theory. Moreover, we could say that any human decision that is theoretically modeled should be proposed in such a way as to maximize together the rational and the emotional that coexist in the human being, in order to reach a real and complete balance; where an alternative, albeit with criticism, could be the following model, by Loewestein and O'Donoghue[48].

In their work, both economists raise both the deliberative (rational, system 2) and affective (emotional, system 1) systems, since both underlie human behavior, and assume that the human being faces a function to minimize, which is the cost of their behavior. One part of the cost is the difference between what the deliberative system wants and what it ultimately obtains and another part of the cost is the effort that the deliberative system (led by the dorsolateral prefrontal cortex) must make to spur the impulse to act certain way (that comes from the affective system).

$$[U(x^D, c(s), a(s)) - U(x^A, c(s), a(s))] + h(W,\sigma)[M(a^A, a(s)) - M(x, a(s))]$$

where U is a utility function, x the chosen course of action, of a set X, the supra-indexes D and A indicate the optimal behaviors for the deliberative and affective systems respectively, s is a vector of stimuli, a(s) and c(s) are the vectors of affective states of the affective and deliberative systems respectively related to these stimuli, h is the effort necessary to correct the desire that comes from the affective system, function of the power of the will, W and elements that weaken it, σ, and M are the courses of action of the affective system.

This model tells us that the deliberative system is subject to two forces: one from the deliberative system itself and another from the affective system. If the first one totally overrides the second one, the behavior followed would be xD, and if only the affective one prevails the behavior would be xA. However, what usually (but not always) happens is that an intermediate point is reached between both extreme positions. And after applying this model to three different problems: intertemporal preference, risk behavior and altruism, they come to the conclusion that the affective system shares the regulation of the behavior with the deliberative system, and that the totally rational behaviors, derived from the deliberative system are not always what we find in reality.

Beyond the simple model of Loewestein and O'Donoghue, it is encouraged to mathematize human behavior in a different way to the neoclassical, this being an alternative modeling direction in Economics; to consider the maximization of both systems (either acting in the form of conflict, as Kahneman argues, or in a unitary way, as Glimcher argues), but not only modeling the deliberative, as has the tradition in economics from the neoclassicals to now (and above an unreal deliberative system, arising from introspection, and not from Neurosciences). Perhaps, in some years, we will see many more models with proposals of this type, without too complex mathematics, and probably more refined, both at the micro level and those that support the macro. This is probably the only way for the neuroeconomic approaches to overcome the Friedman Thesis of epistemological validation, which we will discuss in detail in the last chapter of this book.

ADVANCES IN NEUROECONOMICS

In what is usually not mentioned, Economics started with Psychology (not scientific) in the middle of the XVIII century, hand in hand with the so-called Classics, such as Adam Smith (especially with his "Theory of Moral Sentiments") and David Hume, among others. To be more rigorous, as the (scientific) psychology still did not exist, those founding fathers of economics acted in some way as psychologists, especially through introspection, recognizing in their writings the remarkable influence of emotions - just as the reason- in the decision making; that is to say the conjunction of both, not the separated reason acting in isolation to make the best decision.

However, a few decades later, the economists who followed Adam Smith and the like - the neoclassicals - became skeptical about the possibility that our psychological forces could be measured directly, which led to the adoption by the economic science of the useful tautology between unobserved utilities (originated in the black box of the human psyche) and observed (revealed) preferences.

However, at present, the important advances in Cognitive Neuroscience allow (for the first time in the history of science) to approach a more direct measurement of thoughts and feelings, opening said black box -the human mind-, the basal block of all economic interaction. Undoubtedly, this scientific possibility is disruptive for the Economic Sciences, since it allows to face the generation of economic theory and its subsequent verification / falsification from other methodological paths. We will return to this topic in a later chapter.

Making a very brief historical synthesis of the traditional micro models of decision making, the Theory of Revealed Preferences (in English it was known as WARP) was developed initially in 1930 by the famous economist Paul Samuelson (and later refined, in what it was called GARP), becoming the core of the so-called "neoclassical revolution". The theory, in its GARP version, proposes that if a consumer, when facing the choice between an apple and an orange, chooses the apple, he is revealing his preference for the apple (without necessarily knowing the neuro mechanisms that led him to that decision -It does not matter to the neoclassicals-). Additionally, if the same consumer reveals preferring oranges over pears, this implies that "indirectly" is revealing preferences of apples over pears, that is, which (observed) decisions can be used to predict about the relative desirability of many pairs of other goods, although they have never been directly compared by consumers. Thus, what Samuelson and later authors demonstrated mathematically was that even simple assumptions about this kind of binary choices, revealing stable (albeit weak) preferences, could have powerful implications for economic theory.

After the WARP and the GARP, but within the same idea, came the theoretical refinements of the so-called Expected Utility Theory (von Neumann and

Morgenstern) and Subjective Theory of Expected Profit (Savage), always with the sole purpose of predicting decisions (choices), no matter in the least the internal process in the "human black box", your brain. Undoubtedly, and put into context, the contribution of Samuelson and his followers and refiners was truly ingenious; However, today, with neuro advances, it is clearly insufficient to understand the complexity of the economic decision-making process.

But they do not begin with Neuroeconomics the attacks against the "revealed preferences", but they come already from the decade of '50; for example in 1953, the French economist Maurice Allais demonstrated certain "failures" of that theory, which went down in history as the "Paradox of Allais". In 1963 the so-called "Ellsberg Paradox" was added, with dyes similar to that of Allais, in the sense of discovering faults that violated the main axioms of the Theory of Revealed Preferences and all its later versions. Subsequently, during the '70 and '80 came the Nobel prizes Simon, Kahneman and Tversky (mentioned in detail in a previous chapter), with theoretical and empirical contributions that noted that the range of phenomena that was outside the traditional theory of "Revealed Preferences" and "Expected Utility" was much greater than that implied by the paradoxes of Allais and Ellsberg. Of course, at present, neuroeconomists have joined, with instruments of measurement much more sophisticated than previous critics, and each time discovering "more holes in the neoclassical ceiling", more anomalies, which already cause doubts about their true scientific rigor.

1. Allais's Paradox[49]

In 1952, a few years after the publication of the von Neumann and Morgenstern theory, a meeting was held in Paris to discuss risk economics. Many of the most renowned economists of the time were present. Among the American guests were future Nobel laureates Paul Samuelson, Kenneth Arrow and Milton Friedman, as well as the illustrious statistician Jimmie Savage.

One of the organizers of the Paris meeting was Maurice Allais, who a few years later would also receive the Nobel Prize. Allais set out to show that his guests were susceptible to a "certainty effect", and that, therefore, they violated the theory of expected utility and the axioms of rational choice in which that theory rested.

MAURICE ALLAIS

Allais's paradox was later developed by Maurice Allais in his book "Le Comportement de L'homme

Rationnel Devant le Risque: Critique des Postulats et Axiomes de L'école Américaine", published in 1953. The paradox is generally explained with the following example[50]:

An individual is asked to choose one among the different bets:

- Bet A: 100% probability of receiving 100 million.
- Bet B: 10% chance of receiving 500 million, 89% probability of receiving 100 million, 1% chance of not receiving anything.

And another among the following bets:

- Bet C: 11% probability of receiving 100 million, 89% probability of not receiving anything.
- Bet D: 10% chance of receiving 500 million, 90% chance of not receiving anything.

If the axiomatic of the expected utility were applied, the preference A> B should imply that C> D. However, the experiment shows that more rational individuals would choose A> B, but C <D, although you can easily see that the expected value of each bet is a = 100, b = 139, c = 11 and d = 50.

In the first bet the least risky option is preferable to a higher expected utility, while in the second bet a higher profit is preferable to a less risky option. That ends up being the paradox, based on the fact that in financial risk or betting choices, although people generally prefer certainty to uncertainty, if the bet is presented differently, they will prefer the uncertainty that was previously rejected.

As Allais had anticipated, the well-educated participants in the meeting did not notice that their preferences violated utility theory until the moment they were reminded that the meeting was about to conclude. Allais wanted the ad to fall like a bomb: **that the most outstanding decision theorists around the world had preferences that were inconsistent with their own concept of rationality.** Apparently, he believed that his audience, persuaded, would abandon the approach that he somewhat disdainfully labeled "American school" and adopt its alternative logic of the election he had developed.

However, Allais was going to suffer great disappointment. The majority of economists, little fans to the theory of the decision, ignored the problem of Allais. As often happens when a theory that has been widely accepted and considered useful is challenged, they saw the problem as an anomaly and continued to use the theory of expected utility as if nothing had happened. On the other hand, the decision theorists (a group we can find statisticians, economists, philosophers and psychologists) took Allais' challenge very seriously. When Amos Tversky and Daniel Kahneman began their work, one of our first goals was to find a satisfactory psychological explanation of Allais' paradox.

Most decision theorists, maintained their belief in human rationality and tried to twist the rules of rational choice to allow this pattern. For years there have been multiple attempts to find a plausible justification for the effect of certainty, but none has been convincing. Amos Tversky was little patient with these efforts; he called on theorists who tried to rationalize the violations of the utility theory "lawyers of confusion", since together with Kahneman they went in a different direction. They maintained the theory of utility as a logic of rational choice, but abandoned the idea that humans are perfectly rational in their choices. They set out to develop a psychological theory that would describe the choices people make regardless of whether they are rational or not. In the perspective theory (prospects), the decision values are not identical to the values of the probabilities.

2. The Anomalies

Fortunately, and thanks to all these strong criticisms over the last 50 years, there is now growing curiosity about Neuroeconomics, Behavioral Economics and other "rebellious" branches towards the neoclassical status quo, although still with uncertain credulity about what can change important aspects of traditional economic theory, the neoclassical. It happens that the tradition in economic science of ignoring neuropsychological regularities in making assumptions, both in the micro and macro models, is so strongly rooted-and in fact has proven to be, to some extent, successful, that to know more about the brain and of its underlying neuropsychology seems to be unnecessary for a few colleagues. And it is likely that economists continue a few years more hesitant to give importance to the new neuro findings, beyond the curiosity that they show today, and that they have also shown with Behavioral Economics; but nevertheless, it is difficult to believe that certain neuroscientific regularities are going to be ignored for a long time, especially those that help explain better certain anomalies that have been discussed for years in our discipline.

Mention some of these anomalies, for example, in order to illustrate possible contributions of Neuroeconomics to solve them. They argue Camerer, Loewestein and Prelec[51], that in many areas of economics there are basic or variable constructs that can be usefully thought as neural processes, and in this way, studied using Neuroimaging, Trasncranean Magnetic Stimulation and other related tools (these tools have already been mentioned in a previous chapter). For example, let's take the field of finance, where millions of daily stochastic observations are made in markets, but despite such statistical access, and after decades of arduous academic research, there is still little agreement on basic issues such as why prices of financial stocks are usually so volatile, based on changing risk perceptions. Perhaps knowing a little more about the neural mechanisms that underlie the assessment of risks by human beings, biases and other human "fragilities" can help explain these theoretical riddles better.

Continuing with the enumeration of anomalies in economic theory, let us now turn to labor markets, where a major question is still why wages are rigid to the downside. It is generally said that companies are afraid of such casualties because they want to keep high the "morale of the workers"; and that paying a high salary also induces effort. But probably, this "workers' moral" is not sensitive only to salary levels, but also depends on the feelings of employees towards their employers, and also can be very sensitive to recent experience, to the opinion of other workers, whether the salary cuts are procedurally fair, among others. And there are no reasons why these aspects cannot be described as neural processes and studied in this way, hand in hand with Neuroeconomics.

COLIN CAMERER

Also, within the current theoretical base of economics, there would be an important series of anomalies in terms of intertemporal choices. In the United States, Camerer, Loewestein and Prelec mention, debt with credit cards is quite high at present (about US $ 5,000 average per family) and, as a consequence, a large number of personal bankruptcies are declared annually. There is also the case of low-calorie food, which is cheap and easier to obtain than ever before, but spending on diets and treatments for obesity (no cheap at all) is growing more and more. Surely, understanding how brain mechanisms process reward for what we consume, or how they produce compulsion (shopping, food, etc.), could help explain these facts and shape effective policies on the subject, since analysis based on traditional economic theory (hyper-rationalist) do not fit too much.

But the empirical findings of alleged anomalies crop up everywhere. Let's see additional examples, in this case from the work of the Peruvian economist Ernesto López, which is more based on Behavioral Economics than on Neuroeconomics, but illustrates the current theory-practice disparity in economics with eloquent examples[52]. For example, let's go back to the field of finance and consider investor overconfidence. In theory, rational investors are expected to make periodic contributions and withdrawals from their investment portfolios, which try to keep them balanced in terms of the profitability-risk ratio and carry out some transactions for tax purposes. However, it is difficult that these legitimate needs of the rational investor can justify the high volumes of transactions registered in stock exchanges throughout the world. In a very interesting work, Barber and Odean[53], empirically evaluated the behavior of a sample of 35,000 investors from the United States and came to the conclusion that:

- the volume of transactions was excessive compared to what was recommended and,

- as a consequence of this behavior, agents that carried out the most transactions, in general, obtained worse results than the market average.

Something else: in the same study, investors were classified by sex and it was found that males (who, moreover, are overrepresented in the financial sector worldwide) made 45% more transactions than women and obtained lower net profits by approximately one percentage point, a statistically significant margin.

What explanation can be given to these results? In these cases we speak of overconfidence, which consists of the conviction of an agent, that the accuracy of his knowledge about the value of an action is superior to that of the market and that is reflected in the current price.

In agreement with the empirical findings, psychological studies show an excess of confidence in men with greater intensity than women, especially in what refers to tasks that are perceived as "masculine" - among which finance is counted- and in those situations in which the feedback information is non-existent or ambiguous (again, this is the case of finance). So, even when both men and women show signs of overconfidence, the excess of confidence of the "macho" in an activity that assumes as "his domain" leads him to invest in excess and to obtain worse results than women. That is, again, the neoclassical maximizing cost-benefit calculation seems to fail, and what is worse, we are talking about a large sample of investors, not isolated cases.

Another interesting example is related to household savings. In effect, the theory of the life cycle, widely accepted in the traditional academic world, predicts that people will save during the most productive periods of their lives and will get into debt or consume their savings during the years of lower income. Clearly, this prediction is not supported empirically. On the contrary, it is appreciated that the consumption of people is very closely related to their income and that, in many cases, the consumption of individuals falls drastically when they go to retirement, simply because they do not have enough savings to "soften" their consuming patterns. An analysis conducted for the United States shows that many middle and lower income families simply do not have the capacity to save and, therefore, do not save. And if this happens in the United States, surely similar studies in Latin American countries would lead to results, similar or probably worse.

We can also give as an example the case of those markets characterized by the use of veiled information (hidden): it is verified that there are several markets where companies choose to hide information from consumers. Take as an example banks, which spend large amounts on advertising to express the virtues of their services, but do not sufficiently highlight the various costs that the consumer must assume, such as commissions and expenses of various kinds. In this case, although banks could compete based on these charges (as indicated by conventional economic theory), they decide to hide them, in such a way that most consumers take a long time to understand the cost structure of services associated with their bank accounts. And similarly, in the printer market manufacturers compete intensively for the cost of printing equipment, but they do not compete with respect to the main cost associated with having a printer, namely, ink cartridges only compatible with one type of equipment, that can end up costing ten times the value of the equipment throughout its useful life.

As already mentioned, in these cases, conventional theory would imply that this concealment of information would end up affecting the agent responsible for it, since the veiled information - which is probably not favorable to consumers - would lead to the "rational consumers" discover the information or, at least, establish the conjecture that hidden prices must be high prices and, consequently, be directed towards those suppliers that do not hide information. In balance, all suppliers would reveal the full information relevant to consumers.

However, the results of the analysis show that the existence of "myopic" consumers leads to the emergence and permanence of information hiding behaviors by suppliers, a situation that would configure a market equilibrium in which a part of the information is veiled. These results are consistent with other research that show that consumers give more weight to the sale price of an electrical device than to the cost of the associated electricity consumption during the product's useful life, or that reveal that, in the case of purchases over the Internet, the consumers pay more attention to direct costs than to shipping costs.

Through all these eloquent examples, we have analyzed only six of the many anomalies that the traditional, hyper-rational theory cannot explain today, and that "give rise" to the fact that Neuroeconomics (and also Behavioral Economics) can help to overcome them, with results so far promising. Next, we will analyze more in detail specific findings that different research teams in Neuroeconomics are currently obtaining around the world.

3. Neuroeconomics and Ultimatum Game

In a landmark study in Neuroeconomics, Sanfey, Rilling, Cohen and others[54], applied fMRi (functional magnetic resonance) about nineteen players of the Ultimatum Game, to investigate the neuro fundamentals of the cognitive and emotional processes put into play when making economic decisions. The aforementioned Ultimatum Game (in this case a single shot -one shot game-) consists of two people trying to share a certain sum of money: one player proposes a division and the other can accept it or not.

ALAN SANFEY

Brain images were taken only of the players responding to the proposals (not those who formulated them), where such formulated proposals were sometimes fair and sometimes unfair. The offers considered fair (50/50 distribution of money, or half for each) were all accepted, while unfair offers (all those involving a distribution below 50/50 for the respondent) were more rejected as that increased their degree of injustice (60/40 is not the same as 80/20). And through the neuroimages, it was observed that these unfair offers activated brain areas related to both the emotional (anterior insula) and the cognitive (dorsal-lateral pre-frontal cortex). And in another data that is interesting, it was also observed that the degrees of rejection of unfair offers were greater when the bidder was a human being than when it was simply the computer (who were also used in this experiment as formulators of proposals), illustrating that human beings have a superior emotional reaction to unfair offers from other humans than to the same formulated via some impersonal mechanism (computers in this case).

Ultimatum Game

Player 1 can offer a fair (F) or unfair (U) proposal; player 2 can accept (A) or reject (R).

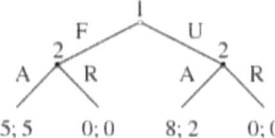

Guth et al. 1982

Nash Equilibrium is at odds: Low offers of less than 20% of the total amount are rejected about half of the time.

Neuroscience has begun to offer clues as to the mechanisms underlying these decisions.

Another interesting finding of this work was given that, in the face of unfair offers that were later rejected, greater activation of the insula than pre-frontal cortex was observed, while the accepted offers showed the opposite, greater activation of the prefrontal cortex than insula. This situation would be reaffirming what is already known in Neurosciences: the rational / cognitive tendency of the pre-frontal cortex and the eminently emotional nature of the insula. But beware... it is not a competition in our brain between the rational and the emotional separately, but it is a performance of both together, related and complementing.

Also, in another interesting finding, it was observed that the activation of the pre-frontal cortex remained constant before less or more unfair offers, perhaps representing how stable the mental representation of a monetary maximization is, while the activation of the insula scale depending on the degree of injustice of the offer.

Finally, Sanfey and other researchers also observed, in the case of unfair offers, an activation of the anterior cingulate, a cerebral area bordering the pre-frontal cortex, normally activated in situations of conflict between the emotional and the cognitive, such as this one experiment.

In this way, we can conclude that the observed activation in the anterior insula (eminently emotional area of the brain) before unfair treatment or offerings, indicates a very important role of emotions in human decision-making processes, despite the attempt of the standard economic theory for suggesting that any sum of money offered to a person - without any cost or consideration - should be accepted, since net income is maximized. This neuroeconomic study then suggests that the human being does not always maximize in his economic decisions, since sometimes, although the economic calculation advises to accept, the emotional influences, making the decision apparently irrational. But such a decision is not irrational, it is simply ... human.

4. Neural Purchasing Predictors

Knutson, Loewenstein and others[55], in one of the first studies that used fMRi (functional magnetic resonance) to examine the consumer's real behavior, "shook the board a bit" of what had been done in Neuromarketing - or in economic terms, in the study of micro-demand functions, and analyzed by brain images people at a time of purchase in concrete form.

Some argue that it is one of the most important Neuromarketing studies published to date.

Twenty-six adults participated in the same, each with $ 20 to spend on certain products, which then would be sent home in case of purchase. And if they chose not to make any purchase, they could keep the money. The products and their prices appeared on a computer screen that participants could see while their brains were being scanned by magnetic resonance.

The researchers found that, as the participants were observing the attributes of each product, a subcortical brain region called nucleus accumbens was activated - this region is usually associated with the anticipation of pleasure or something pleasant, which like-. However, when people were warning about the excessive prices of certain products, two additional things happened: the brain region known as insula (eminently emotional area) was activated and the pre-frontal middle cortex (eminently rational area) was deactivated. We have already mentioned that the insula is a brain area that is activated in situations that the person observes as unfair, or unpleasant; while the pre-frontal cortex is related to the balance of gains and losses, that is, the economic calculation, the eminently rational.

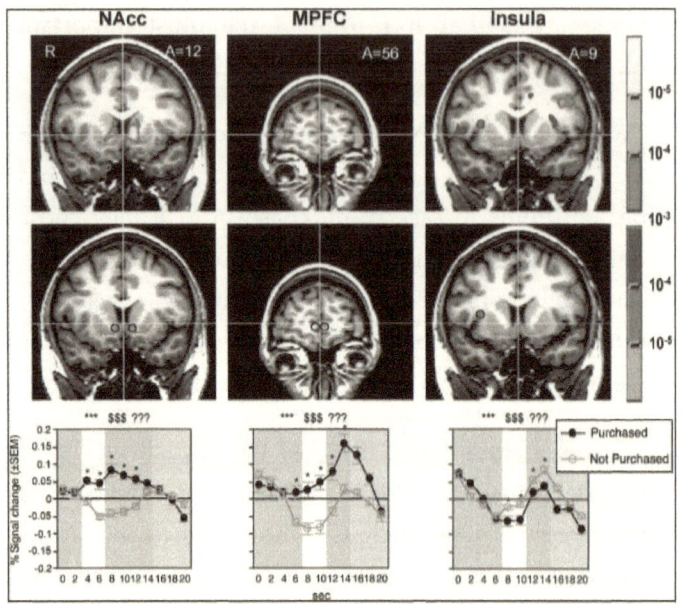

In the upper part of the figure, activation of the nucleus accumbens (NAcc), the middle prefrontal cortex (MPFC) and the insula can be observed. In the middle figure, the geographical location of each of them is observed and in the lower graphs, the changes in the level of activation over time are observed, measured in seconds (product display, price display, decision period) and your confidence intervals.

In this way, by studying which brain regions were activated at the time each person decided to buy, the researchers were able to successfully predict whether the participants would decide to buy or not. Activations of the regions associated with the preference for the product (nucleo accumbens) and the weight of gains and losses (middle pre-frontal cortex) indicated that a person would decide to buy a product. On the contrary, when the region associated with excessive prices (insula) was activated, the participants would choose not to buy said product.

That is to say, a significant aspect of the study is that the brain scan via neuroimaging predicts consumer behavior almost as well as the intentions of the consumers before the experiment, showing that:

- Neuromarketing studies aim to be better than the usual market studies, since they are less biased, although they are more expensive;
- From the econometric point of view, introducing neuro variables allows enriching the demand functions estimated in the traditional way.

5. The Theory of Mind

In this study, Sanfey, Rilling, Cohen and others[56], tried to determine in two different games (Prisoner's Dilemma and Ultimatum), if people who interact socially, receiving feedbacks from other human beings, and intuiting how these feedbacks could be used to infer how our brain works, could predict what others think. Recall that in game theory, one of the most important tasks for participants is to act strategically from what others do or plan to do, and this implies a key role of the so-called Theory of Mind, i.e. those circuits' brain cells that are activated when trying to predict the behavior of our interlocutors.

The so-called "Theory of Mind" studies our social brain. One of the distinctive attributes of human social cognition is our propensity to build models of other minds, that is, to make inferences about the mental states of others. This human capacity has become known in Neurosciences as a theory of the mind and many neuroimaging studies have attempted to elucidate the neural substrates of this natural human ability. Previous studies to the here detailed have already shown the main activable cerebral areas (some more rational, others more emotional) in this type of action.

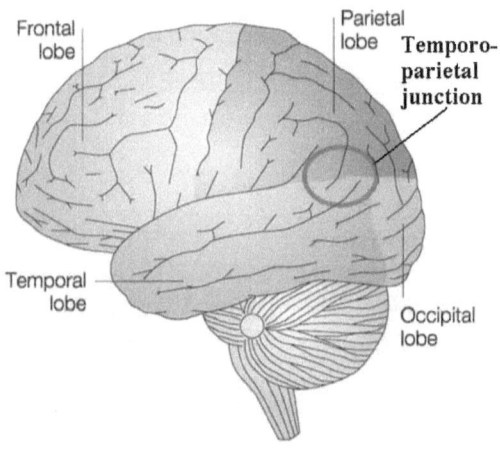

The brains of the participants in this experiment (led by the aforementioned Sanfey) were scanned using fMRi (functional magnetic resonance) while playing two different games: Ultimatum Game (UG) and Prisoner's Dilemma (PDG), both in front of other humans and in front of computer screens. Comparing both games, a striking degree of coincidence was observed between the brain areas that were activated, including both areas already accepted as specific to the Theory of Mind (mentioned above), as well as several other brain areas that had not been previously reported, and that may be related to the immersion of participants in real social interactions. And while the interactions of humans with computers also achieved activation in some of the same areas activated by games between only humans, in the latter case these activations were more notorious and defined.

In both games, the participants witnessed a decision on the part of their partners, in the UG they observed an offer of money that another made them, either fair or unfair, and on which they had to react and in the PDG they observe an election what another did, whether cooperative or selfish, and about which they also had to respond. That is, before deciding the answer to take, in both cases, they witnessed something that revealed the partner's intentions. What brain areas would be activated in both cases? That was the central core of the study.

If in the previous study the activated brain areas were analyzed when responding to a fair or unfair offer, in this new study[57] the previous moment was analyzed, that is to say, the activable brain areas when a proposal was recently known, just or unjust, and it is deliberating what to do, and at the same time, inferring what the other person is like and his true intentions.

Going to the concrete results of the study, for both games (UG and PDG), activation was detected in two of the four classic areas of the Theory of Mind: anterior paracingular cortex and posterior superior temporal sulcus (STS later). Both areas were activated in interactions with both humans and computers, but showed stronger responses to human partners in both games, that is, respondent participants rejected unfair offers from humans to a greater extent than from computers in the UG and cooperated more often with humans than with computers in the PDG.

Following with the results of the study -where we remember there is social immersion of the participants-, brain areas were also found that were activated that had not been noticed in previous studies -without social interaction-. These were:

- precuneus
- upper temporal sulcus (STS) medium
- an area that includes hypothalamus, middle brain and thalamus
- left hippocampus

Both the activation of the posterior cingulate and the hypothalamus can be related to emotional issues when receiving responses from humans, who obviously have less presence when doing studies without human interaction. The activation of the average STS, normally attributable to the biographical memory, may be related to the fact that the participants are learning new information about other people -the ones who make the offers-. Finally, the activation of the hippocampus could be related to the activity of decoding behaviors and intentions of others: are they just or unjust? Are they cooperative or non-cooperative?

In summary, and taking into account that the paper leaves perhaps more questions than answers, the brain areas that can be activated with respect to the theory of the mind (many of them more emotional than rational, without a doubt), would be at least:

- the anterior paracingular cortex
- upper posterior temporal sulcus (posterior STS)
- the posterior cingulate / precuneus
- the average STS
- an area that includes hypothalamus, middle brain and thalamus
- the left hippocampus

6. Oxytocin and Trust

No one can argue, surely, that trust between people is essential to strengthen human societies. Trust is necessary to make friends, form partners, families and organizations and of course play an essential role in economic exchanges and politics. In the absence of trust between people and companies, market transactions are cut, and in the absence of trust in the institutions and leaders of a country, political legitimacy is lost. Recent empirical evidence in humans has identified the role of neuroactive hormones, especially oxytocin, as a facilitator of pro-social behavior based on trust.

Recent neuroeconomic experiments with humans have shown that the reception of a signal of confidence from a stranger is associated with an endogenous release of oxytocin by the brain and also that high levels of oxytocin have been strongly associated with reciprocal behaviors of said signals of trust.

In this work, Paul Zak and Ahlam Fakhar[58], test whether the endocrinological bases of trust between humans (in small groups, that is, at the micro level) can be scaled at the country level (macro level), especially taking into account the statistics on confidence at the national level show substantial disparities (in Norway for example, 65% of respondents answered that they could trust their fellow citizens, while in Peru only 6% responded in that way).

Oxytocin (a type of neuroactive hormone we said), whom Zak calls the "molecule of morality", is synthesized in the hypothalamus (belonging to the limbic system - eminently emotional zone of the brain) and then released into the circulatory system. In humans, certain areas of the brain associated with memory (the diagonal band of Broca and the basal nucleus of Meynert) and areas associated with emotions (hypothalamus and amygdala) present an important accumulation of oxytocin receptors, although there are receptors of oxytocin distributed throughout the brain. This distribution of oxytocin receptors in limbic areas suggests that the decision to trust others has an important emotional component, and therefore a high component of speed and low introspection when deciding.

FIGURE 1

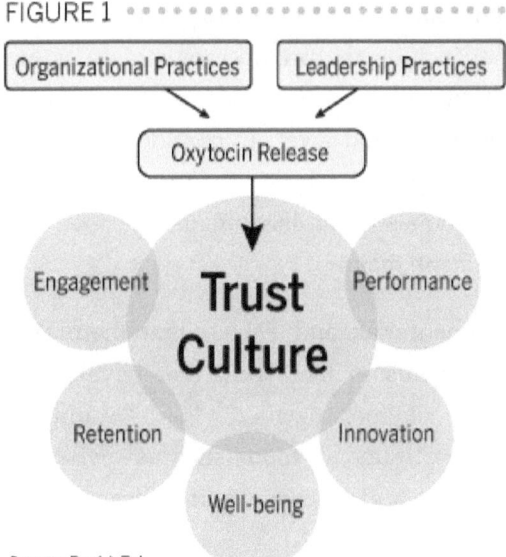

Source: Paul J. Zak.

And, as both studies with animals and humans, indicate that estrogen is highly related to oxytocin levels, the authors of this work used estrogen as a proxy for oxytocin. The hypothesis to be demonstrated in this study was that people who live in societies settled in environments with high levels of oxytocin and / or estrogen are more likely to affirm that their fellow citizens are reliable, that is, to have more confidence in their peers.

Analyzing in detail the work, thirty-one variables were taken (between biological, social and environmental) associated with interpersonal trust for a sample of forty-one countries, where the authors found that two groups of variables are related to trust interpersonal at the country level: the consumption by its inhabitants of plants based on estrogens (phytoestrogens) and the existence of environmental conditions that include the presence of molecules of the estrogen type. In this way, these results provide preliminary evidence that levels of confidence at the country level may be related to the intake of neuroactive hormones by its inhabitants, via food or via the environment, mainly.

They also comment Zak and Fakhar that there are more than 300 plants in the world that have been identified as phytoestrogenic. For example, phytoestrogens are found in foods such as soybeans and derivatives, rye and derivatives, rice, beans, beef and tea / mate, among others.

In summary, this paper shows that endocrinological effects can be a new explanation-independent of the usual institutional causes-for the problem of confidence differentials observed between countries, indicators directly associated with higher or lower levels of investment and economic development of each country. That is to say, this work tries to show that specific environmental / food conditions in some countries, which impact the oxytocin levels of its inhabitants, can lead to higher levels of confidence. Specifically, nations that have high per capita incomes, clean environments and consume more food with phytoestrogens have a good chance of showing high levels of generalized trust among their inhabitants, which facilitates economic transactions in general and investment levels in particular.

This information, Zak and Fakhar conclude, should be useful for politicians, if they are interested in raising the levels of trust among their governed, and therefore the quality of their market systems, especially in developing countries. Also the conclusions of this work give a certain rationality towards the maintenance of clean environments and towards the consumption of healthy foods.

7. Somatic Markers and Decision Making

Based on an interesting work by the Chilean psychologist Claudio Lavin[59], we now analyze the somatic marker hypothesis, developed by Antonio Damasio in 1998, a theory that has been very relevant when understanding the role of emotion in decision making. It is argued that before the consequences of a decision there is a certain emotional reaction that is subjective, that is, it can be "experienced", and at the same time somatic, that is, it is translated into muscular, neuroendocrine or neurophysiological reactions. This emotional response in turn can be associated with consequences, whether negative or positive or sets of stimuli that define a situation, that are repeated with certain constancy over time and that provoke such response. This mechanism of association is what produces what Damasio calls "somatic marker" and that is defined as: "a bodily change that reflects an emotional state, either positive or negative, that can influence the decisions made at a certain time". In this way, it is stated that the emotional reaction goes from being a mere consequence, for example of some negative decision, to influencing the decision making itself, making possible the anticipation of the consequences and guiding the final resolution process.

In this sense, it is affirmed that somatic markers can provide unconscious (or, in general, metaconscious) signals that "facilitate and contribute to decision-making", even without the subjects being able to explain the reason for their strategy (for example, when we buy products that clearly would not suit us from the point of view of the cost-quality ratio, or when businessmen manifest, at certain times, an aversion to risk that seems irrational). One way to study these "somatic marker" effects is shown by the IGT (Iowa Gambling Task), where the word gambling gives us the idea of tests based on bets / games of chance, in which different people must choose between four heaps of cards, and depending on their choice they receive rewards or symbolic monetary punishments, so that in the long run two heaps will lead the participants to lose while the other two win.

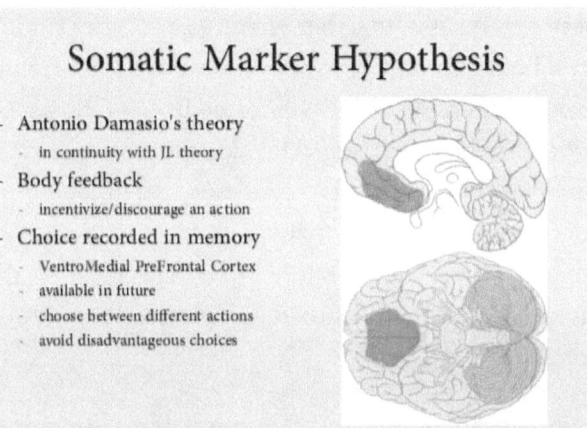

These tests -in their majority- have been carried out through the study of the changes in the electrodermal activity (skin conductance levels and response) produced by the decision-making situation. For example, the works of Bechara - another prominent neuroeconomist nowadays - have shown that normal subjects show greater cutaneous conductance responses when the probable consequences of their choices - gains or losses - are greater. However, the greatest wealth of this research lies in the finding of anticipatory electrodermal responses, that is, they appeared just before the subjects made the choice. The researchers observed that the subjects who chose the heaps of cards with the highest profits showed a greater conductance response before choosing the disadvantageous decks (with lower gains), which has been interpreted as an anticipatory corporal signal that guides the subjects avoid said deck.

These conclusions, together with those of other studies carried out in recent years, have placed the pre-frontal cortex, especially the ventromedial orbitofrontal portion, in the "key region" for decision-making, since it is in this zone where the consequences of long-term actions are evaluated, thanks to the integration of somatic states with information specific to the situation and with stored memories of similar situations.

Lavin concludes that these findings have supported the idea that there are anticipatory somatic responses (supported and reinforced by experience) that guide future behavior and the choices made in similar situations, positioning somatic markers as a relevant variable to consider when evaluating decision making and the relationship between it and emotion. This is also reinforced by the differences between the electrodermal responses of people who achieve optimal performance in the development of tasks and those who achieve poor results and also those who have neurological damage in the brain areas involved in these responses.

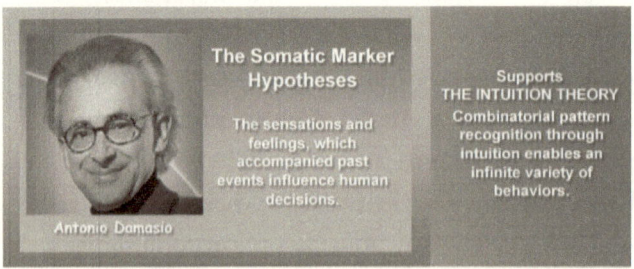

Another interesting study related to the subject is one of Natalie Denburg[60], which analyzes the influence of somatic markers through the different stages in a person's life, especially discriminating between adults under and over 70 years.

Her paper analyzes the correlation that exists between decision making and people's psychophysiological responses, where through the use of the (already mentioned) Iowa Gambling task (IGT), it was observed how they intervene in adults greater changes in skin conductance (SCRs) compared to the anticipation generated prior to the behavioral response. It was found that older adults who obtained negative results in the test (that is, low performance in the bets) presented greater discrimination of the changes in the conductance of the skin during the execution of the test (IGT), reason why it was concluded in which decision-making ability is subject to the interpretation of somatic markers, and that the reduction in decision-making capacity in older adults (over 70 years) would be due to an abnormal functioning of the somatic response against the anticipation of future events.

It was observed that decision making is assisted by emotional processes, signs or somatic markers that originate not only in the body but also in cortical and subcortical areas, including the ventromedial prefrontal cortex (VMPC), the amygdala and the insular cortex, somatosensory cortex, the basal ganglia and the peripheral nervous system. Needless to say, many of the areas mentioned belong to the so-called limbic system, that is, our emotional, meta-conscious and non-rational brain.

In another very interesting aspect of the study, it was also found that, during the game, older adults produced greater amplitude of psychophysiological response to the decks that offered greater reward and that younger adults generated greater amplitude of psychophysiological response to the decks that offered economic disadvantage, which suggests that the pattern of anticipatory discrimination during successful IGT performance differs for older adults and younger adults.

This translates into the fact that decision-making effectiveness in older adults is due to the anticipation of the positive, as opposed to the young adults who sustain their decision making in anticipation of negative responses.

Somatic markers can be positive or negative, although in both cases, they are vital for the action. If positive somatic markers prevail in decision-making in older adults, this suggests that positive somatic states promote approaching behaviors and that younger adults use negative somatic markers to evade options that do not suit them.

But why this difference between young adults and older adults? Some researchers argue that older adults would have greater attenuation of their emotions by experiencing less negative affect than their younger counterparts, presumably for existential reasons[61].

Summarizing then the concept of somatic marker, and beyond the two particular cases analyzed in this section, we can conclude that:

- the somatic marker is "learned" in past experiences;
- the somatic marker is noted in situations in which certain current events are associated with past emotions;
- when the marker is reactivated, either consciously or metaconsciously, the partial or complete replication of an emotional state associated with the current situation to be resolved is promoted;
- the somatic marker, like "memory trace", is recorded in high-order cortical circuits, of which the ventral-medial prefrontal cortex is the most notable example.

In summary, we believe that the hypothesis of the somatic marker, by the hand of Damasio, Bechara and several other researchers in recent years, promises to be of great importance to unite the theory of hyper-rational decisions (on which economics is based on the neoclassical school) with the reality observed in the business world, where very important decisions are made every day, which involve a lot of money, but where the emotional, the intuitive and the metaconscious sometimes end up giving priority to the final decision, improving the success of it, and not the other way around.

8. The Utility of Money

Neuroeconomists usually perform, among other field studies, brain scans while people perform activities where they earn or lose money. The results obtained suggest that the money activates reward areas similar to those that are activated through the consumption of food and drugs, which would imply that the money confers direct utility, instead of being valued only by what can be bought with it.

The standard economic model assumes that the utility of money is indirect, since it is only a means to facilitate the exchange of goods and services, which are those that end up providing utility directly. Thus, the traditional neoclassical economics conceives the pleasure of food or cocaine, for example, and the "pleasure" of obtaining money, as two totally different phenomena. However, neurological evidence[62] suggests that the same dopaminergic reward circuits of the brain are activated for a wide variety of rewards, including attractive faces, funny cartoons, cultural objects, sports cars, drugs, and money). So, according to neuro evidence, it would seem that money, like the other goods and services mentioned, provides a direct reward.

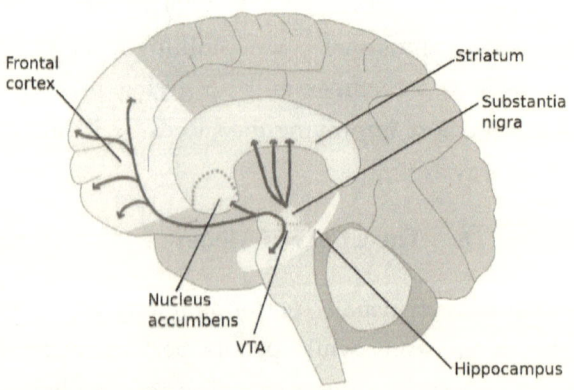

Therefore, the idea that many types of reward (whether by buying goods and services or simply by having money in your pocket, even if it is not spent) are processed in a similar way in the brain, has important implications for economics, that he assumes that the marginal utility of money depends on what it can buy; in this way today it is hypothesized that money would become what psychologists call a "primary reinforcer", which means that people would value money without carefully calculating what they plan to buy with it. And while, we acknowledge, Neuroeconomics is not advanced enough today to categorically affirm this hypothesis, there is a very high possibility that brain valuation for money is loosely linked to the utility of consumption.

But then, if earning money directly provides pleasure, the experience of saying goodbye to him will probably be painful. This would be one of the reasons why many consumers tend to accept purchases in installments (medium and long term financing) to disguise the payments, and in this way reduce our pain by getting rid of liquidity.

9. Deliberative vs Affective

Following a very interesting synthesis made by the Argentine economist Alfredo Navarro[63], in Animal Spirits: Affective and Deliberative Influences on Economic Behavior, Loewenstein and O'Donoghue[64], two eminent North American researchers, maintain that although the neoclassical model supposes an economic agent with a single decision center, the deliberative (the rational part of the brain), this model has worked relatively well to explain the economic behavior, both of the consumer that maximizes its usefulness, and of the businessman who efficiently organizes his company, of the offender who faces to the risk of being arrested if he commits a crime, or of the one who makes the decision to marry or have children.

But Neuroeconomics, as we have commented until the satiety in this book, confirms that there are two decision systems: the affective and the deliberative. The first corresponds to the internal parts of the brain, that is, the most primitive in the evolutionary stage, and the second is located in the cerebral cortex and appears in more recent stages of the evolutionary process. The affective system is related to emotions that have effects on the motivations of human behavior, with a value component always present, either biological (fear, hunger, sexual desire) or social (sympathy, hatred, distrust), and usually operates in meta-conscious form.

Cognitive vs affective processes

Cognitive processes	Affective processes
Concerned with 'yes/no' questions	Concerned with 'go/no go' questions
Work with affective processes to produce action	Work with cognitive processes to produce action
Can control affective processes	Can override cognitive processes

The deliberative system, on the contrary, acts by evaluating what the affective system perceives, with which it is bound by biunivocal nervous connections, and over which it exerts a certain power by having its will power to correct the behavior that would be followed if it existed only the affective system, as it happens with the most primitive animals. The stimuli can affect the affective part only, or also the deliberative part, and depending on the evaluation of both systems, the behavior to be followed will be defined. With these assumptions, which are the basic contributions of Neuroeconomics, Loewenstein and O'Donoghue go a step further, to build a mathematical model that allows them to formalize this relationship. They assume that the human being faces a function to be minimized, which is the cost of his behavior. A part of the cost is the difference between what the deliberative system wants and what it ultimately obtains and another part of the cost is the effort that the deliberative system must make to turn the impulse of acting in a certain way.

$$[U(x_D, c(s), a(s)) - U(x_A, c(s), a(s))] + h(W, \sigma)[M(a_A, a(s)) - M(x, a(s))]$$

where U is a utility function, x the chosen course of action, of a set X, the supra-indexes D and A indicate the optimal behaviors for the deliberative and affective systems respectively, s is a vector of stimuli, $y_a(s)$ and $c(s)$ are the vectors of affective states of the affective and deliberative systems respectively related to these stimuli, h is the effort necessary to correct the desire that comes from the affective system, function of the power of the will, W and elements that weaken it, σ, and M are the courses of action of the affective system.

This model tells us that the deliberative system is subject to two forces: one from the deliberative system itself and another from the affective system. If the first one totally overrides the second one, the behavior followed would be x_D, and if only the affective one prevails the behavior would be x_A. However, what usually (but not always) happens is that an intermediate point is reached between both extreme positions. Subsequently, the authors apply this model to three different problems: intertemporal preference, risk behavior and altruism. In all three cases, they come to the conclusion that the affective system shares the regulation of behavior with the deliberative system, and that totally rational behaviors, derived from the deliberative system, are not always what we find in reality.

Again following a synthesis made by Alfredo Navarro[65], in The Vulcanization of the Human Brain[66], Cohen, renowned American neuroscientist, considers human behavior in terms of its evolution from more primitive forms, in which the cerebral cortex did not yet exist. He considers that the brain is a confederation of mechanisms, which sometimes act together, but at other times they compete with each other (other neuroeconomist, as Paul Glimcher, don't think the same). Cohen describes an experiment in which the behavior of different people is analyzed in the face of the dilemma of avoiding the death of five people by sacrificing a sixth. When the decision must be made at a distance from the facts, we use to accept the suggestion of the cold rationality, avoiding the death of five at the expense of the death of the sixth. But when immersed in the problem, close to the facts, the limbic part of the brain seems to have priority (eminently emotional zone), and we are reluctant to sacrifice that sixth person.

The author, who analyzes the emergence of the human cerebral cortex rationality as something evolutionary, attributes it to the fact that our ancestors did not have the possibility to act at a great distance, due to natural danger the were exposed. The cortex, which would have been the result of a process of vulcanization of the brain, has generated a technological system that has exceeded our emotional capacity. It is a very complicated task to produce a nuclear device, but it is very simple to press a button to throw it. This could imply that the evolution of the human being has led to a crossroads difficult to solve because the cerebral cortex has developed, capable of enormous progress that perhaps would not have occurred in the limbic brain, and that would mean, in that case, and that evolution has taken a bite of the apple of Eden.

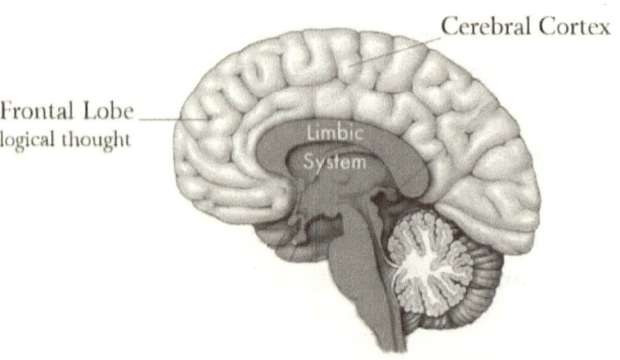

And to finish with the synthesis of neuroeconomic papers made by Alfredo Navarro, let's analyze now the work entitled Damage to the prefrontal cortex increases utilitarian moral judgments, where its authors (Michael Koenings, Liane Young, Ralph Adolphs, Daniel Tranel, Fiery Cushman, Marc Hauser and Antonio Damasio[67]) analyze whether emotions play a causal role in ethical judgments, and how different areas of the brain contribute to that end. They analyze the behavior of six patients who present lesions in the ventromedial prefrontal cortex, (a region of the brain necessary for the control of emotions, and particularly of social emotions), which have an extremely utilitarian behavior when deciding on moral dilemmas. This type of work illustrates the way in which damage to the brain can be an alternative way of studying its functioning.

The research described above constitute only a small sample, in order to illustrate the way in which neuroeconomists work, but there are many other interesting works, which we will not detail in this work for reasons of extension. However, with all those seen in this chapter, we have enough to make a partial assessment of the topic: most of the studies that are being done in Neuroeconomics to date, almost always aim to identify the components of rationality and emotionality that are behind of each economic decision, as if trying to tell traditional theorists, linked to the maximizing and hyper-rationalist models currently in force.

In short, Neuroeconomics is unleashing a theoretical discussion "that brings them", and that surely will reach high decibels in the coming decades, no doubt.

10. Risk and Uncertainty

Following with concrete research results, we will mention the conclusions of other influential neuroeconomic papers. In *The Neural Basis of Financial Risk Taking*, Kuhnen and Knutson[68] tell us that financial investors systematically deviate from rationality when making their portfolio decisions, and in this way, in their study, they try to identify neural mechanisms responsible for such anomalies. Using fMRI (neuroimaging), the authors examined whether, by anticipating investors' neural activity (i.e. by seeing what goes on inside their brain during decision making), optimal and suboptimal financial decisions can be predicted. They characterized two types of deviations with respect to the optimal investment decision (neoclassical):

- risk search errors;
- risk aversion errors.

As for the concrete results, it was found that activation of the nucleus accumbens (eminently emotional area of the brain, activated when the person has a marked preference for something) preceded both risky choices and risk-seeking errors, while activation of the anterior insula (part of the emotional brain, center of disgust-displeasure) preceded choices without risk and risk aversion errors. These findings suggest that:

- different neural circuits, linked to anticipatory effects, promote different types of financial decisions,
- and that excessive activation of these circuits can lead to investment errors (risk and search aversion).

In this way, they conclude that taking into account anticipatory neural mechanisms can add predictive power to the rational decision model of neoclassical economics, which evidently "remains in shame" in the face of empirical evidence.

More about Risk and Neuroeconomics

People react to risks at two different levels. On the one hand, people try to assess the objective level of risk that different scenarios have. But on the other hand, people also react - in situations with a certain degree of risk and uncertainty - on an emotional level, and such emotional reactions can greatly affect their behavior.

The existence in human beings of separate systems for the cognitive and the affective, which respond differently to the risks, is more noticeable when the two systems collide. People often seem to be "two minds" (one deliberative and one more visceral) when facing situations with risk: for example when we have to invite someone to leave, or speak before a certain number of people, or take an important examination, our deliberative mind uses various tactics to propel us to take risks, which perhaps our visceral (emotional, non-deliberative) mind would prefer to avoid. Perhaps the most dramatic illustration of the separation of visceral reactions and cognitive / rational evaluations is found in the various degrees of phobias that people suffer: what distinguishes a phobia is the impossibility of facing a risk that one recognizes - objectively- be little dangerous (move by elevator, by an escalator, to name some of the most scandalous). Moreover, the fact that we humans spend some money on drugs and / or therapies to overcome our phobias, is a clear sign that our deliberative and visceral systems are not in mutual peace usually.

However, today there is much that is known about the neural processes underlying the emotional / affective responses to risks. Most of the risk-averse behaviors are caused by fear responses / fear of risks, where this fear seems to originate in the region called the amygdala (the center of fear, located in the emotional part of our brain). The amygdala constantly monitors new stimuli that indicate potential threat and responds to inputs from both automatic and controlled processes in our brain. However, the amygdala also receives stimuli from the cerebral cortex (the most rational part of the brain), which can moderate or even eliminate the emotional response.

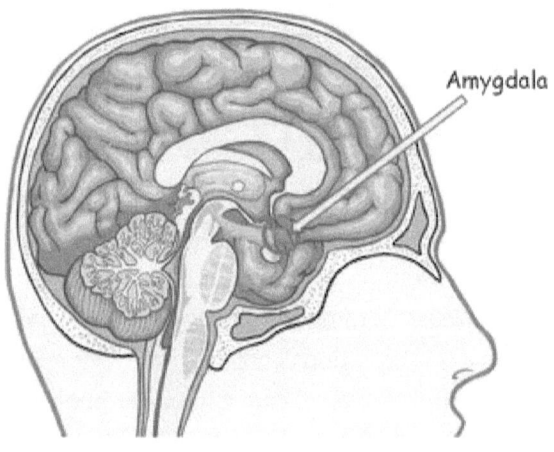

The decision making under risk and uncertainty, as for example the case of intertemporal elections, adequately illustrate both the collaboration and the competition between the emotional and rational systems that exist within us. The case of the difference in risk taking between people with brain damage in the pre-frontal zone (which produces a disconnection between the emotional and rational systems) and normal people is much cited; the former always tend to make decisions that are much riskier than the latter. And while clearly, having pre-frontal damage to the brain in general decreases the quality of our decision-making, there are particular situations in which people with brain damage such as the above can make higher decisions than normal people, for example before very risky scenarios where normal people are usually paralyzed.

The evidence from Neurosciences also substantiates the distinction between risk (known probability) and Knigthian uncertainty (ambiguity). Different studies with neuroimaging show that different degrees of risk and uncertainty activate different areas of the brain. For example Ming Hsu and others[69] found greater activation of the frontal insula and the amygdala (both eminently emotional zones) when people faced ambiguous choices (uncertainty) compared to risky ones.

Once again it can be seen that Neurosciences, and specifically, a consideration of emotional and automatic processes - both long forgotten by economists in dominant economic models - could potentially lead an important line of research and theory, argue Camerer, Loewestein and Prelec in his aforementioned paper[70]. And they add that, if the current theory continues failing to incorporate the affective dimensions of risk, it will be unable to shed light on such important phenomena as the ups and downs in the stock markets, the betting markets and the vicissitudes of public responses to threats as diverse as terrorism and global warming, to name just a few important issues.

11. Game Theory and Neuroeconomics

Game theory is an area of applied mathematics that uses models to study interactions in formalized incentive structures (so-called games) and carry out decision processes. Their researchers study the optimal strategies as well as the predicted and observed behavior of individuals in games. Apparently different types of interaction may, in fact, present similar incentive structures and, therefore, jointly represent the same game.

While economics was one of its first applications (especially for oligopolistic markets), game theory today is used in many fields, from biology to philosophy. It experienced a substantial growth and was formalized for the first time from the works of John von Neuman and Oskar Morgestern, before and during the Cold War, mainly due to its application to military strategy. Since the seventies, game theory has been applied to animal behavior, including the development of species by natural selection. In the wake of games like the Prisoner's Dilemma, in which widespread egoism hurts the players, game theory has been used in political science, ethics and philosophy. Finally, it has also attracted the attention of computer researchers, using artificial intelligence and cybernetics.

But punctually in the field of economics, Neurosciences in general and Neuroeconomics in particular are already well equipped to explore the main assumptions upon which the predictions of game theory rest. These assumptions are:

- players have appropriate beliefs about what others are going to do,
- have no emotions or concerns about what others earn,
- plan forward,
- learn from experience.

In strategic interactions (games), knowing how other people think, and also knowing how other people think you think, is critical in predicting other people's behavior. Nowadays, many neuroscientists think that in the human brain there is an area specialized in "mind reading" (also called Theory of Mind), probably in the pre-frontal zone of our brain, known as area 10 of Brodmann, which generates reasoning about what people who interact with us probably think and then do. In fact, autism is believed to imply a deficit in this area and related circuits. People with autism often have problems imagining what other people think and believe, and therefore are driven to have abnormal behaviors for the common people.

KEVIN McCABE

McCabe and others[71] used neuroimaging to measure brain activity when different people played games involving trust, cooperation, rewards and punishments. They found that those players who cooperated showed significant activation in the aforementioned Brodmann area 10 and in the thalamus. On the contrary, those who cooperated little did not show systematic activation in those areas.

Also interesting is the research by Tania Singer and others[72], who reported an important link between reward and behavior in certain games. These researchers, played the participants of their study, repeated games of the type "prisoner's dilemma", where some players, while they were scanned, faced a series of opponents. First, only the scanned participants were informed that some of their opponents would cooperate intentionally while others would cooperate, but unintentionally. Subsequently - also only the scanned ones - they were shown the faces of those against whom they had played. The faces of the intentional cooperators activated the insula, the amygdala and areas of the ventral striatum, among others. And since striatum is a brain area related to rewards, activations in this region meant that simply seeing the face of people who intentionally cooperated with one is retributive.

More about Theory of Games and Neuroeconomics

In an interesting work on the relationship between Neuroeconomics and Theory of Games, the Argentine economist Alfredo Navarro[73] tells us that, apart from the importance that Neurosciences have for Economics -in particular to redefine the rationality hypothesis-, it is also important to keep in mind that there is a mechanism to export economic methodologies to neuroscience and biology, giving a new perspective to the theory of evolution and allowing analyzing the reciprocal behavior of living beings, where Game Theory plays a very important role. That is, according to this vision, there would be a round trip: Neurosciences impacting Economics, which gives rise to Neuroeconomics (the object of analysis of this work), but also, and this is the novelty, Economics impacting on Neurosciences That is, a soft science impacting a hard science. Let's see how this is. In what follows of this section we will make a review of the work of the aforementioned Navarro, which in turn is based on the very interesting work of the neurobiologist Paul Glimcher[74], where this round trip between Economics, Neurosciences and Biology is analyzed.

Paul Glimcher, who comes from the field of medicine, not economics, in a recent work entitled: Decisions, Uncertainty and the Brain. The Science of Neuroeconomics, analyzes the behavior of living beings based on their effect on other living beings and of these on the first, trying to establish a new paradigm for a better interpretation of the behavior of living beings in general and of humans in particular. Glimcher, after reviewing the ideas about the nature of human behavior of Hippocrates, Galen, Harvey, Bacon and Galileo among others, considers Descartes (1596-1650) as the founder of neuroscience. Divide human behavior into two types, the simple and the complex. The first corresponds to the responses to the impulses of the environment, where there is no free will, as when we perceive the heat of a flame near one hand and quickly remove it. This was revolutionary, because no one before had seriously argued that a phenomenon as complex as behavior could be seen as the product of pure physical interactions in physiological systems.

But the complex behaviors have as characteristic that they are at the mercy of the soul, which supposed lodged in the pineal gland, and that can decide freely according to the circumstances. While the first type of behavior is determined, as is the movement of the planets, whose trajectory we can foresee exactly, it does not occur as well as the second, where free will retains all its validity.

The idea that human behavior, at least that which we call simple, was perfectly predictable took more force at the end of the 18th century with the development of the mathematics of Leibnitz, Newton, Lagrange and Laplace, which allow to predict the future position of the planets every time with better precision. Why then not analyze the behavior of living beings with the same purpose of predicting their behavior? Charles Scott Sherrington, an Oxford neurophysiologist, at the beginning of the last century laid the foundations for the physiological study of reflexes, through a neat description of the processes, but still maintaining the Cartesian distinction between simple, deterministic behaviors and complex behaviors, not deterministic. Subsequently Pavlov generalized the analysis of reflexes to the totality of human behavior and therefore also generalized determinism to all human behavior.

Several reactions against the Sherrington paradigm took place, especially that of Marr, who in the seventies proposed a different hypothesis: behaviors should be analyzed in terms of the organism's objective, which is basically to maximize their "inclusive fitness", meaning that rate at which genes are propagated. But to this must be added the fact that living organisms do not have a full knowledge of the world that surrounds them, for which reason they find themselves in a situation of relative uncertainty. The deterministic mathematics, which was the basis of the theories of reflexes, become insufficient, and it is necessary to resort to the mathematics of the uncertain, that is, to the theory of probabilities, since we rarely have a total knowledge of the circumstances around us. Although the theory of probabilities was born in the eighteenth century with Pascal and Bayes, three centuries pass until it is incorporated into human behavior, both in economics and in neurobiology.

In this way Glimcher, through his historical analysis, presents a way to analyze the behavior of organisms from two different perspectives: simple behaviors, in the Cartesian division, can be solved by applying classical economic theory, because either there is nothing random, or the uncertain is due to our lack of knowledge, so we must use the calculation of probabilities. But in other circumstances -complex behaviors-, we must resort to the theory of games, to analyze behaviors that are unpredictable, not because epistemologically we do not reach knowledge to explain the causes of behavior, as Pavlov maintained, but because they are, necessarily, intrinsically random.

This is a very striking statement for two reasons, firstly because it implies accepting that economic theory explains not only human behavior, but the behavior of all beings belonging to the animal kingdom, and not only economic behavior, but all kinds of behavior, and in second term because, to this affirmation, it is not made by an economist, but by a neurobiologist. According to Pavlov and Laplace, the uncertainty comes from the lack of knowledge of who decides, while what Glimcher says is that the uncertainty comes from outside, from the outside world to who decides, and that the latter must necessarily make a random decision if you do not want your opponent to predict your behavior and gain an advantage from it.

In this way, following the reasoning of the neurobiologist Glimcher, the analysis of the behavior of living organisms can be understood much more fully if we do so from the perspective of game theory, which we remember begins to be applied to the analysis of economic problems with the appearance of the developments of von Neumann and Morgenstern, in 1944, where non-cooperative zero-sum games are analyzed, but more especially after the Nash developments, which analyzes the determination of equilibrium in more generalized situations, such as games cooperatives and non-zero sum.

The analysis of the behavior of organisms that have brains allows Glimcher to argue that there are two types of uncertainty: one that we can call epistemological, which is originated in the lack of information and knowledge of the agent, and that could allow a mechanistic interpretation of the behavior, and another that derives from the need to follow a random behavior.

Suppose a lion is in front of a lamb. You can jump to the right or to the left, trying to guess the behavior of the lamb. Suppose that it can also jump to the right or to the left. If it jumps in the same direction as the lion, it is lost, but if it does it in a different direction, it can be saved. If he always jumped in the same direction, the lion would know in advance what his behavior would be, and he would always be lost. But if he tossed a coin into the air to make his choice, he would be saved, for example, 50% of the time, all on condition that the lion does not know in advance what he is going to do. Therefore, random behavior is essential to pursue what has been defined above as "inclusive fitness".

> **What is game theory?**
>
> - Game theory is a branch of applied mathematics that is used in the social sciences, most notably in economics, as well as in biology (most notably evolutionary biology and ecology), engineering, political science, international relations, computer science, and philosophy.
> - In strategic games, agents choose strategies that will maximize their return, given the strategies the other agents choose.
> - A design tool.
> - The mathematics of human interactions.
> - A promise for the unification of social sciences.

In this way, the mentioned Glimcher reaches its conclusion[75], in the sense that:

We should begin to employ probabilistically based approaches to understand how the brain takes information from the outside world and uses that information in concert with stored representations of the structure of the world to achieve defined computational goals. It has been my central thesis that this goal can be best achieved through the synthesis of economics, biology and neuroscience. The central challenge facing neural scientist is to link behavior and brain...

Economics was designed to be just that, a mathematical corpus which attempts to describe how any goal should be achieved in an uncertain world like the one we inhabit. Behavioral ecologist recognizes this; their field is focused on the study of how animals approximate economically defined goals with regard to the maximization of inclusive fitness.

Experimental economics recognize this; their field is focused on the study of how economic behavior approximate economically defined goals with regard to the maximization of utility. Neurobiologist are also beginning to recognize this, and today it seems natural to assume that some form of Neuroeconomics will play a critical role in explaining how the brain of humans and other animals actually solve the maximization problems this two other disciplines have identified.

In short, Alfredo Navarro, in his great review on the work of Glimcher, illustrates us about something that should fill us with pride to who we come from a soft science such as economics: we are in a position to export analytical tools to tougher sciences such as neurobiology, since it has been discovered that, for example, Game Theory, is a very useful resource to understand the behavior of a large part of living beings, and not only of companies in their economic interactions (such as the theory of the oligopoly).

12. Intertemporal Decisions

Economic analysis defines intertemporal decisions as those with consequences over multiple periods of time, including a wide range of decisions, of varying degrees of complexity and frequency, such as investments in real and financial assets, savings for retirement, purchases with credit cards, purchases of merchandise for the home in advance, etc.

✓ The Traditional Theory

To study and model intertemporal decisions, traditional economics has generally used the theory of discounted utility, based on the idea that economic agents prefer a similar reward more if it is obtained in the present than in the future; and similarly, future costs would be less painful than the costs to be faced today.

To formulate these theories, models have been generally used based on the assumption that the total utility of a series of rewards and / or costs over time can be decomposed into a weighted sum (or integral) of utility flows in each period of time. .

A particular case is the function of exponential discount, which has as its main characteristic that the discount rate is independent of the passage of time, and consequently, the evaluation of a course of action towards the future (project) is independent of the moment in which the project is analyzed. This property of decisions is called dynamic consistency.

However, the problem with this exponential model is that it cannot explain several empirical regularities, that is, it would be incompatible with reality in certain cases. In fact, several field studies show that discount functions decline at a faster rate in the short than in the long term, that is, people are more impatient when they make short-term exchanges (today vs tomorrow), than when they make exchanges in the long term (day 100 vs day 101).

To illustrate, the empirical evidence suggests that if a person is given $ 100 to choose now or $ 110 tomorrow, he may prefer $ 100 now, while the same person may choose $ 100 in two years or $ 110 in two years and one day, he could prefer $ 110 in two years and one day. It seems then that discount rates tend to be higher in the short term than in the long term.

✓ Alternative approaches

At present, some economists familiar with the neuro have studied alternatives to exponential discount functions. The generalized hyperbolic function has the property of declining at a higher rate in the short term than in the long term, adjusting the cases of inconsistent decisions. Ainslie (1992)[76] and Loewenstein and Prelec (1992)[77] have used this type of function in their studies.

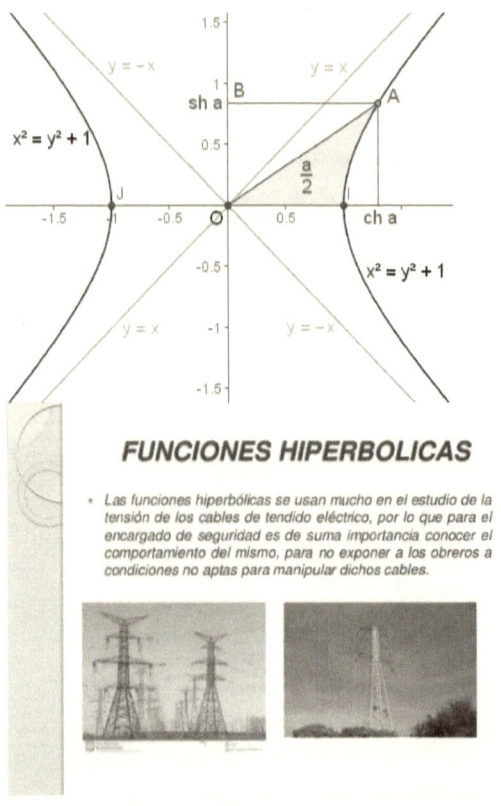

FUNCIONES HIPERBOLICAS

- Las funciones hiperbólicas se usan mucho en el estudio de la tensión de los cables de tendido eléctrico, por lo que para el encargado de seguridad es de suma importancia conocer el comportamiento del mismo, para no exponer a los obreros a condiciones no aptas para manipular dichos cables.

Another highly studied discount function is also the quasi-hyperbolic discount function, which also captures the property that the short-term discount rate is high and the long-term discount rate is low. The quasi-hyperbolic equation is generally referred to as the function biased to the present and was first proposed to model the planning of the transfer of wealth between generations, and then applied to an individual scale by David Laibson (1997)[78] in the model of the golden eggs to study intrapersonal financial decisions.

These models would better capture the dynamic inconsistency of the preferences, that is, the idea that the passage of time changes the preferences of the agents and, consequently, projects that can be positive evaluated with some initial time perspective can be turn negative if they are evaluated from other time perspective.

DAVID LAIBSON

Also models of dynamic inconsistency have been used to study problems of self-control: credit card expenses, drug addictions, etc.

✓ Neuro Fundamentals

As noted above, the quasi-hyperbolic function of discounting time provides a good fit to experimental behavioral data, however few studies have focused their analysis on identifying the causes of this tension between short-term and long-term preferences. Then the following questions arise:

- What is the mechanism behind these intertemporal decisions?

- Do they arise from a single preference mechanism or from multiple systems that interact?

In an attempt to answer these questions, Samuel McLure, David Laibson, George Loewenstein and Jonathan Cohen[79], using functional magnetic resonance imaging (fMRI), examined the neural correlate of time discount while subjects made choices between monetary reward options that varied across time.

The experiment consisted of giving the participants a choice between a sum in the short term and another in the long term, the first being less than the second. Both options were separated by a minimum time lag of two weeks, and in some pairs of options, the earliest option was immediately available.

The hypothesis was that the behavior pattern of the two parameters (β and δ) arises from the joint influence of different neural processes. The β related to the limbic system and the δ related to the lateral prefrontal cortex and other structures associated with higher cognitive functions (the more rational ones).

What results did the researchers obtain? Basically, there would be two systems involved in such intertemporal decisions:

- parts of the limbic system (emotional zone of the brain) associated with the dopamine system of the central brain, including the paralimbic cortex, which would be triggered by decisions involving immediately available rewards;

- regions of the lateral prefrontal cortex and the posterior parietal cortex (eminently rational areas of the brain), uniformly involved in intertemporal decisions independently of the delay in time.

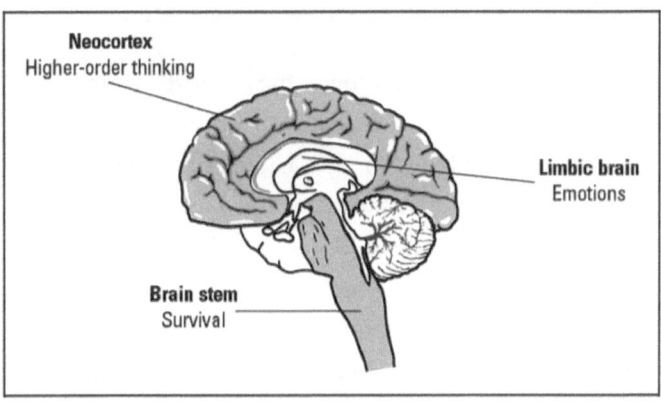

This neuroeconomic finding is consistent with the evidence that consumers act impatient today but prefer to act patients in the future, also supporting the hypothesis that different neuronal systems are activated by intertemporal decisions: the impatience of the short term, which is driven by the limbic system (emotional, not deliberative), and that responds preferably to immediate rewards and to a lesser extent to future rewards; and long-term patience, dominated by the lateral prefrontal cortex and associated structures (the most deliberative parts of our brain), which can rationally evaluate exchanges between abstract rewards, including rewards over longer periods.

Finally, we believe that future research should better assess what kind of discount functions are ideal for predicting real-world economic decisions, and generally improve methods for measuring intertemporal decisions, where Neuroeconomics will undoubtedly play an important role.

13. Glimcher's Two Stages Model

Paul Glimcher, maybe the most important neuroeconomist of the planet at present, from his laboratory at New York University, has made numerous experiments and collected a huge empirical evidence about studies done in other parts of the world, which has allowed him to condense all this material into an interesting theoretical model, published at initial version in 2009[80], then reactualized, where it is hypothesized about the true functioning of the human brain when making decisions. Here is a summary of his model, which in turn is a brief summary of much what it is known in Neuroeconomics so far:

- this model of Glimcher is called "two-stage", because on the one hand, the assessment aspect of decision alternatives is analyzed (something similar to the utility that people give to each object or possible action) -THE VALUATION MAP- and on the other, the concrete decision to be taken is analyzed, that is, the reason for the selection of a single one (among several alternatives) and its subsequent execution -TODAY DECISION-;

- to give a simple example, in the ASSESSMENT STAGE, the model describes the neuropsychological circuits through which human beings value the alternatives A, B, C, D and E that we have for a given course of action (for example where to go on vacation next summer), that is, something similar to the utility (the economic concept) that we give to each alternative in the neoclassical model; whereas in the DECISION STAGE, the model describes in what way (brain circuits that are activated) we end up choosing the "supposed" best alternative, say A, to go on vacation;

- THE ASSESSMENT STAGE has been studied in more detail and depth in recent times, not so much the DECISION STAGE, which in humans is a bit delayed (but not in other mammals, such as monkeys), mainly due to the fact that (in humans) the temporal dynamics of the selection and execution of a given course of action today is difficult to follow via neuroimaging (fMRI);

- in any case, the aforementioned "two systems or stages", VALORATION and DECISION, would not be watertight behavior, since there is some empirical evidence that some characteristics of our valuation process (our preference function) are intrinsically attributable to mechanical processes linked to the decision stage;
- in another interesting feature, today a high number of studies shows that certain areas of the ventral striatum and the frontal cortex "learn" and "represent" valuations (preferences) even when "learning" is passive, that is, even when the person is not faced with an action or specific object on which he has to decide;
- the values (preferences) assigned to objects and actions would be "learned" by means of "trial and error", where the dopaminergic neurons of our mid-brain would play a fundamental role, through the concept of the reward prediction error (the difference between the expected reward of a given course of action and the one actually achieved), an error that would be narrowing down more and more thanks to the aforementioned "learning";

- THE DECISION SYSTEM involves large portions of our parietal cortex, among others; that in turn receive direct and indirect projections from the areas of the ASSESSMENT SYSTEM, and, once the decision has been made, the process is projected directly towards the MOVEMENT CONTROL AREAS, for the concrete execution of the decision;
- in a fact that is quite limiting for those theorists on welfare issues, in Neurosciences today we know a lot about the neuronal circuits involved in the aspects of evaluation of alternatives, only one little about making concrete decisions, but almost nothing about the neural circuits that act in what is called a person's "sense of well-being"; since as we all know, not necessarily the fact of consuming (even though there is a sharp process of weighing rewards and punishments, or costs and benefits) leads us safely to a feeling of well-being;
- in something that is very important, in Neuroeconomics the concept of "subjective value" (VS) is proposed, but in cardinal form, instead of the traditional concept of "utility" of the traditional theory, which is ordinal;
- the VS, in this way, being cardinal, is measured in terms of the rate of "firing of neurons" -neuronal firing rates- that occurs in certain areas of the brain before the perception of each object or alternative action to choose (

for example the options A, B, C, D and E to go on vacation), where the researchers analyze said "neuronal ignition" from the scan of our brain, via neuroimaging;
- the choice of the final alternative when making a decision (the alternative A to go on vacation), would be given after comparing the relative VS between the different options, after a "fouling" of the process by "noise";

- the "reward prediction error" -RPE- of a chosen alternative would be given by the difference between the expected VS and the VS obtained when making the decision (for example, alternative A to go on vacation); and through the delimitation of said RPE is how our brain would improve its rating system, in this way, it is getting less and less wrong;
- the empirical evidence (and working hypotheses) available today suggest that two brain areas seem to contain all the neurons required to extract VS for any object and action: the ventral striatum (member of the limbic-emotional brain) and the middle

prefrontal cortex, and in particular the ventral striatum for actions and the middle prefrontal cortex for objects;
- but one thing is the extraction of SV (that is, granting value to options A, B, C, D and E before making the decision) and another one its storage (once the decision to choose A has been made), the purposes of being used in subsequent decisions;

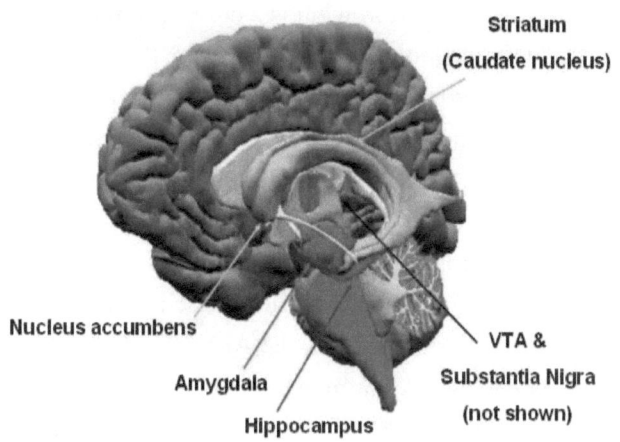

- in this way, the SV calculated in the areas mentioned in the previous item would be stored in a much wider area than the ventral striatum and the middle prefrontal cortex, which we had seen almost exclusively involved when SV is granted for the first time to an option;
- which would lead to the conclusion that when an SV (already stored) is represented in our brain (for example, when deciding where to

go on vacation next year, not this year), it would reflect activity in areas such as the lower frontal sulcus, the insula, the amygdala, the posterior cingulate, the superior temporal sulcus, the caudate nucleus, the putamen, and the dorsolateral prefrontal cortex, and obviously the ventral striatum and the middle prefrontal cortex; that is, a much wider area than the participant in the initial assessment of the option;

- however, and in what is a current limitation of Neuroeconomics, the details (i.e. the how, not only the where) of this assessment process - assignment of VS to objects and actions- are just beginning to be understood, since they are difficult to reach via neuroimaging;
- going to the DECISION STAGE, and as we said at the beginning, it is much less studied than the STAGE OF EVALUATION, always speaking of human beings, not of other mammals, like monkeys, where the empirical evidence is much greater;
- in the DECISION STAGE, the neurons of the lateral intraparietal area (LIP) would seem to play a fundamental role, since they would be responsible for representing the relative VS of each decision alternative (the A, B, C, D and E of our example of holidays);
- remember that the VS of each alternative comes from the ASSESSMENT STAGE, and arose basically from the neuronal activity of two specific areas: the ventral striatum and the

middle prefrontal cortex; but in the DECISION STAGE, the absolute VS of each alternative decision would be transformed into relative VS, and this would occur first in the posterior parietal cortex and then be represented in the LIP area;
- as in the ASSESSMENT STAGE, in the DECISION STAGE there is also internal brain "noise", which affects the quality of decision-making;
- at a certain moment, the set of available options (A, B, C, D and E, with their respective absolute and relative VS) converge to a single alternative, the one chosen (alternative A), which would occur when collicular neurons they exceed their "trigger threshold";
- in what is a very important current limitation, it should be mentioned that the majority of these studies on the DECISION STAGE revolve around monkeys, and in particular decisions made through "generation of movements through the eye", which is not the only possible alternative to generate movements. However, always according to Glimcher, there is some empirical evidence that this type of brain structures would also operate for decisions on more abstract objects than those that a monkey can usually choose (and which are more usual in humans); and less evidence that it would also operate for structures that generate movements other than the eye, in both monkeys and humans;

clarifying that the "lesser evidence" available is temporarily, especially with the advances that are coming in neuroimaging.

Single or Dual System?

To finish with this impressive model, and as we said at the beginning, Glimcher polemizes with Kahneman and affirms that the output of the ASSESSMENT STAGE is not only input of the DECISION STAGE, but also the reverse path would be observed, since there would be numerous decision circuits interconnected with important areas of assessment, such as the aforementioned frontal cortex and basal ganglia; that is, the process would not be linear or additive, but rather more complex, but unitary.

In fact, Glimcher, at the end of the exhibition of his model, attacked fellow neuroeconomists and behaviorists, such as Nobel Prize winner Kahneman, Laibson or Mc Lure, who proposed the existence of two relatively independent systems that would regulate decision-making, one associated with the emotional (the limbic area) and the other more rational (some of frontal and parietal cortex).

To be more specific, Glimcher criticizes the "multiple ego" rationality models, which generally describe the area comprised by the basal ganglia and the prefrontal mid cortex as an emotional module, which interacts (additively) with a second system organized around the posterior parietal cortex and the dorsolateral prefrontal cortex, which would form a rational module.

The mentioned Glimcher indicates that, for example, it would be relatively proven (in monkeys) that neural activity in the posterior parietal cortex (eminently rational) would predict preferences (supposedly generated in emotional areas), under all the conditions that have been studied (immediate reward, future reward, large and small rewards and rewards of high and low probability).

And later Glimcher mentions a lot more empirical evidence, that together, they would be showing a structure globally involved in valuation activities (STAGE OF ASSESSMENT) and not a structure managed exclusively by emotionality;

Of course, concludes Glimcher, the emotions truly influence our decision-making, especially in the ASSESSMENT STAGE, but in no way would there be "multiple selves", that is, the emotional on the one hand determining valuations (utilities) of objects and actions, and the rational on the other side, deciding which is the best option and giving the order to execute.

And here it is convenient to cite the criticism of Kahneman[81], the Nobel Prize in Behavioral Economics, who does not believe that the evidence cited by Glimcher is conclusive to invalidate the argument that decision-making emerges from a conflict between emotions and reason; the opposite of the "unitary" system proposed by Glimcher;

In fact, always according to Kahneman, there would be important behavioral evidence (more grounded in psychology than Neurosciences) about the existence of "multiple selves" in our psyche, and the importance of conflict; however, he concludes that more empirical evidence is needed from Neurosciences to define the winner of this debate; that is to say, it does not attack in definitive form against the Glimcher model, which is logical, since the evidence in Neuroscience is superior to the psychological one;

Finally, Glimcher acknowledges that there are still important aspects to better specify in his model, basically due to lack of empirical evidence, especially in the DECISION STAGE, since we remember that Neuroeconomics is just touching the decade of life and can still be improved a lot plus the instruments available to open our "black box".

In summary, the neuropsychological system that sustains our decision making would seem to be a "little bit" more complex than the simplified version of neoclassical economics, based on ordinal utility curves, faced with the restriction of the income of each consumer, to be able to determine what quantities are consumed of each good and service, deriving from this model the respective demand curves of each of them.

Comparison: Ordinal and cardinal approach

Ordinal Utility	Cardinal Utility
Consumption can't be measured	Consumption can be measured
Utility is used for grading/ranking of the products depending on the preferences of the consumer	Uses utils which help in understanding how much utility is derived from consumption of a product.
Much less compared	Comparative study
Conceptual and practical	Preceded the ordinal approach
Convex function	Concave function
Qualitative measure	Quantitative measure

Undoubtedly this neoclassical model, which is simple and unreal, has been enormously useful for doing science, as we will see in the next chapter, where we analyze whether Neuroeconomics could imply a paradigm shift or not. However, through this model of Glimcher, we have been able to appreciate that today we can measure (via neuroimaging) the true utility that each person obtains from each good or service, the so-called SV (subjective value), which would be observed in our brains depending on the degree of "neuronal firing rate", which is generated when we perceive and evaluate said good or service to acquire it or not; and also that said utility or VS would be cardinal, not ordinal, and that it "learns", that is, it would improve day by day thanks to our "neuronal plasticity". That is, before this new empirical evidence, will continue maintaining the old neoclassical models?

14. Basal Ganglia and Aversion to Change: Criticism to the Extreme Liberal

Is it good to overprotect companies and institutions to endure? According to the renowned economist Nicholas Taleb, overprotection instead of helping to do something stronger, on the contrary, makes it weaker. Like the overprotected children, those organizations that are deprived of elements of stress, in the long run they become weaker. And although the argument seems indisputable, it has an important neuro contradiction, which we develop below.

For Taleb, antifragility goes beyond resilience or robustness. The resilient resists the blows and remains the same, whereas the antifragile becomes better with the blows. Antifragility becomes strong with randomness, uncertainty, the volatile, the unknown, the incomprehensible and the errors. "What does not kill me, makes me stronger", would be a good phrase to exemplify Taleb's concept of antifragility.

According to Taleb, organizations (private, public, NGOs) should tend towards less interventionist patterns, where the natural takes its course, and especially, randomness. For him, the environment of organizations is much more complex than what our memory or historical account can tell. In addition, the educational system and the scientific apparatus would be designed, in their vision, to organize all events in a linear manner, simplifying too much.

In this way, although in nature anti-fragility is the norm, the scientific story rejects antifragility, often preventing interferences with things that it does not understand, confusing the unknown with the non-existent. Impossible to disagree with Taleb in that regard, but of course ... scientists are human beings, flesh and blood like everyone else, whose brains seek assurances and regularities, which limit environmental uncertainty. That is the flaw we notice in Taleb's argument, and on that point is where I want to go deeper.

In the human brain there is a region that participates notably in the formation of routines and habits, since acquiring a routine requires considerable effort, the brain stores in its memory the "template" of the habit, to reactivate it at the slightest sign. These patterns are developed and established in the so-called basal ganglia, whose functions are essential in the acquisition of habits, addictions and learning processes.

Habits help us in our daily lives, because they allow us not to have to decide each of our actions continuously, and thus reduce the consumption of energy in the brain. Constant routines are thus delimited before we get down to work, which saves us time. In this way, the natural thing is that the brain tends more towards the routine than towards the disorder and change, which implies that it has to be trained to achieve what Taleb proposes (in fact, many international companies today pay onerous training for this type of programs for its executives).

What are Basal Ganglia

- The basal ganglia or basal nuclei are group of subcortical nuclei located at the base of the forebrain.
- They are significantly united with the cerebral cortex, thalamus, and brainstem.
- The basal ganglia play a major role in voluntary motor functions, procedural learning, routines or habits, and eye movements.
- They also have contributions in cognition and emotions

In this way, habits arise because our brain is always trying to save mental effort: these fragments of automatic routines are stored in the basal ganglia, so that when we execute an automatic routine, "work" the basal ganglia, and the rest of the brain "rest", simplifying a little. In other words, the permanent change Taleb poses is unnatural to our brain, unless we train it. The tendency is towards order, rigidity and permanence, and not vice versa; and in the end our institutions are the result of our brain format.

Following with his notion of fragile-robust-antifragile, Taleb establishes some comparisons. Curiosity is antifragile, and books have the ability to multiply it. The banking system is fragile, but Silicon Valley, with its permanent innovation, is anti-fragile. Food companies are fragile, restaurants are antifragile. The bureaucrat is fragile, the entrepreneur is antifragile. A person who depends on a salary to live is very dependent on their organization and very fragile for their level of dependence. An artist is antifragile because of his independence from an employer.

In this way, Taleb criticizes all types of state interventionism to save sectors and companies in decline, since that undermines the mechanism that generates anti-fragility, necessary for the system to innovate and be increasingly productive. But of course ... the argument collides with a reality: our brains have a natural tendency towards aversion to change, that is, towards what the renowned economist calls fragile. Such a contradiction!

The Human Basal Ganglia

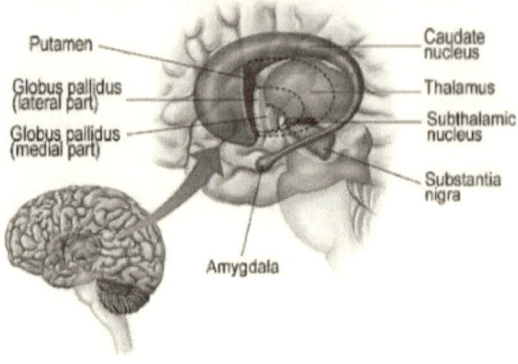

In addition to our natural tendency towards routine and inflexibility, dominated by the basal ganglia in the brain, there is a whole question of errors in our decision-making process, depending on the uncertainty of a complex world (which Taleb describes well), and also of our limited ability to analyze all available information (limited rationality of Simon), which enhance the aversion to change of the average human being.

In general, Neurosciences seem to indicate that our brain is not designed for outstanding performances in relatively complex decisions, including the brains of people who have studied at the university level. It is known that the human brain has been developing for millions of years, but for most of our history as a civilization it served for people who only covered basic needs: find food, reproduce and defend the territory, not much more than that. It was not until the last 200-300 years that the world became exponentially complex, which has implied the need for refined neural connections for decisions that are increasingly risky and / or uncertain, but also a good part of the primitive remnant. Our brain's emotional state has remained almost unchanged.

Paul Glimcher

Paul Glimcher, one of the most reputable neuroeconomists today, argues that the valuations (preferences) we assign to objects and actions would be learned by trial and error, where the dopaminergic neurons of our mid-brain (reward system) would play a fundamental role, through the concept of the reward prediction error (the difference between the expected reward of a given course of action and the one actually achieved), which would be limited by learning. That is, the brain predicts, and is wrong, generating errors, and while they are decreasing with experience, in a world as changing as today, learning is increasingly continuous, and errors too.

That is, there are at least two natural tendencies in the opposite direction to Taleb's antifragility: the action of the basal ganglia (our natural tendency to routines and rigidities) and the computational problems of our brain to predict / decide without mistakes (bounded rationality), in an increasingly complex and changing world.

To conclude, and although we agree with what Taleb raises about the importance of freedom and the search for risks to make robust and anti-fragile people, institutions and economics as a whole, it is a difficult proposal to apply for mental models humans have today, and that, in the end, determines our behavior.

The question is why people, institutions and society tend to fall into rigidities, routines and interventionism, which hinders the dynamism that Taleb mentions as necessary for success, innovation and productivity. And the answer goes through our brain: the human being seeks assurances, low risks, conventions and other rigidities that reassure him and give him certain equilibria that flexibility and permanent randomness do not give him.

In the background, our brain functioning is the result of thousands of years of adaptation of human life to the environment where he lives, with a prominent role to the basal ganglia to build routines and other rigidities that reassure us in the face of so much systemic uncertainty. Adapted brains for permanent change are the minority (and you have to train them), the norm is the routine.

Good book that of Taleb, but with that deep contradiction: it raises certain libertarian conducts as desirable for our modern societies, when our brains, human nature and institutions have adapted to the world doing just the opposite, creating routines and rigidities that moderate the increased environmental uncertainty. The natural tendency of the human being is to seek order, and not disorder; our brains are wired that way, not other way round. That is perhaps the main reason why governments gets so much into economics to temper the changes, our brains seek gradualism, not shock, although that disgusts the most liberal-free traders.

15. Notions in Neurofinance

In an effort to seek better foundations on financial decision making, and using the current boom of Cognitive Neuroscience, a modern area of study has emerged, the Neurofinances, where the use of magnetic resonance images, with people during real risky investment situations (or bets), is essential.

For example, today Neurosciences show that the circumstances that accompany a decision to bet / invest money are seldom independent of the investment / bet itself. The oscillations of stock markets, or the constant variability of betting games (horses, casino, etc.), have a significant impact on the amount of risk that people are willing to take, increasing it.

In this way, observations by brain scanner indicate that the increase in risk taking in bets / investments would be correlated with the emotional reaction caused by being an individual immersed in a situation of volatile bets, which makes the reflective-deliberative activity decrease.

Additionally, and also from Neurosciences, today it is quite clear that the financial choices we make are influenced by our previous experiences, forming what are called somatic markers. The hypothesis of somatic marker, owed to the Portuguese neurologist Antonio Damasio, proposed a way to explain how emotions affect when making complex decisions (including financial investments).

According to Damasio, our previous experiences make us store in the brain a series of sensations (muscular and hormonal responses) pleasant or unpleasant related to certain stimuli. This relationship between stimulus and emotional state is what is called a somatic marker. Faced with the task of making an investment decision in a context of risk or uncertainty, a stimulus similar to that of previous experiences would trigger in our body the release of a certain somatic marker.

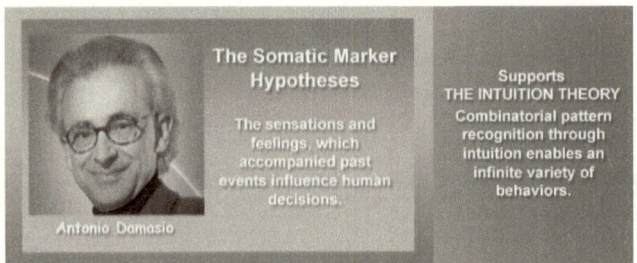

Thus, the options we opt for are those associated with pleasant somatic markers, and we avoid those that the somatic marker associates with adverse results. This process greatly accelerates decision making, being a kind of shortcut for the brain, in order to avoid investing excessive deliberative resources in making decisions that require a rapid response. Needless to say, that in matters of financial decisions in stock markets (or in casinos and places of betting), immediacy is permanent, and these cerebral shortcuts, then, become very useful.

✓ Loss Aversion

An interesting concept, from the hand of Nobel Laureates Kahneman and Tversky, explains the concept of aversion to loss, i.e. the idea that the losses of an amount x make us proportionally more damage than the happiness produced by the profits of that same amount x. That is, it would be more than proportional the pain for the loss of $ 500, than the happiness for winning $ 500.

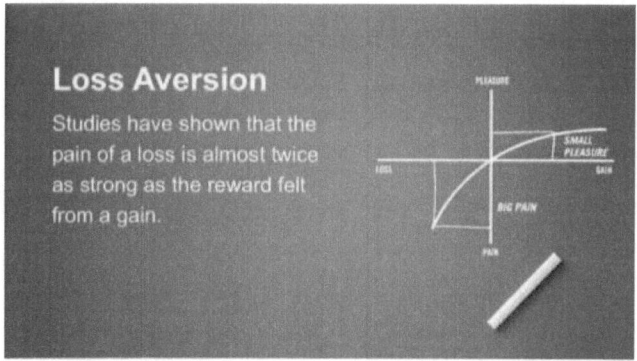

Financial losses are processed in parts of the brain that are responsible for the pain network. One of these areas is the amygdala (the center of fear). For example, patients with this area damaged are proven not to be afraid of losses and often take high financial risks, which normal people do not.

- ✓ Irrational Investors?

There are many aspects of life in which we make mistakes in making decisions, even sometimes very rude. It is proven that, even in areas where we have some experience, we often stumble from time to time, almost inexplicably. According to many economists, in the world of financial betting (stock markets, casinos, etc.), such repetitive errors are usually abundant, which fuels the debate on how rational investors are when designing their portfolios.

In general, Neurosciences seem to indicate that our brain is not suited for outstanding performances in complex financial decisions, including the brains of people who have studied finance at the university level. It is known that human brain has been developing for millions of years, but for most of our history as a civilization, was adapted for people who only covered basic needs: find food, reproduce and defend the territory, not much more than that. It was not until the last 200-300 years that the world became more complex in an exponential way, arising, among others, financial decisions in securities markets, which has implied the need for refined neural connections for increasingly risky decisions, but also, a good part of the primitive remnant of our brain has remained almost unaltered.

Some think that if some investors are too optimistic and others are too pessimistic at the same time, the market should be able to find its middle ground, compensating, and tending towards rationality on average. However, the empirical evidence in Finance seems to show that individual investment errors tend to move in the same direction and also occur more or less at the same time, that is, it is not that irrational investors would be losing money against arbitrageurs more rational, but that the errors, in certain situations, would be generalized (remember the financial panics, with herd behavior, which so often does not rationally justify similar market collapses, or similar bubbles).

That is, it would not be that investors are irrational because they do not know how to calculate future costs and benefits (the most deliberative part of the brain) in controlled situations (a university exam, for example), but that such calculations would cloud, in practice, in environments that are too volatile and risky, generating excessive herd and panic behavior among investors, caused, to a large extent, by brains overly dominated by their more primitive roots (the most emotional parts).

✓ The Brain Predicts

It has also been discovered that the brain works with predictions, contrary to the previously accepted theory, that it reacts to sensations it picks up from the outside world. In this way, human reactions would be just the adaptation of the body to the predictions that the brain makes, based on the state of our body the last time it was in a similar situation (somatic markers).

In this way, the brain tries to find out what a certain sensation means and what is causing it (for example, a strong downturn in the stock market), to then define what to do with it, and thus build thoughts, feelings, perceptions and decisions, that arrive just when it is necessary, and not a second later, but of course, with errors of prediction and biases, which make such decisions may be unsuccessful several times, until the learning improves the perception, and the subsequent action.

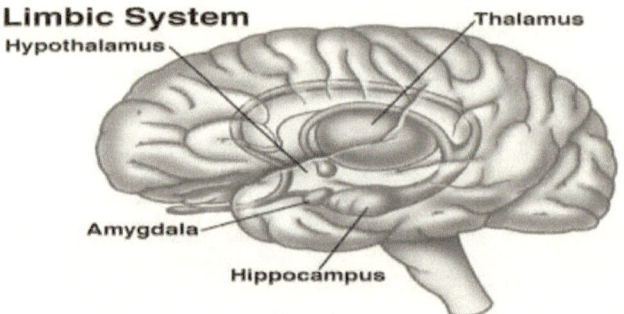

And in this process, it is the limbic tissue (the emotional one) that would dominate, and then direct those predictions to the cortex (the most rational part of the brain). For example, when a person is told to imagine a red apple in their mind, limbic areas of the brain send predictions to visual neurons and cause them to interconnect and fire in different patterns so that the person can actually "see" that apple red The reader can change in this example to red apples for papers that are quoted in the stock market, the conclusions are the same.

In this way, the investors of the market are the architects of their own experiences (somatic markers), which start from the emotional brain, since the limbic regions of the brain send but do not receive predictions. Therefore, our brain would be built so that things work in the reverse of popular knowledge: it is not "seeing to believe", but the other way around, "believing to see". That is, the perceived risk of certain private securities (corporate risk), or of certain countries (sovereign risk), would be mental constructions that arise mainly from the emotional part of the brains of market investors (that is, their limbic parts), explaining in large part the reason for so many financial panics, bubbles, overreactions and mistakes in general, so common in modern stock markets.

16. Reward Prediction Error

Related to the above, Paul Glimcher argues that, in principle, errors arise from an inadequate evaluation of the information available and, in addition, imaginary constructions that do not correspond fully with reality (the predictions we talked about above), overestimating the real possibilities of gambling, or risky financial investments.

Following the aforementioned Glimcher, and as I mentioned in a previous section, in the human brain coexist "two systems or stages", one of VALUATION (where alternatives are compared) and another of DECISION (which chooses an alternative over others), that work related, since some characteristics of the valuation process (our function of preferences -utility-) would be attributable to mechanical processes intrinsically linked to the decision stage.

Within this context, a high number of studies shows that certain areas of the ventral striatum and the frontal cortex "learn" and "represent" valuations (preferences) even when "learning" is passive, that is, even when the person is not before an action or specific item on which you have to decide.

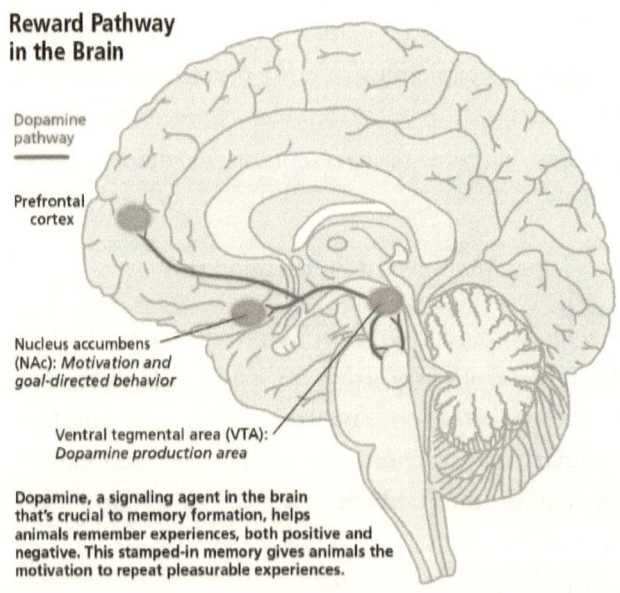

And finally, the valuations (preferences) assigned to objects and actions (for example the portfolios to be inverted) would be "learned" by means of "trial and error", where the dopaminergic neurons of our average brain (reward system) would play a fundamental role, through the concept of reward prediction error (the difference between the expected reward of a given course of action and the one actually achieved), an error that would be limited more and more thanks to the aforementioned "learning".

In short, given the relentless pursuit of improvement in financial decision-making, the emergence of Neurofinance are very welcome, since tools are needed to help understand errors, biases and other usual "irrationalities" in the formation of expectations that then determine the prices of the assets listed on the stock exchange.

In any case, these experiments in controlled environments, with observations via neuroimaging and other analysis tools, only help to begin to understand better the underlying brain mechanisms, although not necessarily to correct them, since it is mainly part of the adaptation from our brain to the complexity of the world that surrounds it, and that is achieved little by little, in a process of permanent trial and error.

Concluding

The results of the studies commented throughout this chapter are only some of the many that have been published in recent years, on the actual functioning of human decision-making processes, both in economics and in management, marketing and other disciplines framed within the so-called "economic sciences"; and it is our main intention to refer them -beyond the specific knowledge they have contributed- to show how this tool works, that we have available since a relatively short time, and which promises advances that we cannot predict yet, but we believe could become important and disruptive to what has traditionally been done in Economics.

As Colin Camerer says[82], in some aspects the contributions will be incremental, in other radicals, with Neuroeconomics advancing at an accelerated pace, continuing the knocking down of the postulates of Jevons 200 years ago:

"I hesitate to say that men will ever have the means of measuring directly the feelings of the human heart."

We must get out of the Friedmanian comfort of the "irrelevance of assumptions" and go to challenge everything we have been saying so far, where some postulates will remain almost unchanged, and others will change, but what is certain is that many economists, in the next few years, are going to study how the brain and our rationality really works, until convince themselves that the maximizing models that we have been using up to now are extremely limited, in light of the new empirical evidence provided by Cognitive Neurosciences.

NEUROECONOMICS AND EPISTEMOLOGY

At this stage of our work, we believe that it is already quite clear what Neuroeconomics is, what neuropsychological techniques it uses to do its research, its latest findings on true human decision-making rationality (not that of neoclassical economics), and some conclusions of concrete studies that are being made in this embryonic field, among the main topics that we have dealt with. But we still need to delve into a matter of extreme importance: how far will these new findings impact the way economic theory is done? Or to put it in epistemological terms, will there be a paradigm shift in our science? And if the answer is affirmative, will it be a change of paradigm to the Kuhn (profound changes) or to the Lakatos (the hard core of science almost does not change)? And if there is any change in the current paradigm, will Friedman's "irrelevance of assumptions" thesis continue to be important, or will this *scientific jugglery* lose meaning, in the words of Paul Samuelson? In short, many important questions still to be answered, on which we are going to try to cast a mantle of light in this chapter.

But first let's start by defining what a paradigm is. The term paradigm was defined by Thomas Kuhn[83] -it is fundamental within his argument-, as "universally recognized scientific relationships that, for a certain time, provide models and solutions to a scientific community". An alternative definition, from Kuhn himself, indicates as scientific paradigm "the complete constellation of beliefs, values, techniques, etc., shared by the members of a given community". That is, within Kuhn's argument, scientists belonging to a certain school of thought (for example the "new classics" in economics) are ascribed to a certain paradigm (we might call it the orthodox in macroeconomics), which fulfills the function to frame or standardize the methodology used in their research, the assumptions from which their models start, etc., since it allows new researchers to adapt to past scientific achievements, achievements that some particular scientific community has been recognizing, for some time, as a foundation for their practices. And continuing with the contribution of the aforementioned philosopher, when the number or magnitude of the anomalies are excessive and the restlessness arises among the researchers, a scientific revolution or change to a paradigm superior to the preceding one takes place. And while Kuhn's ideas have been criticized - Lakatos, another relatively contemporary philosopher of science - is more accepted, his concept of paradigm is generally accepted and in this chapter we will use it as a basis.

In what follows, and before turning fully to deal with the effects that Neuroeconomics could cause in the current paradigm in economic science, we will analyze the way in which that current paradigm was built, where we will first explain general concepts about epistemology and then, in a more detailed way, of epistemology applied to economic science. In this chapter we will mainly follow, among several consulted, the wonderful work of Mark Blaug[84], perhaps the highest authority in epistemology of economics in recent decades.

1. Notions about Epistemology

Although it is not intended, at all, an exhaustive treatment of a topic of great complexity such as the epistemological, in order to justify the dominant methodological position today among economists (which is key to understand the current paradigm) will be useful an introductory reference to the subject, which will be stopped at those most relevant milestones of the last two centuries, a period during which Economics has taken a separate entity as a science.

To give a simple definition, epistemology (from the Greek, ἐπιστήμη or episteme, "knowledge"; λόγος or logos, "theory") is the study of the production and validation of scientific knowledge. It deals with problems such as the historical, psychological and sociological circumstances that lead to its obtaining, and the criteria by which it is justified or invalidated.

Let us start with the analysis of the main epistemological schools in force during the last 200 years, especially those of relevance for economic theory.

✓ Empiricism

It is a philosophical current that exerted a considerable influence on scientists, whose name comes from the Greek *empireia*, which means experience. According to the empiricists, human knowledge begins in sensory experience, and what is more, for many of them sensory knowledge is the only valid type of knowledge.

Caracterización Breve del Empirismo Británico.

Mientras Galileo y Descartes enfatizaban el papel del razonamiento deductivo para la adquisición y defensa del conocimiento, Francis Bacon (1561-1626) enfatizaba una metodología observacional y experimental, con un razonamiento inductivo para adquirir y defender el conocimiento.

De acuerdo con él, "... lo que la ciencia necesita es una forma de inducción que analice la experiencia, tomándola por partes y mediante procesos de exclusión y rechazo, nos lleve a conclusiones inevitables" (The Great Instauration, 1620).

Francis Bacon

This movement flourished in England during the seventeenth and eighteenth centuries, in some way as a form of opposition to continental-inspired rationalism. Francis Bacon is a prominent forerunner of empiricism, especially in his defense of the procedure of observation and induction as a valid method for science; Bacon himself also gave much more relevance to practical knowledge than to speculative nature.

Hobbes, Locke, Berkeley and Hume are the main representatives of British empiricism. Especially the contribution of Locke stands out, which denies the existence of innate ideas, in clear opposition to the Cartesian philosophy. David Hume argues that causality can be interpreted as the mere temporal succession of two phenomena, while John Stuart Mill goes so far as to ground more abstract knowledge, such as mathematics or logic, in sensory experience and in induction.

Due to the influence of the aforementioned authors, the most common vision of scientific research in the mid-nineteenth century is to defend that science must start from the observation of facts, carried out in a free and without prejudice. Then the inductive inference is applied, so that it goes from the particular to the general and universal laws are formulated about these facts. That way, induction is again applied in order to obtain theories or arguments endowed with a greater degree of generality. Finally, it is contrasted whether the laws and theories are true or not by comparing their empirical implications with the observed facts.

In short, it is clear that the empiricists were eminently inductivist, and as we shall see shortly, quite influential among some classical economists such as Adam Smith; However, their methodology little by little was losing sustenance as a way of doing science, especially thanks (or because of) the emergence of the hypothetical-deductive method, much more abstract to do science, and therefore, much more powerful in its scope. This last method is with which economics took the form that even today maintains; it is the method of mathematical modeling, of the assumptions far from reality, of the hypotheses, that although they are not entirely accurate, they are always logically well deduced. Below we detail this method a little more.

- ✓ The Hypothetical - Deductive Method and the Vienna Circle.

Following the philosophy level, in the 2nd half of the 19th century the empiricist inductivism began to decay to give rise to deductivism, under the influence of authors such as Mach, Poincaré and Duhem, and more late (early twentieth century) due to the growing strength of the logical positivism of the Vienna Circle, the latter born around the figure of physicist and philosopher Moritz Schlick, who progressively gave rise to a new philosophy, logical positivism. Among its most prominent members are Carnap, Feigl and Karl Menger (son of the well-known economist).

And while they disintegrated as a group in the late 1930s, logical positivism exerted considerable influence on twentieth-century philosophy of science. Some characteristics of the Vienna Circle and its thinking were:

- received the intellectual heritage of Compte's positivism (opposition to metaphysics, faith in reason, methodological monism and debugging of normative considerations of positive science);
- also with certain influences of English Empiricism (just explained) and Relativism;
- advocated that the inductivist methodology described above (English Empiricism) be replaced by a procedure based on two principles: the hypothetic-deductive method and verification.

At that time (late nineteenth century and early twentieth century), the current epistemological paradigm required a science, to consider it "serious", the following:

- use the hypothetic-deductive method: the logical structure of the scientific explanation should be the following: first, the formulation of a universal law and relevant initial conditions, which were the premise or explanans. The starting point of this universal law is not induction but certain conjectures (as for example that the human being is eminently optimizing). Then the explanandum was deduced by deductive logic. The universal law could consist of a proposition similar to the following: "When A happens, B happens". In turn, it could be deterministic or statistical, in which case the universal law would be qualified in the following way: "When A happens, B happens with probability P".
- use the principle of verification: to understand it, it is necessary to make a classification of the judgments in analytical or synthetic. Analytical judgments are those that contain a truth in the definition of their own terms ("A triangle has three sides") while synthetic judgments provide a truth thanks to practical experience ("swans are white"). However, the synthetic judgments, according to logical positivism, had meaning if and only if they were susceptible of empirical verification, and

> this principle was used to eliminate from the sciences those statements that could be qualified as metaphysical, such as "the paintings of Velásquez are beautiful."

In short, experimental science was conceived as the only valid mode of access to reality. Surely the reader, at this point of the story must already have realized - especially if he is an economist- the enormous influence that this epistemological school has had on economic science, especially because it was decisive at the time when Economics was wrote by the Neoclassicals (Jevons, Walras, Pareto, later Marshall, etc.), creators of the theoretical trunk that even today is almost intact in our science.

In fact, it is at this time when Economics begin to use profusely the mathematical tools (derived, integral, differential equations, etc.) to formulate the hypotheses and hence apply the deductions (hence the hypothetical deductive method), that although they forced "a little" the real human psychology - there were no developments in Neuroscience that there is now, it must be recognized - they gave scientific rigor and predictive power to our nascent science. Later in this chapter we return to the subject.

2. The Logical Deductivism in Economics

Both empiricism (inductivism) and logical positivism (deductivism) had an impact on the way of doing economic theory (the method), the inductivism more in some authors of the Classical School (like Adam

Smith), while deductivism (also called Verificationism) more among the Neoclassical, that is, the economic theory that has survived to this day.

- ✓ Smith, Ricardo and Senior

The classical economists, from the end of the s. 18th and early 19th century, they did not discuss the methodological issues in great detail, but it can be said that, in general, some advocated the use of the inductive method in economics, which was providing so many successes in the natural sciences, but others became quite side of the hypothetical deductive method. The work of Adam Smith (perhaps the most influential economist of all times), integrates diverse influences and, for that reason, its methodology is a complex mixture of many factors, but in the last analysis, it can be described as inductive.

In general, most of Smith's work is an example of the use of the methodology of the so-called Scottish Historical School. According to Blaug[85], it is not easy to characterize the methodology of this school, because neither Adam Smith nor any of its other members used many words to define it: "In any case, such a method seems to consist, on the one hand, of a firm belief in the historical stages, based on the relationship between defined modes or types of economic production and certain principles of human nature; and on the other hand, on a deep commitment to simplicity and elegance as absolute priority criteria of an adequate explanation, both in the field of physical and social sciences. Both his Theory of Moral

Sentiments and The Wealth of Nations can be considered deliberate attempts by Smith to apply the Newtonian method (highly successful in physics, until the appearance of quantum physics), first to Ethics and then to Economics. "

SMITH, RICARDO, MALTHUS

David Ricardo, in a certain contrast to Smith, used deduction and abstract modeling to a greater extent in his works. Another outstanding figure among the classics is Nassau Senior, who in 1827 publishes Introductory Lecture on Political Economy[86] and in 1836 Outline of the Science of Political Economy[87]. In his writings, Senior establishes a distinction between economics as a science and as art, the first what is now considered a positive economics while the second what we now call normative economics. Senior is also credited with the argument that economics rests on very general propositions (the desire to maximize wealth with the least possible effort, the Malthusian principle that the population grows faster than the means of subsistence, and the existence of diminishing returns in agriculture), which are the result of observation and from which certain conclusions are obtained, always according to Senior. That is, somehow, from Senior, among others, the deductive method is gaining strength among economists, from assumptions not necessarily entirely true, such as maximizing rationality.

- ✓ J.S. Mill

John Stuart Mill, in his famous Principles of Political Economy (1848)[88], takes these ideas and gives them their own added value. In the first place, "they are seized" against methodological monism, recommending that economics employ the deductive method, since the inductive method would be harmed by the concomitance of several causes that affect the same phenomenon. In particular, according to J.S.Mill, the economist must begin his research from psychological premises, which are reached by introspection; next, it is necessary to elaborate a theory from the premises, and finally the theories must be contrasted by empirical procedures. That is, with Mill continues to take strength in economics that useful technique of modeling forcing assumptions about our psychology, from introspection, obviously because there was no way to "get inside the black box of the human mind", as now you can, thanks to Neuroimaging and Trasncranean Magnetic Stimulation, among other neuro techniques. Besides, the optimizer was a rationality very easy to mathematize, and in addition, the postulates of the psychologists of that time were not scientifically strong enough to impose themselves "per se".

Stuart Mill also highlights his concept of homo economicus, although it was already exhaustively dealt with in chapter 2, where we analyze the evolution of the concept of rationality in economics. For Mill, although there is a part of human behavior where obtaining wealth is not the main objective, there are other departments of human affairs where the acquisition of wealth is the main purpose: economics deals with this second category, of way that abstracts from all human passions and motives except the desire for wealth and the aversion to work. That is, Mill knows for certain that the man thus described is a fictitious man, in fact he is aware that the economic sphere is only a part of human behavior; nevertheless, he recommends that economics proceed to abstract and work with that fictitious man, who seeks to obtain "the greatest possible amount of wealth with the minimum possible work and self-denial"[89].

> **Four Theses of Utilitarianism**
> - **Consequentialism:** The rightness of actions is determined solely by their consequences.
> - **Hedonism:** Utility is the degree to which an act produces pleasure. Hedonism is the thesis that pleasure or happiness is the **good** that we seek and that we **should** seek.
> - **Maximalism:** A right action produces the greatest good consequences and the least bad.
> - **Universalism:** The consequences to be considered are those of everyone affected, and everyone equally.

As it was already said in a previous chapter, J.S.Mill is one of the greatest precursors of the rationality that the neoclassicals adopted and that has arrived to our days, based on that kind of psychology ad-hoc of homo economicus, so methodologically useful, but false, as Neurosciences demonstrate today.

- ✓ Cairnes

John Elliot Cairnes, another classical economist, in consonance with J.S.Mill, emphasizes that Political Economics is a hypothetic-deductive science, and that the use of a methodology of these characteristics by a science indicates its maturity. In fact, Cairnes affirms that economics must be based on real premises, undoubted facts about human nature and the world (affirmation with which we are in agreement), but that are obtained not by induction but by introspection (there no longer we agree, but of course, at that time there was no Neuroeconomics) as, for example, adds Cairnes, the desire to obtain wealth with the minimum sacrifice, or the Malthusian principle on the population. In short, quite a coincidence between the arguments of Cairnes and Senior; but we repeat, introspection as a scientific mechanism in Social Sciences is not the best tool, and in economics introspection has been used in excess, even far from that which could be justified, based on an ad-hoc psychology, built by economists, not psycologists.

And to make his thinking even clearer, Cairnes does not consider verification as a test of hypotheses, in order to find out if they are true or false, but rather as a method to establish the frontiers of application of the theories, since verification helps to corroborate deductive reasoning. For example, for Cairnes, if a certain theory has been correctly deduced, it will be true. If discrepancies between the facts and the theories are observed, however, it can be attributed to disturbing causes that obscure the theory and show that it has been applied incorrectly, but the theory itself will be true if it has been rigorously obtained through the deductive process.

These ideas, which had already been pointed out by Stuart Mill, and expressed more forcefully in Cairnes, contradict what came later in the field of economic epistemology, the Friedman thesis: "if a theory, even if it has been correctly deduced, does not predict according to the facts, loses scientific support".

In other words, in light of what is accepted today mostly in epistemology of economics - Friedman thesis - the ideas of Mill and Cairnes illustrate the degree of fundamentalism that existed among the first theorists of economics, who went so far as to suppose that divergences between theory and practice were due to "disturbing causes that obscure the theory" and not to the theory being wrong, on top of theories based on dubious premises, emanating from introspection (that is, the occurrence of some) as the principle of rationality, or emanated from observation, as for example the law of Malthus, which fortunately has never been verified true.

It is also interesting to note that the last three authors mentioned (Senior, Stuart Mill and Cairnes) agree that the search for maximum wealth with the least possible effort is one of the driving principles of man, which is not necessarily consistent with the modern Neuroscience findings. But obviously, the coincidence between the three economists is not accidental, but responds to the influence in the England of s. XIX exercised utilitarianism as a philosophical current, which provided key concepts to finish closing the neoclassical paradigm, still current in our science. In particular, the English school of utilitarianism, headed by Bentham, proposes the hedonistic idea that happiness for man is found in well-being, understood as the difference between pleasure and pain. This approach also allows us to obtain the relationship between individual values and social values, since utilitarianism postulates, in terms of social aggregates, the principle of maximum happiness for the greatest possible number of people. The next step was to qualify as useful everything that confers welfare to the human being.

And from these simple postulates, utilitarianism exerted a strong influence on the economic theory elaborated later, facilitating that the assumption of rationality, understood as maximizing pleasure and minimizing pain, was introduced gradually into economics until being described in detail by Stuart Mill (classic) in his characterization of homo economicus, as was recently said. Later, it would reach a more formalized approach thanks to the theory of the marginal utility, of the hand of Jevons, Edgeworth, Sidgwick, Wicksteed and Marshall, which is well-known in Economics History.

At this point in the historical narrative, we will highlight - once again in this book, based on what Neurosciences today, through neuroimaging, "transcranial magnetic stimulation" and other scientifically rigorous techniques, demonstrate that Bentham, Mill, Cairnes, Senior, etc. were not totally true, clearly far from reality. The human being maximizes at times, only sporadically, and does so more in the sense of Simon (limited rationality - already discussed in previous chapters) than in the sense of the utilitarians and the neoclassicals.

BRAIDOT

Even some experts, like Nestor Braidot, often talk about man as "unconsciously rational", the metaconscious may act more strongly than the conscious when defining an economic decision. We repeat, then, some force ideas of Neurosciences applied to the decision making[90]:

- "According to scientists, the brain areas of rationality cannot function isolated from the areas of biological-emotional regulation. The two systems communicate and affect the behavior jointly, and consequently, the behavior of the people".
- "Moreover, the emotional system (the oldest area of the brain) is the first force that acts on mental processes, therefore determining the direction of decisions."
- "The latest advances in Neuroscience have shown that consumer decision-making is not a rational process. That is, customers do not consciously examine the attributes of a product or service to acquire it. "
- "In most cases, the selection process is relatively automatic and derives from habits and other metaconscious forces, among which history, personality, neurophysiological characteristics and the physical and social context that surrounds us all gravitate".
- "The fragrance of a perfume, for example, can evoke different sensations. If the client associates it with painful experiences or with a person with whom he does not sympathize, it is very likely that he will not buy it, even

when the price-quality-brand ratio is reasonable".

It is also interesting to highlight the criticism of utilitarianism by the brilliant historian of economic analysis J. Schumpeter: "the psychology really used [...] was always individual psychology, introspective, and the most primitive type, rarely endowed - if it was ever - of more than a few simple hypotheses about the reactions of the individual psyche. This procedure was called empirical [...]. There was nothing "experimental" or inductive, and in reality it was not very realistic, despite the programmatic statements, the war cries and the invocations of Francis Bacon[91]. "This criticism of Schumpeter does nothing but enhance all that we have been holding in this book, especially our "bold suggestion" that it is already untenable to continue in economics with such rudimentary psychological assumptions, especially after all that has been contributed by Neuroeconomics

✓ John Neville Keynes

It is interesting to analyze the contribution of this English author (father of the famous JM Keynes, although with different thoughts), whose main work is The Scope and Method of Political Economy (1891)[92], where he summarizes the previous tradition - fundamentally represented by Senior, Mill and Cairnes - in the following points:

JOHN NEVILLE KEYNES

- A distinction can be made between positive and normative economics, and it is convenient that this difference appears clear to economists, since the attempt to merge research into what is and what should be is likely to prevent a clear and unbiased response to the two questions.
- The correct methodological procedure of economics consists of starting from some fundamental facts about human nature. Neville Keynes argues that the point of departure for theories must be fundamentally observation, but he asserts that introspection (as Stuart Mill and Cairnes pointed out) can also be useful in this sense, since he considers introspection as a source of obtaining ideas that, in his opinion, can be described as empirical.
- With respect to the concept of homo economicus, Neville Keynes affirms, in an extremely utilitarian way, that the economic behavior that seeks self-interest dominates in reality the motives of altruism and benevolence, that is, for this author the

economist works knowing that man is selfish, unlike others who held that one had to work as if man were selfish.

- The appropriate method for economics must end with the empirical observation relative to the fulfillment of the theory. However, the contrasts of the theories allow to determine their limits of application but not invalidate them: if a test, apparently, contradicts a theory, the researcher must be aware that this result only shows that the test of the theory has been applied incorrectly.

We have made this detail of the ideas of JN Keynes because we believe they synthesize almost perfectly the methodological position that prevailed among most of the economists in the 19th century, that is to say, a good part of the classic and almost all of the neoclassicals, who we remember are the founders of the microeconomic theory, even today almost without fissures. This position is further consolidated with Lionel Robbins, who is usually considered the last verificationist, that is, the last influential economist who wrote before Popper revolutionized epistemology with his concept of "falsificationism", and that gave rise to the epistemological applications of Milton Friedman to Economics, without doubts the most influential economist in the matter of economic methodology during century XX.

✓ Lionel Robbins

Among the most relevant contributions in terms of economic methodology, we find the work of Lionel Robbins, influential English economist, who in 1932 published Essay on the Nature and Significance of Economic Science[93]. In it, the aforementioned author strongly criticizes both inductivism and methodological monism (the same method for both natural and social sciences), showing himself more in favor of the ideas of Senior and Cairnes, that is, in favor of employing a deductive procedure in economics and dualism in the methodology used by the natural and social sciences. For Robbins, the inductive procedure is not successful in economics because there is nothing to indicate that history will be repeated, and thus, historical induction, without the help of analytical judgment, is not a good form of economic methodology.

By criticizing induction so severely in economic theory, it gave way to the justification of the hypothetic-deductive method; for him, the propositions of economic theory are deductions from a series of postulates; and the main postulates are assumptions about simple and indisputable facts of experience in relation to the way in which the scarcity of goods, the object of our science, appears in the world of reality. And from these arguments, he insists again with the highly criticizable foundation of Senior, Cairnes, J.M.Keynes, etc., on the fact that the validity of a theory proceeds, therefore, from the logical derivation of the premises from which it departs. In other words, for Robbins, it does not matter too much to start from correct premises or not, arising from the introspection of some "enlightened ones" or in a more scientific way; while the model is logically well derived, the procedure is valid.

Robbins also criticizes the methodological monism posited by the Vienna Circle, arguing that economics is a branch of knowledge where the uniformity that exists in the natural sciences does not occur, since:

- the subjectivity of the individual has an important role, and
- the complexity of reality prevents the initial conditions remain unchanged in different situations; and this lack of uniformity reduces the effectiveness of purely empirical procedures.

Regarding the interrelation between economics and psychology -one of the most relevant aspects for this work on Neuroeconomics-, this influential English author argues that our science must use the rationality of the utilitarian homo economicus as a premise from which to build models and to make the deductions, in a context where a few economists argued that behaviorism also could provide too a valid starting point for economics in terms of the assumption of rationality. The behaviorists denied the role of introspection - used profusely by neoclassical economists - since, according to them, psychology had to deal only with the external behavior of man; eliminating pernicious metaphysical concepts in the explanation of human behavior.

Robbins argues that in economics concepts that are not observable, such as those of indifference, preference, choice or expectations, adopting Behavioral Psychology as the foundation of Economic Theory would leave the latter incomplete. At this point in our book it is almost redundant to say that, unfortunately for Robbins, today with the help of Neuroeconomics, variables such as indifference, preference, choice or expectations can be measured with enough degree of success, which for economic theory constitutes a true revolution, not yet assimilated by many, by the recent issue.

ROBBINS

And although Robbins says that economics cannot be totally separated from psychology, since the economist must start from psychological concepts to elaborate theories; defends - following the tradition of Senior, Cairnes, etc. - that economic theory maintains a certain independence and autonomy from the psychological principles that ensure the validity of the conclusions of the first, even in cases in which the psychology on which it relies is wrong. In fact Robbins, exemplifies this point with the case of the theory of value, which was constructed - by Jevons,

Edgeworth and Gossen, fundamentally - on the basis of hedonistic principles, which were not however vital for the theory since other economists, like Menger, they could reach the same conclusions based on different assumptions. "The hedonistic borders of the work of Jevons and his followers were incidental to the main structure of a theory which - as its parallel development in Vienna showed - can be presented and defended in non-hedonistic terms at all[94].

That is, Robbins uses an argument very similar to the famous thesis of the irrelevance of assumptions, which Friedman develops more deeply and forcefully years later, where it is stated that starting from unrealistic assumptions does not take away legitimacy to the conclusions of the economic models. We will get back to this point later.

3. Popper and the Falsifiability Condition

Until the appearance of the philosopher Karl Popper, both in economic science and in many others, the hypothetical deductive method (also known as logical positivism or Vienna Circle) was enormously influential. We have already seen the contributions of J.S.Mill, Senior, Cairnes, JNKeynes and to a greater extent Lionel Robbins, all of them founding fathers of our economic theory, among others, and all of them also inspired by this epistemological paradigm of deductivism, which we can basically also call verificationism, different from the more evolved paradigm that will come from the hand of the remarkable philosopher of the 20th century, Karl Popper, called falsificationism. But what was the difference between the two? And in what way did falsificationism impact economics?

First, let's start with the two main criticisms towards the hypothetical-deductive postulates:

- This scientific logic, in the end, means explaining without understanding. The underlying problem that arises at this point is that the hypothetic-deductive method, as it has been described, is implicitly based on Hume's concept of causality, according to which causality is the conjunction of two events A and B that they are contiguous in time and space, so that the previous episode, A, is called cause and the later, B, effect; However, there is no necessary connection between the two episodes, so that causality can simply be a spurious correlation between two phenomena that occur over time. Opponents to the Vienna Circle criticize this Humean notion of causality and postulate instead that scientific explanation and prediction must include a mechanism that connects cause and effect, so as to ensure that the correlation between two events it is necessary and not merely accidental. Returning to the previous example, it would be necessary to know why B happens when A happens, and not only that both events occur in time with a certain sequence[95].

- Secondly, logical positivism - and in particular the verification principle - incurs the well-known problem of induction, which has concerned philosophers since David Hume: no arbitrarily large number of verifications can prove that a theory is true because the inferences from the particular to the general lack a logical justification. In other words, a general statement cannot logically be derived from singular claims, even if the number of these singular claims is high; on the contrary, any universal affirmation can logically be contradicted by a singular affirmation. Using the classic example (which has its origin in Stuart Mill), from the observation of a million white swans the inference "the swan is white" cannot be obtained, but it is enough to see a black swan so that the statement "the swan is white be refuted".

Karl Popper - whose main work is The Logic of Scientific Research[96] - defends the logical rationality and the importance of the hypothetical deductive method in the elaboration of theories. However, Popper knew clearly this asymmetry between induction and deduction, verification and falsification and insisted on the idea that by using the contrast of the theories can show that something is false but cannot be demonstrate that something is true. That is, the change in the validation pattern of the theories is important: the Vienna Circle advocated empirical observation as a verification mechanism, while Popper shows that empirical observation has no verification capacity but falsification. In this way, science, for Popper, is only a set of knowledge susceptible of being empirically falsified, badly despite the devotees of the Vienna Circle.

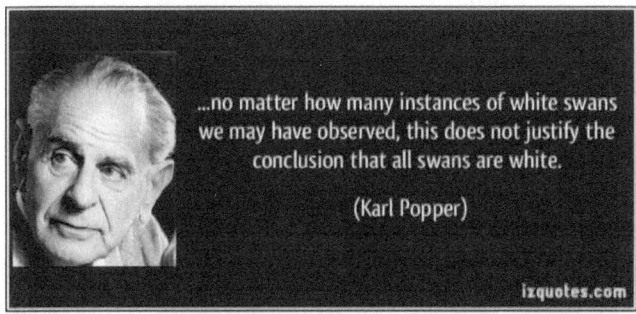

In short, for Popper, the scientific collection is no more than a set of conjectures that have withstood the refutation attempts so far, and in this way the progress of science consists in the progressive substitution of some theories by others, through a process of trial and error. For example, using the Popperian language, today Neurosciences would be falsifying the hypothesis of rationality in force in economics; we will come back to this topic later in this chapter.

Now, how do we obtain the hypotheses from which the theories start, which are then subjected not to verification mechanisms, but to falsification? For Popper, induction is not the appropriate method, since to be able to elaborate generalizations through induction, it is necessary to select some observations from the total of the existing ones (which is an infinite set), that is, an arbitrary mechanism is included. Therefore, for Popper, agreeing with logical positivism and the Vienna Circle, the theories are generated in the understanding of man, anticipate the experience and are not the result of empirical data. In short, for the great Austrian philosopher, when theorizing, one must start from assumptions, not from facts of reality; but these postulates are only conjectures, which can be falsified at any time, contrary to the statement of the verificationist, much more closed in accepting possible failures of their theories.

But of course, not any falsificationism is appropriate, and at this point we must differentiate between naive and sophisticated falsificationism. The naive falsificationism is the one that maintains that a theory can be falsified only by the fact of finding a simple error in a theory, that's why it is naive, since theories are not invalidated in such a simple way. Popper proposes the sophisticated falsificationism as appropriate, where a theory must specify, a priori, the conditions of observation that would falsify it; moreover, the more exact the specification of those conditions in which the theory would be refuted and the more probable its occurrence, the more risks the theory runs but at the same time there will be more guarantees that, provisionally, it is highly confirmed. In synthesis, although for Popper the theories are "simple conjectures", to falsify them is not so simple either, but a series of requirements like those mentioned must be fulfilled, requirements that we believe today fulfills the assumption of neuroeconomic rationality to falsify the neoclassical one. Later in this chapter we will return to this point.

4. The Popperian Falsifiability Criterium in Economics

Economic science could not remain isolated from the influence of Popper's message. Around the decade of the '30 appear strong critics to the "state of the arts" of the time, denoting the influence of falsificationism (the ideas of Popper) in the field of economic methodology. The pioneer in these struggles is Hutchison, a graduate of Cambridge, a teacher from 1935 to 1938 at the University of Bonn, a university where he had the opportunity to become familiar with the ideas of the Vienna Circle, which he would then criticize strongly. We had already commented, in an earlier chapter, that his work The Significance and Basic Postulates of Economic Theory[97] (published in 1938) is one of the first, during the 20th century, that rose up against the deficient ad-hoc premise on human (utilitarian) rationality built on economics; in fact, his work is a criticism of Robbins' 1932 essay, both because of the aforementioned theme of rationality, and because he advocates a greater degree of utilization of empirical procedures in economics. In this way, his thought is considered as a change of tendency with respect to the previous verificationist methodology and as the explicit introduction of certain Popper contributions in the economic methodology.

HUTCHISON

Hutchison directly attacks the ideas of Robbins and his predecessors (Cairnes, Senior, JN Keynes, etc.) by stating that the fundamental difference between science and non-science is that the propositions of the former must "be conceivably capable of being submitted in empirical contrast or being susceptible to being reduced - by logical or mathematical deduction - to testable propositions, recommending economists to stick to these empirical propositions, which are potentially falsifiable.

It is interesting for us, as apologists of Neuroeconomics, to analyze some of the criticisms that Hutchison's contribution received, for example that of Knight[98], which insists - with arguments similar to those of Robbins - on the impossibility of the starting point of Economics are assumptions susceptible to contrast because in human behavior there are important unobservable facets. Knight defends, also, the convenience of maintaining a position of methodological dualism between Social and Natural Sciences, a fact in which we also agree, regardless on the fact that now with Neuroeconomics there will surely be a big approach between the methods of hard sciences and soft. We will come back to this topic later.

We will not go into detail again that the criticisms of Kaldor (and similar Machlup) greatly influence Hutchison, even achieving that, years later, the latter retract, opting for methodological dualism, compared to his monist position externalized in 1938; and that in addition it arrives to affirm that their demands of empirical testing refer primarily to the final propositions, not to the premises. In short, although it is not clear why Hutchison retracted his statements in 1938, he is cited here as well because this work is one of the first important that stand against the "diktat Robbins", the orthodoxy of that time, and it is also the forerunner of one of the most important methodological contributions of the 20th century, Friedman's essay, which managed to attract the attention of professionals of economics from the decade of the fifty.

✓ Milton Friedman: the most influential work in economic epistemology

In 1953, the renowned Milton Friedman, intellectual heir of Alfred Marshall and trained in famous American universities such as Chicago and Columbia, published his article The Methodology of Positive Economics[99], undoubtedly the most influential work in the field of economic methodology of the twentieth century, which would achieve over the years, monopolize the support of the majority of professional economists, and obviously meant the "strong entry" of popperian falsificationism into economic science.

Although we discussed in a previous chapter -as closely related to the concept of rationality- the main postulates of this work, some will be mentioned here again, and analyzed in greater depth, to have a clear vision of Friedman's influence on the history (and in the present) of the methodology in economics. But in general, we can anticipate that Friedman's contribution has influenced to epistemologically consolidate the current neoclassical paradigm in the future, since through his thesis of irrelevance of the assumptions he has put a "protective shield" to this form of theorizing, that can hardly be changed. We will return to the end of this chapter on this point.

In the field of philosophy, Friedman receives a considerable influx of American pragmatism, which include names such as John Dewey or William James. This stream of thought, in short, held the following:

- The objective of science is to dominate and control nature.
- Experience must be the valid way to achieve the previous objective. The starting point of the hypotheses should be the empirical evidence; the point of arrival is also the reality because it is necessary to contrast the implications of the theory. Moreover, the validity of the theory depends on the results it provides. In particular, a theory will be correct if it predicts adequately.

- The validity of a theory, ultimately, derives from the consensus among researchers as to its usefulness, and not from the theory being true or false (these are categories that are no longer considered relevant). In particular, a theory should not be rejected because its assumptions are not realistic.

Following his philosophical influences, we already said that Friedman was a falsificationist, that is to say that he receives from Popper the idea that proceeding to the testing of a hypothesis allows its falsification, and not its verification, as it was defended in the past. Finally, Friedman also has some influences from the Vienna Circle, especially with regard to methodological monism. Below, some reflections on his main ideas in the field of economic epistemology.

✓ Instrumentalism and the problem of induction

You could say that "the instrumentalists (Friedman is) consider that the status of truth of theories, hypotheses or assumptions is irrelevant from the practical point of view as long as the conclusions logically follow from them are successful." And if we take into account that for the pragmatism - current that exerts a considerable influence on Friedman - the starting point of the hypotheses is the empirical evidence, the problem of the induction is latent in the approach of Friedman; let us remember what was said in previous pages when explaining Popper's thought, that induction is not the appropriate method to elaborate the premises, since to be able to elaborate generalizations through induction it is necessary to select some observations from the total of the existing ones (which is an infinite set), and therefore, agreeing with logical positivism and the Vienna Circle, the theories are generated in the understanding of man, anticipate the experience and are not the result of empirical data.

In this way, the instrumentalist position offers an outlet for the problem of induction that came with the philosophy of pragmatics, a problem of which Friedman is fully aware (induction is not a procedure that argues and establishes the veracity of the conclusions in logical terms, unlike the deduction). And since induction does not provide that guarantee, it is necessary to look for an alternative that allows establishing that a theory is valid. This alternative way, for Friedman, is the success in predictions: the ultimate criterion for judging the validity of a theory is the conformity of its predictions with experience.

This argument of Friedman can be interpreted, in a first approximation, in the light of the pragmatic vision that he has of science: science is a theoretical instrument oriented to solve real problems (in particular the Economic Theory should be oriented to the Economic Policy). How to know if the theory will serve in practice in the solution of problems or, in other words, that has reached a sufficient understanding of the phenomenon that allows to manage and control it? For Friedman, the most convincing way to make sure that theory understands phenomena is to prove that it is capable of predicting.

In short, **Friedman tells us: it does not matter in what way the model is generated, if inductively, deductively, or if with realistic or not so realistic premises about the human being and his rationality; but what matters is that predict according to reality.**

✓ The irrelevance of the assumptions

Perhaps more than one economist, especially those who are not too familiar with the topics of epistemology, share Koopmans' vision[100] (to mention only one of Friedman's critics), that observation allows for (by induction) premises that are true and then logic applies the argument by which the truth of the premises generates true conclusions. That is, for Koopmans it is possible to establish the validity of a theory independently of its applications.

Synthesizing the previous paragraph, any layman would say: yes, it should be like that, I take the assumptions out of reality, and put together a model, surely the same (later) will predict reality well. Friedman, in one of his most controversial contributions, argued in a completely opposite way: the realism of the assumptions does not matter, it matters the goodness of the predictions that emanate from the economic models. The historical context of the question is as follows: in the years 1946-48 some articles had been published in the American Economic Review arguing that the assumptions of maximization by companies were unrealistic, since the firms do not know the exact position of the companies, its marginal revenue and marginal cost curves. These were followed by other works that aspired to refute this approach, so that generated a debate about what can be considered one of the foundations of neoclassical economic theory: the premise on hyper-optimizing economic agents. Friedman responds to the controversy by affirming, words more, words less, that it is irrelevant that the assumptions of the theory are realistic or not; **what is important, as noted before, is that the theory is capable of predicting.**

Friedman gets into pure logic to explain this topic, particularly with the ideas of modus ponens and modus tollens. What do we mean by this? These are two argumentative mechanisms used in logic. We have to:

- The argument modus ponens implies that if the assumptions are true, the conclusion is true. In other words, "the truth passes forward", from assumptions to conclusions.
- The argument modus tollens implies that if the conclusion is false, some of the assumptions will be false, that is, "passes the falsehood backwards" of the conclusions to one or more of the assumptions.
- Employing both procedures in the opposite direction gives rise to different fallacies. Thus, the fallacy of affirming the consequent consists in arguing that if the conclusion is true the assumption is true, which is not necessarily true because "the truth cannot be passed back".

- Similarly, the fallacy of denying the antecedent is incurred when it is argued that if the assumptions are false, the conclusion is false, which is not always the case because "falsehood cannot be passed forward".

Modus Ponens	Modus Tollens
Given: $p \rightarrow q$	Given: $p \rightarrow q$
p	$\sim q$
Conclusion: q	Conclusion: $\sim p$

The main argument of Friedman is that if the truth cannot be passed back (fallacy of affirming the consequent), the true conclusions do not require true assumptions. And if an assumption is false, is this a sufficient condition for the falsity of the conclusion? The answer again is negative, because to answer affirmatively would be to incur the fallacy of denying the antecedent. And hence Friedman's main argument, based on the laws of pure logic: **the use of inadequate assumptions does not necessarily generate inadequate conclusions.**

And this is the main protective shield that Friedman gave to neoclassical modeling: according to him, the use of the modus ponens in the right direction (more or less what Neuroeconomics raises when demanding the use of true human rationality in models) it would not be a fruitful procedure for science. In fact, says Friedman, the modus ponens is not applicable because scientists proceed by searching, not from correct assumptions, but from predictions that succeed. In addition, in another aspect also to discuss "long and hard", maintains that the lack of realism is not only an obstacle to science but can be an advantage. For Friedman, **the most accurate theory is the one that explains and predicts more with less: that less refers to the assumptions, which must capture the essential economic relationships but be simple, so that they are not lost in the tangle of accessory details.**

In particular, Friedman is against making 1 to 1 representations of reality when modeling. The key to his argument lies in the trade-off between realism and simplicity: the crucial attribute that a theory must possess is to grasp the essential. In this sense, falsity of assumptions does not mean logical or epistemological falsity for Friedman, but a departure from exhaustive descriptivism. And, in the context of the body of knowledge originally raised by the polemic, the neoclassical theory of the firm - as indicated above - Friedman's ideas fit in the following way:

"It is true that employers do not calculate the cut-off point between marginal cost and marginal revenue to determine the optimal amount offered so that profits are maximized, but even if the agents do not really act like that, supposing that they do it is useful and produces results that they are observed in practice."

At this point of the argument on Friedmanian thought, **we wonder why confuse unrealistic assumptions with lack of simplicity,** the first would be for example build models assuming that human beings are hyper-calculating and always optimize their decision (as has been come modeling traditionally); instead the second would involve building models, with realistic neuropsychological premises, but so full of details that they did not contribute much when it comes to improving the predictive model. **The reality is that they are two very different issues, of course you have to be simple to model, and try to predict more with less, but not from unrealistic assumptions, less now that Neuroeconomics tells us what human rationality is like, and not through introspection, as has been a tradition in our science.** Moreover, following Friedman, what if we assume that all human beings are insane, maybe the models would predict better than with the current hyper-rational. According to Milton Friedman, it would seem that **anything goes, a kind of casino, where one just have to be lucky with the assumptions (the bets), to get predictive success (the winnings bets).**

Deep down, Friedman understands that, although the assumptions are not true hundred percent, they are not so far from reality. That is why the models thus formulated, with a hyper-optimizing logic (for example, the maximization of the net profit of the entrepreneur), predict well. We, the neuroeconomists, perhaps do not agree so much with the "hyper-optimizing mentality" -in fact the current empirical evidence shows it-, but **our models are forced to predict better than the neoclassical ones, otherwise, to the light of Friedman's instrumentalism, will not be an important contribution to science.** We will return later on this point.

✓ The Provisional Character of Theories

We said earlier that Friedman is notably influenced by popperian falsificationism: empirical evidence can refute a hypothesis but not prove it, so that a given paradigm is always provisional, a conjecture, that at some point some other theoretical body will come to refute, partially or totally. Then, in his 1953 work, the American economist tells us his golden rule in epistemological matters, in what is the result of the influences of Popper, the pragmatists and their own added value to economics:

"The hypothesis is rejected if its predictions are frequently contradicted (or more often than the predictions of an alternative hypothesis); He is given great confidence if he has survived many opportunities to be contradicted. The evidence of the facts can never prove a hypothesis, it can only stop disapproving it, not rejecting it, which is what we generally mean when we affirm, somewhat inaccurately, that the hypothesis has been confirmed by experience.[101]"

Finally, Friedman "puts pressure" on those schools that intend to challenge the neoclassical paradigm -as in the case of Neuroeconomics-, stating that there are two additional criteria -with which we fully agree- for the choice between alternative theories, once all of them have shown their consistency with the empirical evidence:

- Simplicity: a theory is simple when less is the initial knowledge necessary to make a prediction within a given field.

- Fertility: a theory is all the more fruitful the more accurate the predictions that result, the greater the area within which the theory offers predictions and the more lines of future research it suggests.

That is to say, in the end, the neuroeconomic models must come out of the trade-off "simplicity versus fertility" that is going to arise; since they will surely be less simple than the neoclassical ones but perhaps more fertile, finer in their contributions, otherwise they will not last in time.

✓ Methodological Monism

Milton Friedman is favorable to methodological monism, at least in regard to positive economics. And while he admits that objectivity is more difficult to achieve in Economics than in other sciences (because of the issue of working with human beings and their free will), it is surprising to state, unlike Robbins, that this fact does not entail a fundamental distinction of economics with other disciplines of a more experimental nature. And in this way, for Friedman the starting point in the construction of hypotheses must be the empirical evidence - just as it happens in the experimental sciences - and not the introspection, far surpassing Robbins and the Neoclassical in this aspect.

To conclude with Friedman's contribution, and after having mentioned the most salient aspects of the correct research method for this influential North American economist, we believe we have made our position as neuroeconomists quite clear: although we agree with several of its postulates, in our opinion its main fault is in confusing simplicity of assumptions (which is desirable) with assumptions unrealism, subject to the model predicting well; this is the great criticism we have for Friedman's thinking. Obviously, we recognize, it is much easier to defend our criticism now than before (for example in the time of Hutchison), when there was no instrument that today provide Neurosciences to refine the assumption of rationality, so it is understandable that the Friedmanian instrumentalism has had so much life, but maybe it's time to stake out again. We will return to this point at the end of the chapter.

- ✓ The Epistemological Triumph of the "Friedman Criterion".

The great victory of Friedman was to change the axis of the discussion. It is no longer established in terms of true or false theories but of useful or useless ones. The premises have already become secondary, if the model predicts well, it must be because this and its initial hypotheses are not so far-fetched. That is why it is already becoming clear, too, that in the light of instrumentalism, the only way for future neuroeconomic models to be accepted as a progress of science is that they surpass those of traditional theory in terms of predictions; in the case that, for example, they only equaled it -and with greater complexity to theorize- traditional modeling would remain fully valid. In this **we must recognize an epistemological triumph for Friedman: theories today are useful or**

useless, beyond their assumptions; and to be more useful than another, a theory must predict better, otherwise there is no progress.

Will it be the triumph of what Paul Samuelson sarcastically calls "juggling F"? For Samuelson[102], the unrealism of assumptions should not be considered a merit of a theory but, rather, a demerit; since theories must, in his opinion, describe reality.

However, when Friedman's argument is coldly analyzed, and although it really sounds like "juggling" at first, we think it is difficult to refute, since he is saying something very clear: "I do not care how you made your model, but if predicts better than all others, is the most valid; and obviously, it is implicit that if predicts well, should not be so preposterous his starting assumptions". And Neuroeconomics should openly accept the Friedmanian challenge, in the sense that if the neuroeconomic models fail to predict better than the current ones, for better assumptions they have, they will hardly imply a progress for economic theory. In this, we believe Friedman has imposed a test to validate the models: either they are useful or they are useless; methodologically, we repeat again, it is a triumph that must be recognized.

But what would happen if, in fact, the neuroeconomic models do not predict better, but only the same as the current ones, but with a greater degree of complexity in the assembly of the models? Should we neuroeconomists cross our arms, and not apply any of the latest findings on the true rationality of the human being making economic decisions? We think not, and while we do not discuss the legitimacy of instrumentalism as a methodology, we cannot be satisfied with the current state of the arts. If Neurosciences allow us to properly model human rationality when making economic decisions, we have the scientific obligation to use said knowledge; Moreover, for Neuroeconomics, it should be a question of "tranquility of scientific conscience" to proceed with more realistic assumptions, whether predictions improve or not.

✓ The Dominant Paradigm in Economics

After all the analysis carried out throughout this chapter, we believe we are in a position to summarize some of the ideas in which today, at the beginning of the 21st century, most mainstream economists coincide, always with respect to the methodological issue. And obviously, in the constitution of this dominant paradigm, Friedman's contribution has exerted a remarkable influence.

- There is a single science, economics, with a double slope, positive and normative; most of the positive propositions are testable, so that, ultimately, their degree of validity can be determined by reference to empirical evidence; on the other hand, normative propositions are not susceptible of empirical testing.

- The demands of logical positivism of the early twentieth century, excessively empiricist, have softened to some extent. Today it is admitted that within economics there can be positive propositions that cannot be verified, but the elaborated conclusions must be testable.
- A branch of knowledge enjoys the status of science if it can submit its conclusions to the contrast offered by the facts of the real world, here we can clearly see the influence of Popper's contribution; but without falling into naive falsificationism (admit that a single test can refute a theory). What is accepted today, on the contrary, is sophisticated falsificationism, according to which refuting a theory is a little more complicated.
- The discrimination between rival theories is carried out mainly in terms of empirical evidence, since, due to sophisticated falsificationism, it is difficult to prove and / or refute the theories in a definitive way.
- There is an interaction between empirical evidence and deductive reasoning in the elaboration of economic theory. Theories rest on assumptions, and in regard to the realism of the assumptions, in general, the

contributions of Friedman already described are accepted. In the development of the theory careful attention is given to its logical structure and deductive rigor, so that in the contributions of economists a degree of mathematical complexity can be found increasingly. In recent years the controversy has grown over the desirability that the mathematical content of economic theory were so high.
- It is commonly accepted that human behavior lacks the determinism found in the behavior of the inanimate world, therefore a perfect methodological monism is impossible.

5. Change of Paradigm with Neuroeconomics?

We had started the chapter arguing that it was only at the end of the chapter that we were going to try to "throw some light" on the intricate theme of the paradigm shift, since the issue is not simple and we have to extrapolate too much into the future; remember that Neuroeconomics as a field is still very embryonic. In order to analyze this topic, throughout this chapter we stopped first in the concept of paradigm (Kuhn's, one of the most accepted at present), then we made a brief detail of the main epistemological schools that have influenced Economics in the last 200 years, to finally take the time to review the historical evolution of the method in economics, that is, how the main theorists were working to build our influential science.

That is, along the way traveled to here (we believe) has been relatively clear who were the most influential over the past two centuries, so that the paradigm currently in force (the original neoclassical, although more refined) has triumphed the way he did it. Without fear of being wrong, methodologically there are two names that stand out: Lionel Robbins and Milton Friedman. Can we say the same thing, about thirty years, of Glimcher, Kahneman, Thaler, Camerer, or Paul Zak, to name just a few of the most reputable neuroeconomists today? That is, **can Neuroeconomics revolutionize the current method in our science, the "Friedman Thesis" for example? Will this novel field change the prevailing neoclassical paradigm?**

And if the answer is affirmative, will it be a strong change in the Kuhn's sense? Or more limited in Lakatos' sense? In what follows, we will try to sketch some ideas on this issue, starting with a brief summary of the ideas of Kuhn and Lakatos, two influential epistemologists of the late twentieth century, with specific writings on the subject of paradigm's change.

✓ Kuhn

The main writing of Thomas Kuhn is *The Structure of Scientific Revolutions*, whose first edition is published in 1962[103]. About this work, which is based on an analysis of the historical evolution of several sciences, there is quite a coincidence that:

- for Kuhn, the historical evolution of science is characterized by abrupt changes from one

paradigm to another, as opposed to soft changes;
- however accepted the current paradigm is, there will always be certain inexplicable anomalies in the context of said paradigm; but when the number or magnitude of the anomalies are excessive and the restlessness emerges among the researchers, a scientific revolution or change towards a superior paradigm to the preceding one takes place.

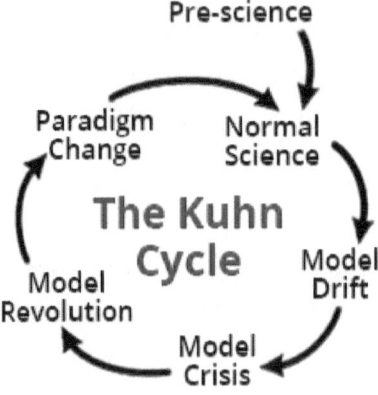

Scientific progress, for Kuhn, would occur in the following steps:

- Be part of a situation of agreement among scientists, of any science, on the problems to be solved and the general forms of the solution (for example, the neoclassical paradigm in economics).
- At a given moment, certain theories that introduce the controversy appear, especially highlighting certain "theoretical anomalies", so that the prevailing consensus is breaking

down (in economics, all criticisms of the concept of rationality listed in chapter 3 could be), among them Hutchison, J.M.Keynes, Simon, Kahneman, and finally Neuroeconomics).
- A new theoretical approach is consolidated, offering a solution to the problems that until then had been neglected (for example, if Neuroeconomics were consolidated, with its new hypothesis on human rationality).
- Finally, there is a conversion in the scientists to the new framework (there would be a paradigm shift in economics), which becomes the normal science of the next generation, until the process starts again.

However, the main critics of Kuhn argue that revolutions in science have been much slower and less dramatic than he maintains, where it can be said that, at any moment, science consists of paradigms that overlap and they influence each other, and that the new ones do not replace the previous ones in a sudden but gradual way, which leads Schwartz to describe this vision of science (Kuhn's) as "funny, but false"[104]. However, his paradigm concept is quite accepted:

- "universally recognized scientific relationships that, for a certain time, provide models and solutions to a scientific community"
- "the complete constellation of beliefs, values, techniques, etc., shared by the members of a given community"

✓ Lakatos and the Research Programs

Lakatos, contrary to Kuhn's ideas, focuses its contribution around the concept of the Research Program:

- In science, more than paradigms, there are research programs, with a central core and a protective belt.
- The central core is composed of assumptions, premises or beliefs that are considered irrefutable, largely due to their metaphysical nature (there would enter the concept of optimizing rationality that we have criticized so much in economics).
- Positive heuristic or partially articulated set of suggestions or indications on how to change, the refutable variables of the research program.
- Negative heuristics or methodological rules that tell us which research paths we should avoid.
- The protective belt is formed by auxiliary hypotheses that are modified as they are falsified, as a result of the suggestions of the positive heuristic.
- For Lakatos: the hard core remains relatively stable;
- The advance of science, meanwhile, occurs when one research program is considered better than another because it is able to explain all the facts of the second and, in addition, make other predictions, some of

which are confirmed empirically. The history of science, therefore, can be conceived, in part, as the abandonment of degenerate research programs and their progressive substitution by other progressive ones;
- Lakatos is widely accepted today among economics theorists.

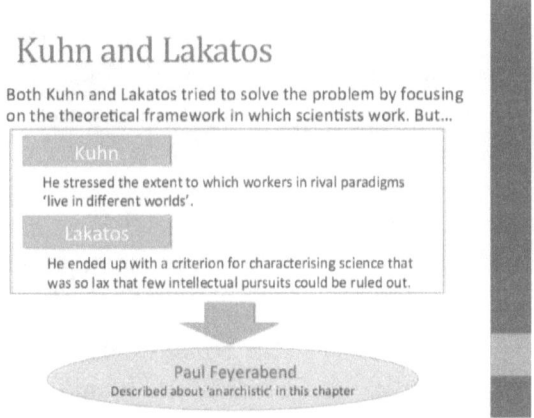

6. **Neuroeconomics Change to Lakatos: Hard Core or Protective Belt?**

If we take the Keynesian research program (or paradigm), in the middle of the last century it seemed that it was going to modify part of the neoclassical hard core (the Keynesians argued that economics was full of rigidities, that they contradicted the neoclassical optimizing premises, and their forecasts of fully flexible variables), plus other changes in the protective belt. However, there is some agreement among economists that Keynes' ideas have been discredited a bit in recent decades, at least among the theoreticians, due to the large number of intrinsic contradictions present in their models, and the need of micro fundamentals for macro models. Perhaps Keynes, if he lived now, with the advances in Applied Neuroscience, would be remarkably more influential than he could be in theoretical matters; since in the end Keynes, like the majority of the theoreticians until not long ago, resorted to the so criticized "introspection" to construct the premises of their theoretical models, the hard core in terms of Lakatos.

Currently, Behavioral Economics and Neuroeconomics are also strongly attacking the dominant research paradigm / program, although not as broadly as Keynes (due to the variety of topics), but with a lot of hardness and strong scientific arguments against the most basic metaphysical premise of neoclassical thought, the hypothesis of ultra-optimizing rationality, which is no small thing, because from there all models start, the micro and today also the macro. That is, today the hard core of our science is the one that could be modified, with Neuroeconomics and Behavioral Economics. And from this possibility emerges the following question: would we be closer to a paradigm shift to the Kuhn than to the Lakatos, for the radical of the eventual change? The answer is not easy, however at the end of the chapter we propose one; but first let's review the current epistemological critiques for Neuroeconomics.

7. Apologists and Detractors of Neuroeconomics

The birth of Neuroeconomics has created one of those rare historical moments in which economists stop to reflect on the fundamental questions of our science, that is, the epistemological, as for example the interdisciplinary approach to the economic problem, the borders of economics, the objectives of our science, questions of validity or refutation of theories, among others. The debate is hot today, and is on the agenda of many important economic congresses around the world, and the waters are quite divided, although generally with a nod in favor of this novel branch.

On the side of the detractors, we have the already famous Gul and Pesendorfer[105], for whom Neuroeconomics is and will be irrelevant to economics, both in empirical evidence and in explanatory power, since Economics and Neuroeconomics ask different questions and as a result, they use different abstractions. For both authors, economic models should not make assumptions about the physiology or psychology of the brain; giving Neuroeconomics only the modest role of inspiration for economists, as new neuro studies unravel new issues related to decision-making, and as long as the models include variables about what an economic agent chooses and not about how an economic agent chooses. But the maximizing modeling, and the hyper-rational homo economicus will never be dethroned, in the particular vision of these respected and at the same time highly criticized economists, who join some (very few) who believe that Neuroeconomics is a branch with a lot of marketing and very little scientific rigor.

Luckily, today practically no one in the profession thinks that Neuroeconomics is irrelevant to economic theory, in fact there are those who think that Neuroeconomics will allow economics, traditional social science, to approach the methods of natural sciences, which use inductive behavior much more than the deductive one (tradition in economics), and they tend to be more rigorous from the epistemological point of view than social ones.

However, Neuroeconomics will certainly not be what Camerer, Loewestein and Prelec said in 2004-05, when they thought this new branch would serve to expose all the theoretical anomalies of traditional Economics and its hyper-rational models, and would help the profession in a forceful way to refute or accept models and explanations in economics, that is, to facilitate the adequate popperian falsificationism in economic science. Today we know that the epistemological triumph of Neuroeconomics is not guaranteed at all, and that still remain many years of battle to see certain achievements, but perhaps not as optimistic as those that were believed ten years ago.

In fact, at that time, Camerer, Loewestein and Prelec came to affirm that "Neuroeconomics would allow direct measurement of thoughts and feelings", replacing the weak theories of marginal utility and revealed preferences, which now reign in microeconomics and that date more than 100 years. And they also affirmed that the new branch "would not only increase the realism of the current models, but also eventually replace the traditional constructs, with new models," the neuro models". In short, an excess of optimism that was wasted at that time by these three founding fathers of Neuroeconomics.

In this way, in recent years Camerer, Loewestein, Prelec and several other enthusiasts of the first period have been reducing the volume of their claims, since they have found several difficulties with neuro field research, especially with econometric deductions from functional magnetic resonances (fMRI), among some of the methodological limitations found in Neuroeconomics.

However, the latter does not invalidate at all the future of this novel branch of economics, since it is truly helping to improve the traditional economic theory, and not only as a source of inspiration, according to Gul and Pessendorfer. Neuroeconomics will undoubtedly improve particular explanations of economic phenomena, and thus also of aggregate markets in which these phenomena occur; but it is not so sure that the paradigm of traditional hyper-rational modeling changes strongly, because of the Friedman Thesis, already widely commented.

Who can have doubts that Neuroeconomics, in a short period of time, will help us understand economic issues as psychologically intricate as the phenomena of monetary illusion, Keynesian sticky prices and strategic interaction in game theory, among other issues; all issues that today maximizing mathematics does not leave well-founded at all. However, probably Microeconomics, Macroeconomics or Theory of

Games, as complete bodies of theory, do not change much thanks to Neuroeconomics.

In any case, today it is difficult to find theoreticians who strongly criticize the neuroeconomic project, and most still see it as "a hope for the future", rather than as a "passing fad". And undoubtedly, behind the acceptance of Neuroeconomics as a promise, is that of all its branches derived in Business and Administration: Neuromanagement, Neuromarketing, and Neuroleadership, among others.

For example, among moderate critics, we find Kuorikoski and Ylikoski[106], that argue that the idea of a direct connection between Economics and Neuroscience is wrong, and that both fields can only be integrated via psychological theories of decision making. The central thesis of them is that the neuro findings only provide primary evidence for **psychological research, which should link the neuro with the economic,** to be able to explain the economic behavior of agents with greater wealth than traditional modeling.

In line with the above, we also find moderate criticism from Alessandro Antonietti[107], emphasizing that several of the correlations neuro-mind reported by neuroeconomists do not serve much as empirical evidence, given the technical problems still present to identify the exact role played by the different brain structures behind the decision process. And Antonietti also ends up agreeing with Kuorikoski and Ylikoski on **the important role that psychological theories** must play in the connection between neuro findings and economic theory.

KUORIKOSKI-ANTONIETTI

Particularizing a little more, today the authors already speak of two different Neuroeconomics, or rather, of two different research programs within the same field:

- Behavioral Economics in the Scanner (BES)
- Neurocellullar Economics (NE)

With regard to BES, it is the branch of Neuroeconomics that tests via neuroimaging (among other techniques) the main postulates of Behavioral Economics; while the other branch (NE), follows the opposite way: apply economic models to understand the functioning of the brain, and that at the hand of Paul Glimcher, is collecting more and more scientific respect. In fact, one of the most promising research of Glimcher focuses on its so-called "subjective value" (the "utility" of economists), based on the dopaminergic signals detected in the ventral striatum and the middle prefrontal cortex of our brain, constituting a "common zone" of reward or satisfaction (valuation) in the individual decision-maker. Undoubtedly a very interesting research program of the NE branch, and with less criticism than the BES, although the latter is the most profusely developed in this last decade (and also the most analyzed in this work).

But when we say that there are almost no total critics of Neuroeconomics, let's take the case of a famous detractor such as Glenn Harrison[108] (although not as much as Gul and Pesendorfer), who criticizes the BES Neuroeconomics, but not the Neuroeconomics of Glimcher (NE). It happens that Harrison criticizes the lack of methodological rigor of BES, especially by the econometric limitations of neuroimaging in humans, and not so much of the NE, since this mainly examines rats and monkeys, with the technique of "single sells", and not so much neuroimaging.

HARRISON

In particular, Harrison and Ross criticize that the BES branch consists of repeating protocols that permanently demonstrate human irrationality under neuroimaging, but in studies carried out with few people, who apply valuations to different alternatives, but always isolated from the ecological-environmental context that surrounds. Subsequently, according to both authors, these irrationalities will try to be shown as anomalies within the theory of "rational choice", which does not take into account that the architecture of the brain determines that our decisions are a variable mixture of rationality and emotionality. And finish Harrison and Ross, arguing that this way of approaching studies in the BES branch ignores the ecological nature of economic rationality, that is, ignore the way in which people approach that hyper-rationality that illustrates the theory, given by the external structures that exist in the environment, which include especially the cultural issues that limit and condition our decision making.

In short, we see that both authors (Harrison and Ross), in order to criticize the BES branch of Neuroeconomics, resort to the postulates of the American Institutionalist School, an old school, but in a renewed boom within the current theory; but they do not do so using the macro institutions (Federal Reserve, concrete legal structures, etc.) as is usually done, but the cultural institutions (habits, traditions, customs, etc.) that have generally been exempt in traditional economic models, such as also in the neuro. And finally, they recommend for the new models neuro BES, the modern concept of ecological rationality of the Nobel Prize Vernon Smith (School of Experimental Economics)[109], which has been growing more and more in scientific acceptance at present. What does this concept of ecological rationality say? That economic regularities, understood as ecological properties of the context surrounding economic agents, can dominate the normal neuropsychological processing that occurs in controlled laboratory experiments, invalidating them.

And later, Harrison and Ross also criticize the econometrics derived from brain neuroimaging, in the first place due to the lack of precision of their estimates, which is a topic that technological progress will probably help to improve, but which today is a problem. Recall that the unit of analysis of Neuroeconomics is the brain, emitting signals per unit of time, from precise and specific points, that are captured by different techniques, especially neuroimaging. Secondly, they mention the problem of "reverse inference", that is, when activations in certain regions of the brain make it possible to presume the identification of specific cognitive processes. So, these authors argue that high correlations between well-identified psychological patterns and their neural counterparts are the exception and not the norm in most experiments, and that most of the time the interpretation of neuroimaging is captious. For example, the amygdala and insula, which have been mentioned in several BES studies as playing a central role in making economic decisions, from the emotional point of view, have also been identified, in other studies outside economics, as playing other roles, not exactly emotional roles. And thirdly, they criticize the problem of blood flow in anticipation of some event, which finally does not end up happening and that disregards the expected relationship between blood flow and neural activity, which helps to confuse the identification of neuropsychological processes applied to decision economic making.

And while we believe that the criticisms of Harrison and Ross towards the BES branch are important, they do not invalidate it at all, since on the one hand technological progress will improve neuroimaging (Neuroeconomics is a project for the future, not something for the very short term), and on the other hand, these authors fall into a problem that Michiru Nagatsu[110] identifies very well: the neuroeconomists of the BES branch pose questions conceptually different from those of the traditional economists; the first ones consider how the individual economic agents (considered as physical and biological beings) take decisions, while the latter consider the same thing but with ultra-rational beings, that is, the traditional homo-economicus. And Nagatsu concludes that the two approaches can lead to different models of decision making, and that they are not necessarily incompatible with each other. What is not clear is which of the two types of models will end up adopting economic theory, that is, the epistemological theme will be in full debate for the next years.

And this must necessarily be the case, since it will be the epistemology of economics that finally decides the scientific validity of Neuroeconomics, in any of its two branches. In the opinion of Bernheim[111], a scholar and critic of Neuroeconomics at the same time, **only when this novel and hybrid discipline provides us with a model derived from research in this field, that improves our measurement of the causal relationships studied by traditional models, the necessary proof will have been passed for its full acceptance.** This is what has been called **the Bernheim**

Challenge, which is exactly the same thing that we are proposing with our thesis: **the chance that the current and future neuroeconomic models are accepted as a progress of science is that they surpass in terms of predictions to those of the traditional theory; otherwise, traditional modeling would remain fully valid, because it is simpler than the neuroeconomic model.**

This is the result of the epistemological triumph of Milton Friedman, back in the mid-twentieth century, to establish the armor that still today scientifically supports the traditional economic theory, hyper-rational and hyper-unrealistic, and that gave entry into economics from theories by Karl Popper, the remarkable twentieth-century philosopher of science:

- Between the years 1946-48 some articles had been published in the American Economic Review that argued that the assumptions of maximization by companies were unrealistic, since firms do not know the exact position of their marginal income and cost curves, generating a debate about what can be considered one of the foundations of neoclassical economic theory. Friedman responds to the controversy by affirming it is irrelevant that the assumptions of the theory are realistic or not; the important thing is that the theory is capable of predicting accurately.
- According to Friedman[112], it is verifiable that truly important and significant hypotheses have premises / assumptions that are clearly

inadequate representations of reality and, in general, the more significant the theory is, the less realistic these assumptions will be. For him, the reason is simple, since a hypothesis is important if he explains a lot with little, that is, if he abstracts the important elements of the accessory.

The penetration of this thesis in the standard methodology of economics is so great, that **the only way that the current and future neuroeconomic models are accepted as a progress of science is that they surpass in predictions those of the traditional theory;** since in case they only equaled it, the traditional modeling would remain fully valid, because it would surely be simpler than the neuroeconomic model. In this we must recognize an epistemological triumph for Friedman: he changed the axis of the debate and the theories today are useful or useless, beyond their assumptions; and for a new research program (such as Neuroeconomics) to be more useful than the dominant program, it must predict better, otherwise there will be no scientific progress.

But suppose that the neuroeconomic models do not manage to overcome the traditional ones in predictive capacity and only equals them, the neuroeconomists cannot be satisfied with the triumph of "Juggle F" with the assumptions, with a "anything goes while predicting the model well". If Neurosciences allow us to correctly model human rationality when making economic decisions, we neuroeconomists have the scientific obligation to use such knowledge, although there is a possibility that the models become more complex. **In this sense, we share with Antonio Rangel that Neuroeconomics can very well become a field of specialization within economics, regardless of whether or not it meets the Bernheim challenge.**

Summarizing

Synthesizing Friedman's thought, with his famous thesis of "irrelevance of assumptions", we believe that he confuses something desirable (the simplicity of the model, explaining much with little) with something undesirable (unreal premises, to predict reality almost by chance - for a success of the lottery type with the chosen assumptions-). In fact we have already mentioned before that we fully share Samuelson's qualification to this thesis: Juggling F.

But the penetration of this thesis in the standard methodology of economics is so great, that the possibility that the current and future neuroeconomic models are accepted as a progress of the science is that they surpass in predictions those of the traditional theory; since in case they only equaled it, the traditional modeling would continue in full force, for its simplicity superior to the neuroeconomic one.

In fact Bernheim, a scholar and critic of Neuroeconomics already mentioned in this chapter, agrees with our central thesis for this chapter, when he argues that only when this new and hybrid discipline provides us with a model derived from research in this field, to improve our measurement of the causal relationships studied by traditional models, we will have passed the necessary test for their full acceptance[113].

In short, we recognize that there is a possibility that the current paradigm in economics does not change at all with this neuroeconomic boom; that will depend, in the light of "Friedman Thinking", on the new models predicting better. But one thing we are sure: all those scientists of economics who are familiar with the neuro are going to develop over the next few years many models based on postulates about true human rationality (not the one used now), and although they may not predict better than the traditional ones -we still do not know- they will enrich the debate significantly, helping to explain many of the current neoclassical anomalies.

CONCLUSIONS

The methodologically disruptive irruption of Neuroeconomics has come to stay. We are not talking about a passing fad, or a new fetish that economists are going to love for a while and then it will remain in the trunk of memories, as it has happened more than once. Advances in Neurosciences are now available for all Social Sciences, and impacting and modifying theoretical traditions in fields as varied as Education, Marketing, Management, etc., aiming to cross transversally each and every one of the Social Sciences, which economics is hardly immune.

Now, to speak of a paradigm's shift in Kuhn's sense is unlikely, being in the sense of Lakatos much more pertinent, as we argued in the previous chapter. In this way, throughout this work, we have been analyzing several of the lines of research where today Neuroeconomics most promises, in order to solve the main anomalies of the current neoclassical model. For example, Neuroeconomics is today trying to explain (among many others):

- the phenomenon of rigid wages falling;
- the anomalies in regards to intertemporal elections (excess of indebtedness at the family level, scarcity of savings for our retirement, etc.);
- strategic decisions;
- the influence of emotional aspects on individual demand functions;

- decisions in contexts of risk and uncertainty;
- and in general, specific aspects in each of the main fields of the traditional Economics, where the hypothesis of full rationality fails.

It happens that the irruption of Neuroeconomics and the Economics of Behavior, put in check the assumption of the neoclassical rationality (theory of the expected utility), underlying in almost all the base models of our science. We refer mainly to that cluster of ideas (long described throughout this book) that already at the end of the 19th century was entirely captured by the hand of Jevons, Walras, Marshall, etc.), and that were very well summarized by John Neville Keynes (the father of John Maynard Keynes, paradoxically a great critic of these postulates) of the following form:

- The correct methodological procedure of economics consists of starting from some fundamental facts about human nature. The point of beginning of the theories must be fundamentally observation, but introspection can also be useful, since it is considered as a source of obtaining ideas that can be described as empirical.
- The economic behavior that seeks self-interest dominates in reality the reasons for altruism and benevolence, so the economist must work knowing that man is selfish.
- The appropriate method for economics must end with the empirical observation relative to the fulfillment of the theory. However, the

contrasts of the theories allow to determine their limits of application but not invalidate them: if a test, apparently, contradicts a theory, the researcher must be aware that this result only shows that the test of that theory has been applied incorrectly.

This brief summary, made by J.N. Keynes (father J.M. Keynes, as we said) synthesizes almost perfectly the methodological position that prevailed among most economists in the 19th century, who we remember are the founders of the microeconomic theory, even today in force almost without fissures. This methodological posture will be further refined during the 20th century, starting with Lionel Robbins, and especially Milton Friedman, undoubtedly the most influential economist in the field of economic methodology during the 20th century.

With Friedman, in turn based on the remarkable Austrian philosopher Karl Popper, the theoretical shielding of traditional economic theory is finished, especially through the thesis of "irrelevance of the assumptions", where it is stated that it does not matter that the assumptions of a theory are realistic or not; the important thing is that the theory is able to predict accurately". Moreover, for Friedman it is verifiable that truly significant theories have premises that are clearly inadequate representations of reality and, in general, the more significant the theory, the less realistic their assumptions will be (as is the case of the imperfect hypothesis of rationality used in Economics for more than two centuries). For Friedman, the reason is simple, a hypothesis is important if explains a lot with little, that is, if it abstracts the important elements of the accessory.

And although at this point Friedman confuses something desirable (the simplicity of the model) with something undesirable (unrealistic premises), the penetration of this thesis in the standard methodology of economics is so great, that for current and future neuroeconomic models are accepted as a progress of science, is that they surpass in the matter of predictions to the traditional ones; otherwise, traditional modeling will continue in a certain way, despite many of its inconsistencies, since it is simpler than the neuroeconomic one.

In this way, there is a possibility that the current paradigm in economics does not change too much with this neuroeconomic boom; that will depend on that new models "predict better" than traditional ones. But why content ourselves with explaining the economic behavior of individuals based on false assumptions, in a time where neuroimaging and "transcranial magnetic stimulation", among other modern neurotechnics, allow us to specify with some approximation the real substrate of our decision making.

In the past, all those "discontented" with neoclassical rationality (J.M.Keynes, Simon and Hutchison, etc.) had no choice other than to appeal also to introspection to refute traditional thought; but now there are much more scientific instruments, such as those used by Neuroeconomics, impossible to ignore with the argument of "simplicity of the model".

Thus, throughout this book, we have mentioned several of these "dissatisfied" with the triumphant paradigm. For example, a "non-conformist ex ante" with the assumptions of the Neoclassical Economics is the very Adam Smith, the so-called "father of economics", who with his "Theory of Moral Sentiments" (written in the year 1756) expressed:

> *When I endeavor to examine my own behavior, when I endeavor to pronounce judgments on it, either to approve it or to condemn it, it is evident that in such cases it is as if I were divided into two different persons, and that I, the examiner and The judge embodies a man other than the other me, the person whose conduct is examined and judged. The first is the spectator... The second is the agent, the person that I designate as myself, and from whose behavior I tried to form a feeling, as if it were a spectator's. The first is the judge, the second the person who is judged.*
>
> *When we are about to act, the avidity of passion will rarely allow us to consider what we do with the dispassion of an intelligent person...*

We also saw, in previous chapters, the critical thinking of another of the "discontented" with the current paradigm, Hutchison, who in 1938, with his work *The Significance and Basic Postulates of Economic Theory*, sharply criticizes neoclassical conventional wisdom:

> *Simply to rely on **dogmatic assertions**, even when supported by phrases like "inner feelings of necessity" or "a*

> *priori facts", is to commit* **scientific suicide**. *It must really be explained in what precise way this "inner feeling of necessity," with which psychological method justifies its propositions, differs from the "inner felling of necessity" which* **political fanatics** *and the like always discover in support of their doctrines...*

> *We have seen that within Economics the "optimistic procedure of beginning with highly simplified "isolated" abstractions, in the hope of gradually making more realistic by removing the simplifying assumptions, is apt to come to a dead end, and that if one wants to get beyond a certain high level of abstraction one has to begin more or less from the beginning with extensive empirical research...*

And also, throughout this work, we have analyzed the thinking of the contemporary Simon, who from a series of works that made him creditor to the Nobel Prize (not many years ago), gives an account of his questions to the principle of rationality in the decisions of businessmen, through his idea of "bounded rationality", where he states that, instead of optimizing in the way that neoclassical theory assumes, economic agents set a goal. When they achieve it, even if it is not optimal, they feel satisfied with it and do not seek to optimize. The men of flesh and bone have limited capacities to acquire knowledge and to make calculations, and to predict their behavior, from the theoretical point of view, it would be necessary the participation of psychologists and sociologists, in addition to the economists.

But in spite of its remarkable critical power, it is easy to see that both Adam Smith, Hutchison and Simon (the three just mentioned), as well as JM Keynes, among others of the critics profusely quoted throughout this work, ran into the great difficulty of not having scientific mechanisms of stem, superior to simple introspection, to refute neoclassical thought. However, now the question has changed, there are the neuroimages and the "trasncraneal magnetic stimulation", among other available techniques, so modeling and debating with more theoretical support becomes easier. In fact, these advances are allowing Behavioral Economics, with the Nobel Kahneman at the head, to base much better a lot of research previously backed only on Psychology, but now also of Cognitive Neurosciences.

We believe that modeling in economics should involve considering the maximization of the affective and deliberative systems at the same time (either acting in a conflict or in a unitary form), but not only modeling the deliberative, as has been the tradition in Economics from the Neoclassical until now.

In short, the challenge for the coming decades is to create simplified neuroeconomic models that aim to consider the true neuropsychological aspects that underlie our decision making (something forgotten by economic science for more than two centuries), and with the objective that they can effectively be considered by the theoretical tradition in economics as useful, and in this way help to correct the many existing anomalies and theoretical inconsistencies. The challenge is great, but we believe not impossible, the tools are (still perfectible) and the anomalies of the traditional theory as well. Doing so is almost a scientific obligation, whether or not the Friedman-Bernheim thesis is overcome.

BIBLIOGRAPHY

1. ADOLPHS R, TRANEL D, DAMASIO H, DAMASIO A. *Fear and the human amygdala.* Neuroscience, 1995; pág: 5879-91.
2. AHARON Itzhak, ETCOFF Nancy, ARIELY Dan, CHABRIS Chris F., O'CONNOR Ethan, and BREITER Hans C. 2001. "Beautiful Faces Have Variable Reward Value: fMRI and Behavioral Evidence." Neuron, 32(3): 537–51.
3. Akerlof, G.A. (1991), Procastination and obedience, American Economics Review, 8(2), 1-19.
4. ALEXANDER MP, BENSON DF, STUSS DT. Frontal lobes and language. Brain Lang 1989; 37: 656-91.
5. ANSLIE, G. (1992), Psicoeconmics, New York: Cambrigde University Press.
6. ANTONIETTI, Alessandro, Do Neurobiological Data Help Us to Understand Economic Decisions Better? Journal of Economics Methodology, Volume 17, Issue 2 June 2010, pages 207-218.
7. ARCHIBALD, G. C. (1959) "The State of Economic Science". *British Journal for the Philosophy of Science,* 10. Reimpreso en Marr, W.L. y Raj, B. (eds.), *How Economists Explain. A Reader in Methodology.* University Press of America, Lanham.
8. AUMANN, R. (2005) "War and Peace". Prize Lecture. http://nobelprize.org/nobel_prizes/economics/laureates/
9. **AYDINONAT, N. EMRAH; Neuroeconomics: More Than Inspiration, Less Than Revolution; Journal of Economics Methodology, Volume 17, Issue 2 June 2010; pages 159-169.**

10. BARBER, B. y T. ODEAN (2001). "Boys Will Be Boys: Gender, Overconfidence and Common Stock Investment", The Quarterly Journal of Economics.
11. BARON-COHEN S, LESLIE A M, FRITH U. *Does the autistic child have a 'Theory of Mind'?* Cognition 1985; 21: 37-46.
12. BARON-COHEN S. *Theory of Mind and autism: a review*.Special Issue of the International Review of Mental Retardation, 23, 169, (2001).
13. BERNHEIM B., "Neuroeconomics: A Sober (but hopeful) Appraisal"; Working Paper N° 13954; National Bureau of Economic Research; 2008.
14. BERRIDGE, Kent C. 1996. "Food Reward: Brain Substrates of Wanting and Liking." Neuroscience and Biobehavioral Reviews.
15. BHATT, Meghana and CAMERER, Colin; "Self-Referential Strategic Thinking and Equilibrium as States of Mind in Games: Evidence from fMRI." Games and Economic Behavior Journal.
16. BLAIR, R. James and CIPOLOTTI Lisa. 2000. "Impaired Social Response Reversal: A Case of 'Acquired Sociopathy.'" Brain, 123(6): 1122–41.
17. BLAUG, M. (1976) "Kuhn versus Lakatos o paradigmas versus programas de investigación en la historia de la economía pura". *Revista Española de Economía* 6, (primera época), enero-abril, 9-50.
18. BLAUG, M. (1992), *The Methodology of Economics*. (Segunda edición), Cambridge University Press, versión pdf.
19. BOEREEGeorge, Psicología General "Neurotransmisores", Universidad de Shippensburg.
20. BOLAND, *Critical Economic Methodology*. Routledge, Londres, 1997.

21. BRAIDOT, Nestor "Neuromarketing, Neuroeconomía y Negocios", Editorial Puerto Norte-Sur 2005.
22. BRAIDOT, Nestor, artículo en Revista "Entorno Económico", Mendoza, Argentina, febrero 2006.
23. BREITER, Hans C., AHARON Itzhak, KAHNEMAN Daniel, DALE Anders, and SHIZGAL Peter. 2001. "Functional Imaging of Neural Responses to Expectancy and Experience of Monetary Gains and Losses", Revista Neuron.
24. CAIRNES, J.E. (1875) "The Character and Logical Method of Political Economy". MacMillan, Londres.
25. CALDWELL, B.J. (1994) *Beyond Positivism*. (Edición revisada), Routledge, Londres.
26. CAMERER C. F., Behavioral Game Theory Experiments in Strategic Interaction, Princeton University Press, 2003. http://press.princeton.edu/titles/7517.html
27. CAMERER C. F., THALER R.H., Anomalies: ultimatums, dictators and manners, Journal of Econ. Perspect.1995.
28. CAMERER, C. y LOEWENSTEIN, G. (2004). "Behavioral Economics: Past, Present, Future." Princeton: Princeton University Press.
29. CAMERER, C., LOEWENSTEIN, G. y PRELEC, D. (2005), "Neuroeconomics: How Neuroscience can inform Economics", *Journal of Economic Literature*. Vol. XLIII. No. 1.
30. CAMERER, C.; L. BABCOCK; G. LOEWENSTEIN y R. THALER (1997). "Labor Supply of New York City Cabdrivers: One Day at a Time"; The Quarterly Journal of Economics, 112(2), 407-441.
31. CARDONA HERRERO, Sergio; "Neuromanagement. Los Conocimientos sobre el

Cerebro Aplicados al Mando en las Organizaciones" Editorial Almuzara, 2008.
32. CARSTENSEN, L.L., ISSACOWITZ, D M., CHARLES, S.T., 1999, *Taking time seriously: a theory of socioemotional selectivity*, American Psychologist 54, 165-181.
33. CARTER, Rita. El nuevo mapa del cerebro. Guía ilustrada de los descubrimientos más recientes para comprender el funcionamiento de la mente. Editorial Integral. Ediciones de Librerías S.A. Barcelona, España, 1998.
34. CHABRIS, Christopher, LAIBSON, D. and SCHULDT, J., Decisiones Intertemporales, diciembre 2006, artículo publicado en Durlauf, S. y Blumen L, (Eds) (2007) The New Palgrave Dictionary of Economics (2nd edition), London: Palgrave Macmillan.
35. CHIC GARCÍA Genaro Neuroeconomía: Nuevas Orientaciones en los Estudios de Historia Económica. 2006.
36. CHORBAT, T. y McCabe, K. (2005). "Neuroeconomics and Rationality". *George Mason University School of Law". Working Paper Series. Paper 29*.
37. COHEN, J. (2005). "The Vulcanization of the Human Brain". *Journal of Economic Perspectives.* Vol 19. No. 4.
38. COOPER, R.W. y JOHN, A. (1988) "Coordinating Coordination Failures in Keynesian Models". *Quarterly Journal of Economics* 103, agosto, 441-463.
39. DAMASIO, Antonio "En busca de Spinoza. Neurobiología de la emoción y los sentimientos", Editorial Crítica, 2005.
40. DAMASIO, Antonio R. "Descartes' Error: Emotion, Reason, and the Human Brain", 1994, New York.

41. DE WAAL F. Good natured: the origins of right and wrong in humans and other animals. Cambridge: Harvard University Press; 1996.
42. DELGADO, Mauricio R., LEIGH E. NYSTROM, C. FISSELL, D. C. Noll, and Julie A. Fiez. 2000. "Tracking the Hemodynamic Responses to Reward and Punishment in the Striatum." Journal of Neurophysiology.
43. DELLA Vigna, Stefano and ULRIKE Malmendier. 2003, "Overestimating Self-Control: Evidence from the Health Club Industry," Berkeley Working Paper.
44. DENBURG, Natalie L., Psychophysiological anticipation of positive outcomes promotes advantageous decision-making in normal older persons, Elsevier. 2006.
45. DÍAZ ATIENZA Joaquín "Funciones Ejecutivas y Aprendizaje: I) Neuroanatomía y Evaluación" Extraído de: http://www.tdah-andalucia.es
46. ERK, Suzanne, SPITZER Manfred, WUNDERLICH Arthur P., GALLEY Lars, and WALTER Henrik. 2002. "Cultural Objects Modulate Reward Circuitry." Neuroreport.
47. FEHR Ernst, FISCHBACHER Urs and KOSFELD, Michael "Neuroeconomic Foundations of Trust and Social Preferences" 2005 Institute for the Study of Labor (IZA)
48. FISCHER, S. (1977) "Long-Term Contracts, Rational Expectations, and the Optimal Money Supply Rule". Journal of Political Economy 85, 1, 191-205.
49. FLETCHER, Paul C., HAPPE Francesca, FRITH Uta, BAKER S. C., DOLAN Ray J., FRACKOWIAK Richard S., and FRITH Chris D. 1995. "Other Minds in the Brain: A Functional Imaging Study of "Theory of Mind" in Story Comprehension." Cognition, 57(2): 109–28.

50. FLORES SÁNCHEZ, María de Lourdes "El aprendizaje acelerado".
51. FRIEDMAN, M. (1953); The Methodology of Positive Economics. En *Essays on Positive Economics*, University of Chicago Press, Chicago, 3-43. También disponible en: http://www.ppge.ufrgs.br/giacomo/arquivos/eco02036/friedman-1966.pdf
52. FRIEDMAN, M. (1968) "The Role of Monetary Policy". *American Economic Review* 58, marzo, 1-17.
53. FRIEDMAN, M. (1990) *Teoría de los Precios*. Alianza Editorial, 2da edición.
54. FRITH, Uta. 2001. "Mind Blindness and the Brain in Autism." Neuron.
55. FRITH, Uta. 2001. "What Framework Should We Use for Understanding Developmental Disorders?" Developmental Neuropsychology, 20(2): 555–63.
56. FUMAGALLI, Roberto; The Disunity of Neuroeconomics: a Methodological Appraisal; Journal of Economics Methodology, Volume 17, Issue 2 June 2010; pages 119-131.
57. GLIMCHER P. W. "Decisions, uncertainty, and the brain: The science of neuroeconomics" 2003. Cambridge, MA: MIT Press.
58. GLIMCHER Paul W. and RUSTICHINI Aldo "Neuroeconomics: The Consilience of brain and Decision" 2004 Science Vol 306
59. GLIMCHER, P. (2003), *"Decisions, Uncertainty and the Brain. The Science of Neuroeconomics"*, Cambridge, Mass.: The MIT Press.
60. GLIMCHER, P.; CAMERER, C.; FEHR, E; POLDRACK, R.; *Neuroeconomics. Decision Making and the Brain. Editorial Elsevier, año 2009.*
61. GLIMCHER P., Choice: Towards a Standard Back Pocket Model, incluido en Neuroeconomics, Decision Making and the Brain, Elsevier, 2009.

62. GÓMEZ LÓPEZ, R., Evolución Científica y Metodológica de la Economía: Escuelas de Pensamiento, versión pdf, disponible en http://www.eumed.net/cursecon/libreria/rgl-evol/rgl-metod.pdf
63. GREENE JD, SOMMERVILLE RB, NYSTROM LE, DARLEY JM, COHEN JD. An fMRI investigation of emotional engagement in moral judgment. Science 2001.
64. GUL F. y PESENDORFER W., "The Case for Mindless Economics", Working Paper, Princeton University, 2005.
65. HAPPÉ F, BROWNELL H, WINNER E. Acquired 'Theory of Mind' impairments following stroke. Cognition 1999.
66. HAPPE, Francesca, EHLERS Stefan, FLETCHER Paul, FRITH Uta, JOHANSSON Maria, GILLBERG Christopher, DOLAN Ray, FRACKOWIAK Richard, and FRITH Chris. 1996. "'Theory of Mind' in the Brain: Evidence from a PET Scan Study of Asperger Syndrome." Neuroreport, 8(1): 197–201.
67. HARRISON, Glenn y ROSS, Don, "The Methodologies of Neuroeconomics", Journal of Economics Methodology, Volume 17, Issue 2 June 2010.
68. HSU, Ming; CAMERER, Colin y otros; 2005, "Ambiguity Aversion in the Brain: FMRI and Lesion Patient Evidence.", Caltech Working Paper.
69. HUANG Peter H. "Law and Human Flourishing: Happiness, Affective Neuroscience, and Paternalism".
70. HUME, D. (1980) [1748]. *"Investigaciones sobre el conocimiento humano"*. Madrid: Alianza Universidad.

71. HUTCHISON, T.W (1938) *The Significance and Basic Postulates of Economic Theory*. Edición de 1965: Augustus M. Kelley, Nueva York.
72. IUDICA, Valentina (1993), *Metodología y Epistemología de la Ciencia Económica*, Facultad de Ciencias Económicas, Universidad Nacional de Cuyo, Mendoza, Argentina.
73. JEVONS, W.S. (1871) *La Teoría de la Economía Política*, 1998, Editorial Pirámide
74. KAHNEMAN, D. (2003). "Maps of Bounded Rationality: Psychology for Behavioral Economics. American Economic Review. Vol 93. no. 5.
75. KAHNEMAN, D. and A. TVERSKY (1974). "Judgement Under Uncertainty: Heuristics and Biases", Science, Vol. 185, pág. 1124-1131.
76. KAHNEMAN, Daniel: "Maps of bounded rationality: psychology for behavioral economics", American Economic Review, 93, 5, 2003.
77. Kahneman D., *Remarks on Neuroeconomics*, incluido en *Neuroeconomics, Decision Making and the Brain*, Elsevier, 2009.
78. KEYNES, J.M. (1936); Teoría General del Empleo, el Interés y el Dinero, Fondo de Cultura Económica, 3ra edición 2001, disponible en la web en: http://www.listinet.com/bibliografia-comuna/Cdu332-38FB.pdf
79. KEYNES, J.N. (1890), *The Scope and Method of Political Economy*. 4ta Edición de 1915, University of Cambridge, disponible en: http://socserv.mcmaster.ca/econ/ugcm/3ll3/keynesjn/Scope.pdf
80. KIYOTAKI, N. (1988) "Multiple Expectational Equilibria under Monopolistic Competition". *Quarterly Journal of Economics* 102, noviembre, 695-714.

81. KNIGHT, F. (1940) "What is Truth in Economics?"; University of Chicago Press, 1956, p 151-178, disponible en Google Books, http://books.google.com.ar/books?id=rCyFf7vnH0UC&printsec=frontcover&dq=KNIGHT+Frank+What+is+Truth+in+Economics&hl=es&sa=X&ei=DrXvUtTCMIulsASKioC4Dw&ved=0CCoQ6AEwAA#v=onepage&q=KNIGHT%20Frank%20What%20is%20Truth%20in%20Economics&f=false.
82. KNUTSON, B., Rick S., WIMMER, G., PRELEC, D., LOEWENSTEIN G. (2006). Neural predictors of purchase. Neuron 53, 147–156
83. KNUTSON, Brian and PETERSON Richard. In Press. "Neurally Reconstructing Expected Utility." Games and Economic Behavior.
84. KNUTSON, Brian; WIMMER, G. ELLIOTT; KUHNEN, Camelia M.; WINKIELMAN, Piotr "Nucleus accumbens activation mediates the influence of reward cues on financial risk taking", 2008.
85. KNUTSON, LOEWENSTEIN y otros, Neural Predictors of Purchases, en Revista Neuron, enero de 2007.
86. KOENIGS, M., YOUNG, L., ADOLPH, R., TRANEL, D., CUSHMAN, F., HAUSER, M., DAMASIO, A. (2007) "Damage to the prefrontal cortex increases utilitarian moral judgemets". *Nature.* Vol 446.
87. KOOPMANS, T. (1957) *Three Essays on the State of Economic Science.* McGraw-Hill, Nueva York.
88. KUHN, T. (1977) *La estructura de las revoluciones científicas.* Fondo de Cultura Económica, México.
89. KUHNEN, C. y KNUTSON, B. (2005). "The Neural Basis of Financial Risk Taking". *Neuron.* Setiembre.
90. KUORIKOSKI, Jaakko y YLIKOSKI, Petri, Explanatory Relevance Across Disciplinary

Boundaries: The Case of Neuroeconomics, Journal of Economics Methodology, Volume 17, Issue 2, June 2010, pages 219-228.
91. LAIBSON. D. (1997), Golden eggs and hyperbolic discounting. Quaterly Journal of Economics, 112, 443-477.
92. LAKATOS (1975) "La falsación y la metodología de los programas de investigación científica". En Lakatos, I. y Musgrave, A., (eds.) *La crítica y eldesarrollo del conocimiento*, Grijalbo, Barcelona, 203-343.
93. LAKATOS, I. (1971) "History of Science and Its Rational Reconstruction". En Cohen, R.S., Buck, C.R., Dordrecht-Holland, D. (eds.), *Boston Studies in Philosophy of Science* VIII.
94. LAKATOS, I. y MUSGRAVE, A. (eds.) (1975) La crítica y el desarrollo del conocimiento. Grijalbo, Barcelona.
95. LAMBRECHT, Anja and SKIERA Bernd. "Paying Too Much and Being Happy About It: Causes and Consequences of Tariff Choice–Bias." 2006. Johann Wolfgang Goethe-University Frankfurt.
96. LAVIN, Claudio, Emociones y decisión: marcadores somáticos, publicado en www.neuroeconomia.cl, año 2007.
97. LAZA, Sebastián, artículos públicados en blog ECONOMÍA APTA PARA TODO PÚBLICO: www.seblaza.blogspot.com.ar :
98. LESLIE A M.; Presence and representation: the origins of 'Theory of Mind'. Psychol Rev 1987; 94: 412-36.
99. LIEBERMAN Philip, Human Language and our reptilian Brain, Harvard Uniersity Press, Cambridge, 2002. http://books.google.com.ar/books?id= VyLdaH Jw 0C

100. LIPSEY, R.G. (1974), Introducción a la Economía Positiva. Novena edición castellana: Vicens Vives, Barcelona. p. 15.
101. LIPSEY, R.G. (1991) Introducción a la Economía Positiva. Décimo segunda edición castellana: Vicens Vives, Barcelona.
102. LOEWENSTEIN, George F. 1994. "The Psychology of Curiosity: A Review and Reinterpretation." Psychological Bulletin.
103. LOEWENSTEIN, George F., WEBER Robert, FLORY Janine, MANUCK Stephen and MULDOON Matthew. 2001. "Dimensions of Time Discounting." Conference on Survey Research on Household Expectations and Preferences.
104. LOEWESTEIN, G. and PRELEC, D. (1992) Anomalies in intertemporal choice: evidence and an interpretation. Quaterly Journal of Econnomics, 107, 573-957.
105. LOEWESTEIN y O'DONOGHUE "Animal Spirits: Affective and Deliberative Processes in Economic Behavior" 2005.
106. LÓPEZ, Ernesto, "Todos tenemos nuestro cuarto de hora: Economía Conductual, Neuroeconomía y sus implicancias para la protección al consumidor", mimeo, año 2005, INDECOPI.
107. MACHLUP, F. (1978) "Operationalism and Pure Theory in Economics". En *Methodology of Economics and Other Social Sciences*. Academic Press, Nueva York.
108. MÄKI, Uskali; When Economics Meets Neuroscience: Hype *And* Hope; Journal of Economics Methodology, Volume **17**, Issue **2** June 2010; pages 107-111.
109. MANKIW, N.G. (1990) "A Quick Refresher Course in Macroeconomics". *Journal of Economic Literature* 28, diciembre, 1645-1660.

110. MARCHIONNI, Caterina y VROMEN, Jack; 'Neuroeconomics: Hype or Hope?', Journal of Economics Methodology, Volume 17, Issue 2 June 2010, pages 103-106.
111. MAS-COLELL, A., WHINSTON, M. y GREEN, J. (1995). "Microeconomic Theory". Oxford: Oxford University Press.
112. Mc LURE, Samuel, LAIBSON David, LOEWENSTEIN George and COHEN Jonathan, Separate neural system value inmediate and delayed monetary rewards, Science, octubre de 2004.
113. McCABE, K., HOUSER, D., RYAN, L., SMITH, V. y TROUARD, T. (2001) "A functional imaging study of cooperation in two person reciprocal exchange". *Proceedings of the National Academy of Sciences of the United States of America"*. www.pnas.org/cgi/doi/10.1073/pnas211415698.
114. McCLURE, Samuel M., LAIBSON David, LOEWENSTEIN George, and COHEN Jonathan D. "Separate Neural Systems Value Immediate and Delayed Monetary Rewards" 2004.
115. MELITZ, J. (1965) "Friedman and Machlup on the Significance of Testing Economic Assumptions". *Journal of Political Economy* 73, 37-60.
116. MENDOZA Lara Elvira y LÓPEZ HERRERO Paz Consideraciones sobre el desarrollo de la Teoría de la Mente (TOM) y del Lenguaje. Dpto. Personalidad, Evaluación y Tratamiento Psicológico. Universidad de Granada
117. MILL, J.S., *Principles of Political Economy* London: Longmans, Green and Co., ed. William J. Ashley, (1909, 7ma edición), disponible en: http://www.gutenberg.org/files/30107/30107-pdf.pdf

118. MILL, J.S. (1967) *Collected Works, Essays on Economic and Society*. J.M. Robson (edit). University of Toronto Press, Toronto, p. 323; también disponible en: http://files.libertyfund.org/files/244/Mill_0223-04_EBk_v7.0.pdf
119. Mobbs Dean, Greicius Michael D., Eiman Abdel-Azim, Vinod Menon, and Allan L. Reiss. 2003. "Humor Modulates the Mesolimbic Reward Centers." Neuron.
120. MOLL J, ESLINGER P, OLIVEIRA-SOUZA R. Frontopolar and anterior temporal cortex activation in a moral judgment task: preliminary functional MRI results in normal subjects. Arq Neuropsiquiatr 2001.
121. MONTAGUE, P. Read and Gregory S. BERNS. 2002. "Neural Economics and the Biological Substrates of Valuation." Neuron, 36(2): 265–84.
122. MORA TERUEL Francisco Neurocultura: todo está en el cerebro.2007 www.abc.es
123. MORALES, Raúl, Una nueva ciencia, la Neuroeconomía, estudia las decisiones económicas humanas, publicado en: http://www.secyt.unc.edu.ar/Temas/Boletin/articulos/BoletinV1N10_neuroeconomia.html, agosto de 2003, originalmente publicado en Tendencias Científicas (21/06/03) http://www.tendencias21.net
124. MOTTERLINI Mateo "Economía emocional, En qué nos gastamos el dinero y por qué" Editorial Paidós Ibérica.2008
125. MULLAINATHAN, S. y R. THALER (2000). "Behavioral Economics", Working Paper 7948. National Bureau of Economic Research.
126. MUTH, J. (1961) "Rational Expectations and the Theory of Price Movements". Econométrica 39, julio, 315-334.

127. NAGATSU, Michiru, Function and Mechanism: The Metaphysics of Neuroeconomics, Journal of Economics Methodology, Volume 17, Issue 2 June 2010, pages 197-205.
128. NAVARRO, Alfredo Martín, De SCHANT, Fermín y MARTÍN, Jorge Marcelo, Neuroeconomía y Metodología: Algunas Reflexiones Iniciales, año 2007, mimeo.
129. NAVARRO, Alfredo, Neuroeconomía y Teoría de Juegos. Implicancias Metodológicas, mimeo (2007).
130. OLDS, James and MILNER Peter. 1954. "Positive Reinforcement Produced by Electrical Stimulation of Septal Area and Other Regions of Rat Brain." Journal of Comparative and Physiological Psychology
131. PATINKIN, D. (1959), *Dinero, Interés y Precios*, Editorial Aguilar.
132. PEYROLÓN, Pablo, Neuroeconomía o la Economía del Prozac, Profesor Asociado Universitat Pompeu Fabra y ESCI, publicado en http://www.eumed.net/ce/pp-neuro.htm.
133. PHELPS, E. (1967) "Phillips Curves, Expectations of Inflation and Optimal Unemployment over Time". *Economica* 34, agosto, 254-281.
134. POPPER (1991), *Discurso de Investidura como Doctor Honoris Causa*, Universidad Complutense, Madrid.
135. POPPER, K. (1962) La lógica de la investigación científica, Tecnos, Madrid, disponible en: http://ifdc6m.juj.infd.edu.ar/aula/archivos/repositorio//0/103/Karl R. Popper - La Logica de la Investigacion Cientifica.pdf
136. PRELEC, Drazen and Duncan Simester. 2001. "Always Leave Home without It." Marketing Letters.

137. PRELEC, Drazen and George F. LOEWENSTEIN. 1998. "The Red and the Black: Mental Accounting of Savings and Debt." Marketing Science.
138. RABIN M., A perspective on psychology and economics, Eur. Econ. Rev. 46 (2002).
139. RAMÓN, José María (2004), *La Epistemología de Khun, Lakatos y Feyerabend: un análisis comparado*, Universidad Nacional de la Patagonia, pág 53-62, disponible en: http://josemramon.com.ar/wp-content/uploads/Ram%C3%B3n-Jos%C3%A9-Mar%C3%ADa-La-epistemolog%C3%ADa-de-khun-Lakatos-y-Feyerabend.pdf
140. RILLING, J., GUTMAN, D., ZEH, T., PAGNONI, G., BERNS, G., y KILTS, C. (2002). "A Neural Basis for Social Cooperation". *Neuron*. Vol 35. No. 2.
141. ROBBINS (1971) *Autobiography of an Economist*. Macmillan, Londres.
142. ROBBINS, L. (1932) *An essay on the Nature and Significance of Economic Science*, MacMillan, Londres, disponible en: http://mises.org/books/robbinsessay2.pdf y reeditado por The Mises Institute, Alabama, 2007, disponible en Google Books: http://books.google.com.ar/books?id=nySoIkOgWQ4C&printsec=frontcover&dq=lionel+robbins&hl=es&sa=X&ei=Y7DvUr7-AcipsQTolIDgBw&sqi=2&ved=0CC0Q6AEwAA#v=onepage&q=lionel%20robbins&f=false
143. ROBBINS, L. (1934) "Remarks on the Relationship between Economics and Psychology". The Manchester School of Economics and Social Science.
144. ROTWEIN, E. (1959) "On the Methodology of Positive Economics, *QuarterlyJournal of Economics* 73, 554-575.

145. ROWE, Andrea D., BULLOCK Peter R., POLKEY Charles E., and MORRIS Robin G.. 2001. "'Theory of Mind' Impairments and their Relationship to Executive Functioning Following Frontal Lobe Excisions." Brain.
146. SAMUELSON (1963) Problems of Methodology: Discussion. *American* Economic Review Papers and Proceedings 53, 2, 231-236.
147. SAMUELSON, P.A. (1948) *Foundations of Economic Analysis.* Harvard University Press, Cambridge, Mass.
148. SÁNCHEZ-ROBLES, Blanca, La Economía. Concepto y Método, disponible en: personales.unican.es/sanchezb/web/La%20economia.pdf sitio de la Universidad de Cantabria, España.
149. SANFEY, Alan G., James K. RILLING, Jessica A. AARONSON, Leigh E. NYSTROM, and Jonathan D. COHEN. 2003. "The Neural Basis of Economic Decision-Making in the Ultimatum Game." Science,
150. SANFEY, Rilling, COHEN y otros, The Neural Basis of Economic Decision Making in the Ultimatum Game, en Revista Science, junio de 2003.
151. SANFEY, Rilling, COHEN y otros, The neural correlates of Theory of Mind within interpersonal interactions, en Revista Science Direct, año 2004.
152. SARGENT, T. y WALLACE, N. (1975) "'Rational Expectations', the Optimal Monetary Instrument, and the Optimal Money Supply Rule". *Journal of PoliticalEconomy* 83, abril, 241-254.
153. SAXE, Rebecca and KANWISHER Nancy. 2003. "People Thinking about Thinking People: The Role of the Temporo–Parietal Junction in 'Theory of Mind.'" Neuroimage, 19(4): 1835–42.
154. SCHULTZ, Wolfram. 2002. "Getting Formal with Dopamine and Reward." Neuron.

155. SCHUMPETER, J. (1971) *Historia del Análisis Económico*. Fondo de Cultura Económica, México.
156. SCHWARTZ, P. (1997) "Invitación a la economía". En Febrero, R. (edit.) *Qué es la Economía*, Pirámide, Madrid, 65-100.
157. SEN, A. (1987). "Rational Behavior"; Macmillan Press Limited.
158. SENIOR, N. (1827) Introductory Lecture on Political Economy. En Selected Writings on Economics. A Volume of Pamphlets 1827-1852. Kelley, Nueva York, disponible en: http://mises.org/books/selected_writings_senior.pdf
159. SENIOR, N. (1836) *Outline of the Science of Political Economy*, edición de 1951: Kelley, Nueva York, disponible en http://digamo.free.fr/senior36.pdf
160. SIEGAL M, CARRINGTON J, RADEL M. Theory of Mind and pragmatic understanding following right hemisphere damage. 1996. Brain and Language.
161. SIMON, H. (1997). *"An Empirically Based Microeconomics"*. Raffaelle Mattioli Foundation. Cambridge: Cambridge University Press, version pdf.
162. SINGER Tania and FEHR Ernst "Neuroeconomics of Mind Reading and Empathy " 2005 University of Zurich and IZA
163. SINGER, Tania, KIEBEL, Stefan y otros, 2004, "Brain Responses to the Acquired Moral Status of Faces", Neuron, 41 (4): 653-62.
164. SINGER, Tania; KIEBEL, STEFAN J.; WINSTON, Joel S.; DOLAN, Ray J. and FRITH, Christopher D. "Brain responses to the acquired moral status of faces". Neuron, February 2004a
165. SMITH, A. (1941) [1759]. "Teoría de los Sentimientos Morales". México: Fondo de Cultura Económica.

166. SPERRY, GAZZANIGA y BOGEN "Interhemispheric relationships, the neocortical commisures: syndromes of hemisphere disconnection", en Handbook of Clinical Neurology, 1969, vol 4, pág 273-290, Amsterdam, North Holland.
167. STROZT, R. H. (1956) Myopia and inconsistency in dynamic utility maximization, Review of Economics Studies, 23, 165-180.
168. THALER, R. (1985). "Mental Accounting and Consumer Choice", Marketing Science, Vol. 4, pág. 199-214.
169. TIRAPU-USTÁRROZ J., PÉREZ-SAYES G., EREKATXO-BILBAO M., PELEGRÍN-VALERO C. ¿Qué es la teoría de la mente? 2007. Revista de Neurología.
170. TRAIN, Kenneth E. Optimal Regulation: The Economic Theory of Natural Monopoly. 1991 Cambridge: MIT Press.
171. TRAIN, Kenneth E., Daniel L. McFADDEN, and Moshe BEN-AKIVA. 1987. "The Demand for Local Telephone Service: A Fully Discrete Model of Residential Calling Patterns and Service Choices." Rand Journal of Economics.
172. TURNER, Jonathan H; On the origins of Human Emotions, Stanford University Press, 2000.
173. VARIAN Hal R; "Microeconomía intermedia"; 4ta Edición, Editorial Antoni Bosch 1996.
174. VARIAN, Hal R; "Microeconomic Analysis"; 1978.
175. VERCOE, Moana y ZAK, Paul; Inductive Modeling Using Causal Studies in Neuroeconomics: Brains on Drugs; Journal of Economics Methodology, Volume 17, Issue 2; June 2010.
176. VerLEE, W.L.; Aprender con todo el cerebro; Ediciones Martínez Roca; 1986.

177. WINNER E, BROWNELL H, HAPPÉ F, BLUM A, PINCUS D.; *Distinguishing lies from jokes: Theory of Mind deficits and discourse interpretation in right hemisphere brain-damaged patients.* Brain Lang 1998; 62: 89-106.
178. VROMEN, Jack; Where economics and neuroscience might meet; Journal of Economics Methodology, Volume 17, Issue 2 June 2010; pages 171-183.
179. ZAK Paul J. "Neuroeconomics" 2004 The Royal Society
180. ZAK y FAKHAR, Neuroactive hormones and interpersonal trust: international evidence, Elsevier, año 2006.
181. ZALTMAN Gerald, Cómo Piensan los Consumidores, Ediciones Urano, S.A. Editorial Empresa Activa. 2004.

NOTAS

[1] Kahneman, (2003): "Maps of Bounded Rationality: Psychology for Behavioral Economics", American Economic Review, 93.
[2] Zak, (2004), "Neuroeconomics". Paul Zak is one of the most renowned neuroeconomists today, specialized in the relationship between oxitocyn and trust.
[3] Glimcher Paul W. and Rustichini Aldo "Neuroeconomics: The Consilience of Brain and Decision", (2004), Science Vol 306.
4 Neuroeconomist of the George Washington University.
5 Extracted from Tom Wolfe, Hooking Up (2000).
[6] Schumpeter, J. (1971) History of Economic Analysis. Fondo de Cultura Económica, Mexico, p. 167.
[7] Braidot, Nestor; article in "Entorno Económico" Magazine, Mendoza, Argentine, February 2006.
8 C.F. Camerer, G. Loewenstein, D. Prelec, ««Neuroeconomics: How Neuroscience can Inform Economics", Working Paper, UCLA Department of Economics, (2003).
[9] NAVARRO, Alfredo Martín, De SCHANT, Fermín and MARTÍN, Jorge Marcelo, Neuroeconomía y Metodología: Algunas Reflexiones Iniciales, (2007), mimeo.
[10] Knutson, Brian; Wimmer, G. Elliott; Kuhnen, Camelia M.; Winkielman, Piotr; "Nucleus Accumbens Activation Mediates the Influence of Reward Cues on Financial Risk Taking". Neuroreport, 19 (5): 509-513, March 26, (2008).
[11] These authors are eminent researchers on interhemispheric brain relations and connections. See, for example, "Interhemispheric Relations, the Neocortical Commissures: Syndromes of Hemisphere Disconnection," in Handbook of Clinical Neurology, 1969, vol. 4, p. 273-290, Amsterdam, North Holland.
[12] NAVARRO, Alfredo Martín, De SCHANT, Fermín and MARTÍN, Jorge Marcelo, Neuroeconomics and Methodology: Some Initial Reflections, 2007, mimeo.
[13] Damasio, Antonio R. Descartes' Error: Emotion, Reason, and the Human Brain. 1994. New York.
[14] The pioneering study applied to Neuroeconomics was led by Sanfey, Rilling, Cohen and others, and published under the title: The Neural Basis of Economic Decision Making in the Ultimate Game, in Science Magazine, June 2003.
[15] KNUTSON, LOEWENSTEIN and others, Neural Predictors of Purchases, Neuron, January 2007.
[16] Camerer, C., Loewenstein, G. and Prelec, D. (2005), "Neuroeconomics: How Neuroscience Can Inform Economics", Journal of Economic Literature. Vol. XLIII. No. 1.

[17] Blaug, Mark, The Methodology of Economics (2nd Edition, Cambridge University Press, 1992), pdf version.
[18] Neuroeconomía y Metodología: Algunas Reflexiones Iniciales, by Alfredo Martín Navarro, Fermín De Schant and Jorge Marcelo Martín. Dr. Alfredo Navarro is a prominent Argentine economist, titular member of the National Academy of Economic Sciences of the Argentine Republic, and with scientific writings in various fields of economic science.
[19] Great work available in:
http://personales.unican.es/sanchezb/web/La%20economia.pdf
[20] Hume, D. (1980) [1748]. "Investigations on human knowledge". Madrid: University Alliance.
[21] Smith, A. (1941) [1759]. "Theory of moral feelings". Mexico: Fondo de Cultura Económica.
[22] Simon, H. (1997). "An Empirically Based Microeconomics". Raffaelle Mattioli Foundation. Cambridge: Cambridge University Press, pdf version.
[23] MILL, J.S. (1967) Collected Works, Essays on Economic and Society. J.M. Robson (edit). University of Toronto Press, Toronto, p. 323
[24] JEVONS, W.S. (1871) The Theory of Political Economy, 1998, Editorial Pirámide, p.101.
[25] Braidot, Nestor, article in "Entorno Económico" Magazine, Mendoza, Argentina, February 2006.
[26] ROBBINS, L. (1932) An essay on the Nature and Significance of Economic Science, MacMillan, London, reissued by The Mises Institute, Alabama, 2007, available in Google Books.
[27] HUTCHISON, T.W (1938), The Significance and Basic Postulates of Economic Theory; 1965 edition: Augustus M. Kelley, New York.
[28] KNIGHT, F. (1940) "What is Truth in Economics?", Chicago University Press, p 151-178, available in Google Books.
[29] KEYNES, J.M., General Theory of Employment, Interest and Money, Fondo de Cultura Económica, 3rd edition 2001, available on the web at: http://www.listinet.com/bibliografia-comuna/Cdu332-38FB.pdf
[30] PATINKIN, D. (1959), Money, Interest and Prices, Editorial Aguilar.
[31] FRIEDMAN, M. (1968) "The Role of Monetary Policy". American Economic Review 58, March, 1-17.
[32] PHELPS, E. (1967) "Phillips Curves, Expectations of Inflation and Optimal Unemployment Over Time". Economica 34, August, 254-281.
[33] FRIEDMAN, M. (1990) Theory of Prices. Alianza Editorial, 2nd edition.

[34] FRIEDMAN, M. (1953), The Methodology of Positive Economics. In Essays on Positive Economics, University of Chicago Press, Chicago, 3-43. Also available at: http://www.ppge.ufrgs.br/giacomo/arquivos/eco02036/friedman-1966.pdf

[35] FRIEDMAN, M., 1953, The Methodology of Positive Economics, Essays on Positive Economics, University of Chicago Press, Chicago, p.19)

[36] MUTH, J. (July 1961) "Rational Expectations and the Theory of Price Movements", Econometrica 39, 315-334.

[37] SARGENT, T. and WALLACE, N. (1975) "'Rational Expectations', the Optimal Monetary Instrument, and the Optimal Money Supply Rule". Journal of Political Economy 83, April, 241-254.

[38] Braidot, Nestor, article in "Entorno Económico" Magazine, Mendoza, Argentina, February 2006.

[39] MANKIW, N.G. (1990) "A Quick Refresher Course in Macroeconomics". Journal of Economic Literature 28, December, 1645-1660.

[40] Simon, H. (1997), "An Empirically Based Macroeconomics," Raffaelle Mattioli Foundation. Cambridge: Cambridge University Press, pdf version.

[41] See Kahneman, D. (2003). "Maps of Bounded Rationality: Psychology for Behavioral Economics. American Economic Review. Vol 93. N° 5, where you summarize the results of your investigations.

[42] Camerer, C. and Loewenstein, G. (2004). "Behavioral Economics: Past, Present, Future" in Camerer C. and Lowenstein G. (ed.) "Advances in Behavioral Economics", Princeton: Princeton University Press.

[43] López, Ernesto, "We all have our quarter of an hour: Behavioral Economics, Neuroeconomics and its implications for consumer protection", mimeo, year 2005, INDECOPI, p. 119-120.

[44] MULLAINATHAN, S. and R. THALER (2000). "Behavioral Economics", Working Paper 7948. National Bureau of Economic Research.

[45] KAHNEMAN, D. and A. TVERSKY (1974). "Judgment Under Uncertainty: Heuristics and Biases", Science, Vol. 185, p. 1124-1131.

[46] THALER, R. (1985). "Mental Accounting and Consumer Choice", Marketing Science, Vol. 4, p. 199-214.

[47] CAMERER, C.; L. BABCOCK; G. LOEWENSTEIN and R. THALER (1997). "Labor supply of New York City cabdrivers: One day at a time", The Quarterly Journal of Economics, 112 (2), 407-441.

[48] Loewenstein, G. and O'Donoghue, T. (2004). "Animal Spirits: Affective and Deliberative Influences on Economic Behavior". Working Paper.

[49] Extracted from: http://racionalidadltda.wordpress.com/2013/05/26/la-paradoja-de-allais/

[50] Excerpted from: http://policonomics.com/en/paradoja-allais/

[51] Camerer, Loewestein and Prelec (2005); Neuroeconomics: How Neuroscience Can Inform Economics; Journal of Economics Literature, Vol. XLIII, N°1.

[52] López, Ernesto, "We all have our quarter of an hour: Behavioral Economics, Neuroeconomics and its implications for consumer protection", mimeo, year 2005, INDECOPI, p. 114-116.

[53] BARBER, B. and T. ODEAN (2001). "Boys Will Be Boys: Gender, Overconfidence and Common Stock Investment", The Quarterly Journal of Economics.

[54] Sanfey, Rilling, Cohen and others, The Neural Basis of Economic Decision Making in the Ultimatum Game, in Science Magazine, June 2003.

[55] Knutson, Loewenstein and others, Neural Predictors of Purchases, in Revista Neuron, January 2007.

[56] Sanfey, Rilling, Cohen and others, The Neural Correlates of Theory of Mind within Interpersonal Interactions, in Science Direct Magazine, 2004.

[57] Sanfey et al, The Neural Basis of Economic Decision Making in the Ultimatum Game, in Science Magazine, June 2003.

[58] Zak and Fakhar, Neuroactive Hormones and Interpersonal Trust: International Evidence, Elsevier, 2006.

[59] Lavín, Claudio, Emotions and decision: somatic markers, year 2008, published in the blog www.neuroeconomia.cl

[60] Denburg, Natalie L., Psychophysiological anticipation of positive outcomes promotes advantageous decision-making in normal older persons, Elsevier, 2006.

[61] Carstensen, L.L., Issacowitz, D.M., Charles, S.T., 1999, Taking time seriously: a theory of socioemotional selectivity, American Psychologist 54, 165-181.

[62] Aharon, Itzhak, Nancy Etcoff, Dan Ariely, Chris F. Chabris, Ethan O'Connor, and Hans C. Breiter. 2001. "Beautiful Faces Have a Variable Reward Value: fMRI and Behavioral Evidence." Neuron, 32 (3): 537-51. Mobbs, Dean, Michael D. Greicius, Eiman Abdel-Azim, Vinod Menon, and Allan L. Reiss. 2003. "Humor Modulates the Mesolimbic Reward Centers." Neuron. Erk, Suzanne, Manfred Spitzer, Arthur P. Wunderlich, Lars Galley, and Henrik Walter. 2002. "Cultural Objects Modulate Reverse Circuitry." Neuroreport. Schultz, Wolfram. 2002. "Getting Formal with Dopamine and Reward." Neuron. Breiter, Hans C., I. Aharon, Daniel Kahneman,

A. Dale, and Peter Shizgal. 2001. "Functional Imaging of Neural Responses to Expectancy and Experience of Monetary Gains and Losses." Neuron. Knutson, Brian and Richard Peterson. In Press. "Neurally Reconstructing Expected Utility." Games and Economic Behavior. Delgado, Mauricio R., Leigh E. Nystrom, C. Fissell, D. C. Noll, and Julie A. Fiez. 2000. "Tracking the Hemodynamic Responses to Reward and Punishment in the Striatum." Journal of Neurophysiology.

[63] Navarro, Alfredo Martín, De Schant, Fermín and Martín, Jorge Marcelo, NEUROECONOMY AND METHODOLOGY: SOME INITIAL REFLECTIONS, mimeo, year 2007, p. 23-25.

[64] Loewenstein, G. and O'Donoghue, T. (2004). "Animal Spirits: Affective and Deliberative Influences on Economic Behavior". Working Paper.

[65] Navarro, Alfredo Martín, De Schant, Fermín and Martín, Jorge Marcelo, NEUROECONOMY AND METHODOLOGY: SOME INITIAL REFLECTIONS, mimeo, 2007.

[66] Cohen, J. (2005), "The Vulcanization of the Human Brain", Journal of Economic Perspectives, Vol 19. No. 4.

[67] Koenigs, M., Young, L., Adolph, R., Tranel, D., Cushman, F., Hauser, M., Damasio, A. (2007) "Damage to the prefrontal cortex increases utilitarian moral judgemets". Nature, Vol 446.

[68] Kuhnen, C. and Knutson, B. (2005), "The Neural Basis of Financial Risk Taking", Neuron. September.

[69] Hsu, Ming; Camerer, Colin and others; 2005, "Ambiguity Aversion in the Brain: FMRI and Lesion Patient Evidence.", Caltech Working Paper.

[70] Camerer, C., Loewenstein, G. and Prelec, D. (2005), "Neuroeconomics: How Neuroscience can inform Economics", Journal of Economic Literature. Vol. XLIII. N° 1.

[71] McCabe, K., Houser, D., Ryan, L., Smith, V. and Trouard, T. (2001) "A functional imaging study of cooperation in two person reciprocal exchange". Proceedings of the National Academy of Sciences of the United States of America, www.pnas.org/cgi/doi/10.1073/pnas211415698

[72] Singer, Tania, Kiebel, Stefan and others, 2004, "Brain Responses to the Acquired Moral Status of Faces", Neuron, 41 (4): 653-62.

[73] Alfredo Navarro, Neuroeconomics and Game Theory. Methodological Implications, mimeo (2007). The author is a Full Member of the National Academy of Economic Sciences.

[74] Glimcher, P. (2003), Decisions, Uncertainty and the Brain. The Science of Neuroeconomics, Cambridge, Mass.: The MIT Press.

[75] Glimcher (2003), "Decisions, Uncertainty and the Brain. The Science of Neuroeconomics", Cambridge, Massachussets: The MIT Press, p. 321.

[76] Anslie, G. (1992), Psychoeconomics, New York: Cambrigde University Press.
[77] Loewestein G. and Prelec D. (1992) Anomalies in intertemporal choice: evidence and an interpretation. Quaterly Journal of Econnomics, 107, 573-957.
[78]Laibson. D. (1997), Golden eggs and hyperbolic discounting. Quaterly Journal of Economics, 112, 443-477.
[79]Mc Lure, Samuel, David Laibson, George Loewenstein and Jonathan Cohen, Separate neural system value immediate and delayed monetary rewards, Science, October 2004
[80]Glimcher P., Choice: Towards to Standard Back Pocket Model, included in Neuroeconomics, Decision Making and the Brain, Elsevier, 2009.
[81]Kahneman D., Remarks on Neuroeconomics, included in Neuroeconomics, Decision Making and the Brain, Elsevier, 2009.
[82] Camerer, C., Loewenstein, G. and Prelec, D. (2005), "Neuroeconomics: How Neuroscience can Inform Economics", Journal of Economic Literature. Vol. XLIII. No. 1
[83]KUHN, T. (1977), The structure of scientific revolutions. Fondo de Cultura Económica, Mexico D.F, p. 13, Ibídem, p. 269.
[84]Blaug, Mark (1992), The Methodology of Economics. (Second edition), Cambridge University Press, pdf version.
[85] Blaug, Mark, The Methodology of Economics. (Second edition), Cambridge University Press, pdf version, p. 52.
[86] SENIOR, N. (1827) Introductory Lecture on Political Economy. In Selected Writings on Economics. A Volume of Pamphlets 1827-1852. Kelley, New York, available at: http://mises.org/books/selected_writings_senior.pdf; can also be found at: http://www.eumed.net/libros-gratis/2013/1252/nassau-william-senior.html
[87] SENIOR, N. (1836) Outline of the Science of Political Economy, 1951 edition: Kelley, New York, available at: http://digamo.free.fr/senior36.pdf
[88] MILL, J.S., Principles of Political Economy London: Longmans, Green and Co., ed. William J. Ashley, (1909, 7th edition), available at: http://www.gutenberg.org/files/30107/30107-pdf.pdf
[89]MILL, J.S. (1967) Collected Works, Essays on Economic and Society. J.M. Robson (edit). University of Toronto Press, Toronto, p. 323; also available in: http://files.libertyfund.org/files/244/Mill_0223-04_EBk_v7.0.pdf
[90]Braidot, Nestor, article in "Entorno Económico" Magazine, Mendoza, Argentina, February 2006.
[91] SCHUMPETER, J. (1971) History of Economic Analysis. Ariel, Barcelona, p. 167

[92] KEYNES, J.N. (1890), The Scope and Method of Political Economy. 4th edition, 1915, University of Cambridge, available at: http://socserv.mcmaster.ca/econ/ugcm/3ll3/keynesjn/Scope.pdf

[93] ROBBINS, L. (1932) An essay on the Nature and Significance of Economic Science, MacMillan, London, available at: http://mises.org/books/robbinsessay2.pdf

[94] ROBBINS, L. (1934) "Remarks on the Relationship between Economics and Psychology", The Manchester School of Economics and Social Science 5, 2, 89-101.

[95] BLAUG, M. (1992), The Methodology of Economics. (Second Edition), Cambridge University Press, pdf version, page 14.

[96] POPPER, K. (1962) The Logic of Scientific Research, Tecnos, Madrid, available at: http://ifdc6m.juj.infd.edu.ar/aula/archivos/repositorio//0/103/Karl R. Popper

[97] HUTCHINSON, T.W (1938), The Significance and Basic Postulates of Economic Theory, 1965 Edition: Augustus M. Kelley, New York.

[98] KNIGHT, F. (1940), "What is Truth in Economics?" Journal of Political Economy, reissued in On the History and Method of Economics. Selected Essays. University of Chicago Press, 1956, 151-178.

[99] FRIEDMAN, M. (1953), The Methodology of Positive Economics. In Essays on Positive Economics, University of Chicago Press, Chicago, 3-43.

[100] KOOPMANS, T. (1957) Three Essays on the State of Economic Science. McGraw-Hill, New York.

[101] FRIEDMAN, M. (1953), The Methodology of Positive Economics. In Essays on Positive Economics, University of Chicago Press, Chicago, p. 9.

[102] Samuelson (1963) Problems of Methodology: Discussion. American Economic Review Papers and Proceedings 53, 2, 231-236.

[103] KUHN, T. (1977) The structure of scientific revolutions. Fondo de Cultura Económica, Mexico D.F.

[104] SCHWARTZ, P. (1997) "Invitation to economics", in What is economics, Pyramid, Madrid, 65-100, p. 93.

[105] GUL, F. and PESENDORFER, W.; "The Case for Mindless Economics", Working Paper, Princeton University, 2005.

[106] KUORIKOSKI, Jaakko and YLIKOSKI, Petri, Explanatory Relevance Across Disciplinary Boundaries: The Case of Neuroeconomics, Journal of Economics Methodology, Volume 17, Issue 2, June 2010, pages 219-228.

[107] ANTONIETTI, Alessandro, Do Neurobiological Data Help Us to Understand Economic Decisions Better? Journal of Economics Methodology, Volume 17, Issue 2 June 2010, pages 207-218.
[108] HARRISON, Glenn and ROSS, Don, "The Methodologies of Neuroeconomics", Journal of Economics Methodology, Volume 17, Issue 2 June 2010.
[109] SMITH, Vernon, Rationality in Economics, Cambridge University Press, year 2007.
[110] NAGATSU, Michiru, Function and Mechanism: The Metaphysics of Neuroeconomics, Journal of Economics Methodology, Volume 17, Issue 2 June 2010, pages 197-205.
[111] BERNHEIM B., "Neuroeconomics: A Sober (but hopeful) Appraisal"; Working Paper No. 13954; National Bureau of Economic Research; 2008.
[112] FRIEDMAN, M. (1953); The Methodology of Positive Economics. In Essays on Positive Economics, University of Chicago Press, Chicago, 3-43.
[113] Bernheim B., "Neuroeconomics: A Sober (but hopeful) Appraisal"; Working Paper No. 13954; National Bureau of Economic Research; 2008.

www.ingramcontent.com/pod-product-compliance
Lightning Source LLC
Chambersburg PA
CBHW020629220526
45464CB00001B/70